D0350359

Glass Houses

Glass Houses

Congressional Ethics and the Politics of Venom

Susan J. Tolchin and Martin Tolchin

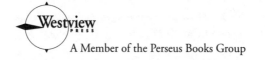

Westview
PRESS
A Member of the Perseus Books Group

HOUSTON PUBLIC LIBRARY

R01259 39839

All rights reserved. Printed in the United States of America. No part of this publication may be reproduced or transmitted in any form or by any means, electronic or mechanical, including photocopy, recording, or any information storage and retrieval system, without permission in writing from the publisher.

Copyright © 2001 by Westview Press, A Member of the Perseus Books Group

Westview Press books are available at special discounts for bulk purchases in the United States by corporations, institutions, and other organizations. For more information, please contact the Special Markets Department at The Perseus Books Group, 11 Cambridge Center, Cambridge, MA 02142, or call (617) 252-5298.

Published in 2001 in the United States of America by Westview Press, 5500 Central Avenue, Boulder, Colorado 80301-2877, and in the United Kingdom by Westview Press, 12 Hid's Copse Road, Cumnor Hill, Oxford OX2 9JJ

Find us on the World Wide Web at www.westviewpress.com

Library of Congress Cataloging-in-Publication Data
Tolchin, Susan J.
    Glass houses : congressional ethics and the politics of venom / Susan J. Tolchin and Martin Tolchin.
        p.   cm.
    Includes bibliographical references and index.
    ISBN 0-8133-6760-3
    1. United States. Congress—Ethics.   I. Tolchin, Martin.   II. Title.

JK1121.T65 2001
328.73'0766—dc21   2001035491

The paper used in this publication meets the requirements of the American National Standard for Permanence of Paper for Printed Library Materials Z39.48–1984.

10   9   8   7   6   5   4   3   2   1

To Dr. Mila Chernick

By the Authors

Selling Our Security:
The Erosion of America's Assets

Buying into America: How Foreign
Money Is Changing the Face of Our Nation

Dismantling America: The Rush to Deregulate

Clout: Womanpower and Politics

To the Victor: Political Patronage
from the Clubhouse to the White House

By Susan J. Tolchin

The Angry American: How
Voter Rage Is Changing the Nation

Contents

Preface and
Acknowledgments

"To do good is noble, but to teach others to
be good is nobler—and no trouble."
—Mark Twain

There were two predictable reactions whenever we mentioned we were writing a book on congressional ethics. "Oxymoron," was the most frequent reaction to the term "congressional ethics." The runner-up was, "it must be a short book." Evidently, folks still don't think too highly of Congress, although judging from the regularity with which they vote for incumbents, they continue to harbor great affection for the individual lawmakers who represent them. Americans resist change, even as they grow more cynical about politics.

The truth will take a long time to catch up with reality: that lawmakers are more honest and more ethical today than ever before. That doesn't mean that they are inherently better people or that "faith-based" politics has raised them to a new level of virtue. The fact is that our current environment has become more transparent, more partisan, and more focused on ethics. This new era of "Glass Houses" has made politicians more sensitive to ethical lapses; with so much out in the open, what they fear most of all is a picture of themselves on the front page of the morning newspapers. Any doubters can easily find a list of what lawmakers can and cannot do in the thick rule books governing ethical behavior published by the House and the Senate. Members of Congress often request advance approval from the ethics committees when they are uncertain.

Many thanks go to all the people who helped us understand the complex field of congressional ethics and who so generously shared their insights, knowledge, time, and experience. The book focuses on data compiled from a variety of primary and secondary sources, including interviews with former and current members of Congress, scholars, journalists, lawyers, and lobbyists. All direct quotes in the text that are not cited in the endnotes are drawn from these interviews and include Nan Aron, Richard Baker, Robert Bennett, Tony Blankley, Stanley Brand, Howard Berman, Rex Brown, Pat Choate, Byron Dorgan, Nadia Fam, Barney Frank, Stuart Gilman, Newt Gingrich, Howell Heflin, Marcy Kaptur, Carl Levin, Chuck Lewis, Andrew Maguire, Mark Mansfield, Howard Metzenbaum, David McIntosh, Bob Packwood, Robert Pear, Alan Platt, John Rohr, Gary Ruskin, Michael Seyfert, Louise Slaughter, Jacob Stein, Robert Torricelli, Leroy Towns, Tim Weiner, and Jim Wright.

Susan's professional home at the School of Public Policy at George Mason University has been very supportive in a number of ways. Her students in a course in Ethics and Public Policy have critiqued drafts of selected chapters, with a sharp eye to readability and content; several of the papers from these classes have found their way into the text. A grant from the Provost's office paid for research assistance, as did another grant from the School of Public Policy. Many thanks to Dean Kingsley Haynes, Provost Peter Stearns, Senior Associate Dean James Finkelstein, and Vice Provost Christopher Hill for making these resources possible.

At George Mason University, Susan's research assistant, Kenneth Cox, did a superb job tracking down leads, checking facts, and reading successive drafts of the manuscript. He became a whiz at computer research, employing the same skills and indefatigability that made him such a successful captain of a nuclear submarine in his earlier career in the U.S. Navy: diligence, integrity, and patience. Jennifer Arnold, administrative assistant at the School of Public Policy, worked hard and cheerfully at the onerous task of meeting deadlines.

Many of our friends, colleagues, and relatives read the manuscript in a short time and were especially helpful in offering their criticisms. They are Nan Aron, Linda Cashdan, Pat Choate, Adam Clymer, Robert Dallek, Al Eisele, Martha Kessler, Connie L. McNeely, Robert Pear, James P. Pfiffner, Richard Reeves, John Rohr, Donna Shalala, Paul Simon, Charles Tolchin, and Karen Tolchin Vance.

We are also grateful to our editor, Leo Wiegman, for his vision of the book, close attention to detail, and incisive editing. Melissa R. Root, who copyedited the book, also did a splendid job and provided us with valuable editorial suggestions.

Many thanks, too, to our agent, John Wright, for his continued dedication, persistence in getting the best out of us, and steadfast good humor.

This book is dedicated to Dr. Mila Chernick, a great physician and close family friend.

Susan J. Tolchin
Martin Tolchin

Acronyms

ACLU (American Civil Liberties Union)
CIA (Central Intelligence Agency)
CNN (Cable News Network)
FBI (Federal Bureau of Investigation)
FCC (Federal Communications Commission)
FDR (Franklin Delano Roosevelt)
GAO (General Accounting Office)
GOPAC
HHS (Health and Human Services)
HMO (health maintenance organization)
IOB (Intelligence Oversight Board)
IRS (Internal Revenue Service)
LBJ (Lyndon B. Johnson)
NARAL (National Abortion Rights Action League)
NASA (National Aeronautics and Space Administration)
NEA (National Education Association)
NOW (National Organization for Women)
NSA (National Security Agency)
PAC (political action committee)
SEC (Securities and Exchange Commission)
SID (Status-Income Disequilibrium)
YMCA (Young Men's Christian Association)

1

The Ethics Wars

*"The system was always political.
It was always a political weapon."*
—Stan Brand, former counsel to the chief
clerk of the House of Representatives

THE GINGRICH ERA

He was an unlikely revolutionary, a former history professor, often un-
kempt, with an unruly shock of white hair across his forehead. A dedicated
conservative, intense and articulate, he sought the limelight by hurling
charges at his foes. In a losing campaign for Congress in 1974, he stood
outside a Georgia prison and, borrowing from Mark Twain, characterized
members of Congress as a bunch of "criminals."[1]

Elected to Congress on his third try in 1978, Newt Gingrich brought
his own special spirit of combativeness to Washington. He used all available
means, especially the ethics process, to lead what would become known as
the Republican Revolution of 1994. But Gingrich's ethics crusade involved more than just personalities or ambition; it included a policy thrust
as well. His vision was key to his scorched earth strategy that wrested control of the chamber from the Democrats and installed a conservative
agenda, known as the "Contract with America," which made Congress
subject to the same laws it enacted for the rest of the country. Gingrich
climbed to the pinnacle of power as the first Republican Speaker in forty
years. In the course of his ascent, Gingrich unleashed forces that toppled a
Democratic Speaker, destroyed several careers, and ultimately claimed him
as a victim.

"Ethics was not political until Gingrich," reflected Rep. Barney Frank, a
brilliant, cantankerous ultraliberal Massachusetts Democrat who was himself
a victim of Gingrich's vendettas. "He invented the politics of venom. Newt

saw that Republicans could only take power by demonizing Democrats. . . . The Democrats responded in kind. Gingrich told Republicans to treat Democrats as 'corrupt.'"

In fact, the ethics process always had political overtones, but Gingrich took it to new heights. The ensuing frenzy of charges and countercharges helped explain why the public's opinion of Congress plummeted at the turn of the new century. It was Congress itself that repeatedly diverted attention from substantive issues to focus on the foibles and follies of its own members, sometimes exacting draconian penalties that seemed far in excess of what they deserved. On the other hand, few would disagree that members of Congress should be held to the highest ethical standards, lest their lapses corrupt the legislative process and the very fabric of our democracy.

To Gingrich, the ethics process was a long-neglected political weapon, as well as a legitimate one. Gingrich was appalled by the extent to which collegiality led lawmakers to ignore flagrantly unethical conduct. "It always fascinated me that when I got there, the basic attitude was, 'Unless it was a public relations nightmare, you didn't deal with it,'" Gingrich recalled in a recent interview. Although Congress has the sole authority to discipline its own members, that power had been used so sparingly that some critics, including Gingrich, felt that there were virtually no limits on a lawmaker's behavior.

What bothered Gingrich initially was the long-time practice of allowing convicted felons to enjoy the full privileges of the House while their cases were on appeal. Gingrich immediately targeted Rep. Charles Diggs (D-Mich.), a dour Detroit undertaker who was convicted in 1978 on twenty-nine felony counts involving the diversion of congressional employees' salaries to his personal use. "I said if he voted," recalled Gingrich, "I would move to expel him. Now, members can't vote after their convictions while their appeals are pending."

Despite Gingrich's efforts, which included leading a Republican motion to expel Diggs, House members dropped their investigation following Diggs's admission of guilt and applied the lesser sanction of censure. Even a censure vote would never have occurred without Gingrich's initiative because Democrats as well as Republicans typically preferred to cover up their colleagues' problems until forced to act. Diggs was the first representative censured since 1921.

Several years later, in 1982, Congress and Gingrich confronted a massive scandal involving congressional pages that finally became impossible to ignore. Two lawmakers—Rep. Dan Crane, a flamboyant Illinois Republican, and Rep. Gerry E. Studds, a studious Massachusetts Democrat—were accused of having sexual relations with teenaged pages. Crane was charged with having an affair with a young woman and Studds with a young man. Democrats said that Gingrich attacked Crane as well as Studds in an effort to appear evenhanded. Crane was defeated for reelection, while Studds was reelected seven times from his district in eastern Massachusetts until he voluntarily retired in 1996. "Ethics problems hurt Republicans at the ballot box far more than they hurt Democrats," Gingrich reflected. "Republicans are perceived as having higher moral standards, as being more upright. With Democrats, voters don't care as long as they [their representatives] are effective."

Gingrich accelerated his campaign to invigorate the congressional ethics process. After Diggs, he attacked Rep. Fernand St Germain, a high-living Rhode Island Democrat and chairman of the House Banking Committee. St Germain was found to have repeatedly violated disclosure provisions of both the House Code and the Ethics in Government Act. But the Ethics Committee concluded that the "identified improprieties do not rise to a level warranting further action by this committee." Gingrich was appalled but not surprised that St Germain received only a mild slap on the wrist from the Democratic-controlled House in 1987.

In his boldest move, Gingrich leveled charges in 1987 against the Speaker of the House, Jim Wright, a Texas Democrat. The tall, red-headed Wright, a decorated combat pilot in World War II, began his career in politics as an unabashed liberal. As mayor of Weatherford, Texas, he had hired Craig Raupe, who lost his teaching job at the University of Texas because he had run afoul of a Red-hunting committee of the state legislature. Wright installed Raupe as director of recreational programs, and Raupe promptly desegregated the town's swimming pools. Elected to the state legislature, Wright was considered that body's most liberal member. When he came to Congress in 1955, Wright maintained his liberal credentials and installed Raupe as his chief of staff. At the same time, however, Wright also wooed the conservative oil, gas, and banking interests that were so powerful in his state.

Wright needed money and devised a scheme that caught Gingrich's attention. In strong headline-grabbing language, Gingrich attacked Wright for privately publishing a book of speeches and memoirs, *Reflections of a Public Man*, that was purchased in bulk by several of Wright's supporters.[2] Since the book's sales netted Wright a sum of approximately $71,000, Wright was charged with using the book to circumvent House restrictions on outside income.

A master of vitriolic rhetoric, Gingrich called Wright a "crook" and the "worst Speaker of the twentieth century." Gingrich went on to accuse Wright of sixty-nine ethics violations, including improperly taking gifts from a real estate developer.[3] Gingrich also charged that Wright had lobbied U.S. and Egyptian officials on behalf of the Neptune Oil Company shortly after the company had given Wright the chance to invest in a lucrative gas well. Wright countered that he was merely lobbying on behalf of a constituent, an argument that has been used in many other ethics cases. Wright was also accused of using the book as a campaign fund-raising tool, as well as a vehicle for funneling corporate money into his own pocket.

As the furor mounted, embarrassed Democratic elders finally persuaded Wright to resign. In a long and emotional speech before Congress, Wright predicted that Gingrich would eventually be consumed by his own "mindless cannibalism." In 1998, Gingrich unintentionally closed the loop when he notified Republican leaders of his own resignation: he declared he was not willing to "preside over people who were mindless cannibals."

Gingrich asserted that "Wright had clearly worked explicitly to violate the rules," said he pressed charges against Speaker Wright because "no Democrat was likely to bring those charges." In retrospect, Gingrich admitted Wright's punishment may have been excessive, but he noted that, "Members of his [Wright's] own caucus told him he had to leave. He had caved on a pay raise, and his members were really angry at him."

Wright's resignation emboldened his partisan attackers. "I retired in the mistaken belief that by resigning, I would so shock and shame everybody they would abandon the politics of disparagement," Wright recalled. "I was wrong."

"The poisoning of the well of civil discourse lingers on," he continued. "There's arsenic in the water, even today."

Wright said it cost him $500,000 in legal fees to defend himself against Gingrich's charges. "That nearly busted me," he said, noting that "people not wealthy can't afford a defense."

Ethics occupied a critical role in Gingrich's ambitious plans for himself and for his fellow Republicans. He used the ethics process frequently—some would say relentlessly—to transform it from a sleepy, humdrum set of procedures into a real *force de frappe* feared by lawmakers in both the House and the Senate. The pursuit of ethics also speeded Gingrich's rise from an obscure backbencher to Speaker, helped the Republicans seize Congress from the Democrats for the first time in forty years, and made the new Speaker a national hero and an object of constant media attention. At the time of his stunning victory in 1994, he became one of the most renowned stars of national politics, accompanied everywhere by batteries of cameras and crowds of admirers. His face beamed out from the cover of *Time* magazine, and even the most trivial of his activities received extensive news coverage.

But the fabled Gingrich was not immune from the forces that he had unleashed. He reinvigorated the ethics process only to find it used against him. As he knew all too well, the ascension to power did not immunize him against partisan attack; on the contrary, it made him more vulnerable. Swollen by his new power, his insensitivity made him an easy target.

The first charges against Gingrich involved a book advance of $4.5 million that he had accepted from a publishing house owned by Rupert Murdoch immediately after becoming Speaker. The ethical problem was obvious to everyone but Gingrich. An international media mogul who owned a chain of newspapers and television stations, Murdoch stood to gain substantially from his relationship with the Speaker. Only after confronting a torrent of negative publicity did Gingrich give up the advance and agree to accept earned royalties instead. In fact, the book proved to be a bestseller although it earned far less than $4.5 million in royalties.

Gingrich contends that the two cases are not comparable even though Wright's $71,000 earnings paled in comparison to Gingrich's $4.5 million advance. Unlike Wright, Gingrich argued, "My books always had regular publishers and were sold in regular bookstores." Gingrich, now a private citizen, compared the furor that greeted his $4.5 million advance with what he regarded as "the silence with which lawmakers and the media have accepted Hillary Clinton's $8 million book advance," negotiated on the eve of her being sworn in as the junior senator from New York in January 2001. "No honest person thinks it is not a double standard," Gingrich declared. In retrospect, Gingrich's accusation against the media's treatment of Senator Clinton did not ring quite true: Persistent criticism of her book advance appeared for at least a month after it was made public; she also withstood—some say ignored—attacks from enemies and supporters alike for the "gift registry" that brought her thousands of dollars worth of china and silverware before January 3, 2001, when Senate ethics rules would take effect.

As payback for his attacks on Wright and other Democrats, Democratic leaders launched a fusillade of charges against Speaker Gingrich. In April 1989, Rep. Bill Alexander of Arkansas, the deputy Democratic whip, filed a 490-count complaint against the Speaker. "The only thing they found I did that was wrong was failure to disclose that I co-signed a loan for my daughter," Gingrich claimed. "My attorney had written a letter that was not technically correct, and I overlooked the mistakes."

More devastating were the more than five hundred charges involving GOPAC, a political action committee run by Gingrich to raise money for Republican candidates. Gingrich was accused of diverting funds from GOPAC to finance a course he taught at two small Georgia colleges, Kennesaw State College and Reinhardt College, on the subject of "Renewing American Civilization." The course was primarily financed by GOPAC via the tax-exempt Progress and Freedom Foundation. Democrats called it a tax-scam. The charges were leveled for the most part by House Democratic Whip David Bonior of Michigan. Other charges were also brought by Democrats: Rep. John Lewis, from Georgia, accused Gingrich of engaging in a "massive tax-fraud scheme"; George Miller, of California, said Gingrich's actions were designed to "defraud the tax laws of the country"; and Colorado Rep. Pat Schroeder said, "We might as well rip up all the laws, rip up all the rule books, if the guy at the head can thumb his nose at them."[4] GOPAC had served Gingrich well: as his personal political action committee; as a fund-raising vehicle; and as a wellspring for the body of ideas that became the "Contract with America." But Gingrich was not protected from the newly invigorated ethics process. Even his fellow Republicans, unable to protect him from charges of ethics violations, voted decisively against him. After a bruising, partisan battle on January 21, 1997, the House of Representatives voted 395–28 to reprimand Speaker Gingrich.

The Speaker pleaded guilty, acknowledged that he had failed to seek detailed advice from a tax lawyer before proceeding with the course, and also admitted that he had provided "inaccurate, incomplete, and unreliable" information to Ethics Committee investigators. In return, the House not only reprimanded Gingrich, in January 1997, it levied an unprecedented and humiliating $300,000 fine against him that was agreed upon by leaders of both parties. "I had filed information that was wrong," Gingrich recalled, "but it was not intentional." He dismissed the charges against him as "99 percent partisan."

Gingrich saw nothing wrong with borrowing some of the money to pay the penalty from former presidential candidate and Senate Majority Leader Bob Dole, who had just left the Senate in 1996 to become a lawyer-lobbyist with Verner Liipfert Bernhard McPherson and Hand, a Washington, D.C., law firm.

Gingrich may have touched a public chord with his revival of ethics as a viable, politically potent issue. But at the same time, he was out of sync with public opinion when it came to his own activities. Roper polls recorded that 48 to 51 percent of the public considered his loan from Dole "inappropriate."[5] But Gingrich's reluctance to pay the fine also indicated that he must have regarded the penalty as inappropriate. Nevertheless, he submitted his final payment a year later.

The congressional charges touched off a three-year Internal Revenue Service investigation that concluded that Gingrich had acted within the law. There was no tax fraud, said the IRS. James Cole, the Ethics Committee's outside counsel, reached the same conclusion. But he warned the committee not to be fooled by the content of the classes, which included lectures on the uniqueness and diversity of the United States and praised leaders including Franklin Roosevelt, Harry Truman, and Ronald Reagan. "There was an effort to have the material appear to be nonpartisan on its face," Cole told the committee, "yet serve as a partisan political message for the purpose of building the Republican party." The course was basically a way to have Gingrich spread his political views, Cole said. "The idea to develop the message and disseminate it for partisan political use came first," Cole said. "The use of the 501C(3) [the Progress and Freedom Foundation]) came second as a source of funding."[6]

The IRS found that people affiliated with GOPAC "were involved in the development of the course content, fund-raising, and other logistics." But the agency noted that Gingrich took care to keep GOPAC separate from the course by "the prompt establishment of the Progress and Freedom Foundation as a broadly funded, fully separate entity from GOPAC."

In view of his vindication by the IRS, the question is why Gingrich pleaded guilty and agreed to pay the $300,000 fine. "To grasp the answer, one has only to remember the white-hot environment of the months following the Republican takeover of Congress," wrote Byron York, describing the public furor surrounding questions of ethics in public life.[7]

Tony Blankley, Gingrich's press secretary and key adviser, recalled that, "I was struck by the ability of an allegation that was untrue and venomous to stick. Why do some things connect, and others don't? Who are the judges who determine whether behavior is scandalous?"

In a curious twist of fate, GOPAC became the Speaker's undoing as quickly as it had become his benefactor. By the mid–1990s, political action committees (PACs) were a well-established institution on the national landscape, used and exploited by ambitious politicians from both parties. Gingrich joined the bandwagon and argued he was only doing what every other politician did to achieve political success: taking advantage of new interpretations of election laws that allowed for the development of PACs. But the issue soon arose, as it did with every other ethics case before and after the Gingrich era—such as Packwood, Keating, and Abscam—as to what constituted legitimate political activity and what raised questions of ethical misconduct. No answers were readily forthcoming, to the consternation of politicians caught in the middle. "Traditionally," wrote John Rohr, one of the nation's most learned ethics scholars, "the study of ethics has focused on two questions—doing good and avoiding evil. Just what is meant by 'good and evil' is, of course, the very stuff of the history of ethics."[8]

Quarrels over the meaning of elections laws affected both political parties with no resolution in sight. At the same time Gingrich was battling the vagaries of election laws, Vice President Al Gore was fending off Republican charges that he had accepted illegal campaign contributions from Buddhist monks and nuns at a fund-raiser in a California monastery. He was also accused of making telephone calls to contributors from the White House instead of using a telephone that was not located on government property. Some of these battles looked just plain silly and, if carried out to the letter, were considered a colossal "waste of time" for busy public servants, according to Sen. Carl Levin (D-Mich.). Levin found it hard to discern the rationale for requiring members of Congress to "leave their Capitol offices just to make fund-raising calls. It takes an hour out of their lives, instead of five minutes."

Was GOPAC a conduit for personal use or a genuine service to constituents? And if it were political, who were the beneficiaries? All roads led back to Gingrich, whom his accusers had charged had personally benefited from GOPAC far more than had the party, the voters, or the district.

Ethical difficulties seemed to stalk Gingrich. As astute as he was politically, he failed to recognize that the sea change that he had helped to bring about in congressional ethics had taken hold with the American public. Many attributed his lapse to just plain bad judgment, the arrogance that invariably accompanies power; others pointed to the heightened scrutiny that comes with excessive media attention.

To the consternation of many of his fellow Republicans, Gingrich's reign was short-lived. He suddenly resigned from the Speakership and gave up his congressional seat in 1998, after only four years as Speaker. But in that relatively short time, he had altered the political landscape of Congress and implemented far-reaching changes, such as applying equal employment laws to Congress, that had eluded his Democratic predecessors.

He was a hero to many, albeit a fallen hero. At the same time he was revolutionizing Congress, Gingrich was fighting ethics charges at every turn. Shortly after he resigned, the real reason for his departure emerged—yet another ethics issue, this one involving sex. He divorced his second wife,

Marianne Gingrich, and married a congressional aide, Callista Bisek, who had been his mistress. His estranged wife sued the Speaker for divorce, naming Bisek as the cause of the split. Critics noted the irony of Gingrich's faithful advocacy of the family values plank of the Republican agenda at the same time he was violating his marriage vows. The incident also occurred during the heat of the Clinton impeachment battle, and Gingrich may have feared that his infidelity would be revealed. Republicans had also lost seats in the 1998 election.

PARTISAN POLITICS

The seriousness of an ethics breach is usually determined by the public's reaction to the charges. Sometimes a lawmaker's errant behavior will prompt his or her peers, especially those from the opposite party, to generate a public relations blitz and start a drumbeat for a full inquiry. At other times, the public relations nightmare will explode on its own and prompt an ethics investigation. Whether a member has brought discredit to Congress often depends not on any inherent wrong involving the member, but on whether the "sin" has reached the public, and only then, on the public's reaction.

Intense adverse publicity, even for practices long tolerated, nearly always fuels voter outrage, which often means political death to the offender. Lawmakers will even turn their backs on Speakers as powerful as Wright and Gingrich if their actions attract publicity sufficiently negative to call attention to their ethical lapses. And the public will also turn its back on legislators who violate current norms, which are in a constant state of change. Dueling was acceptable in the early nineteenth century, whereas today's combatants fortunately favor verbal weapons.

Congressional ethics before the Gingrich era often involved a system of quiet collusion—some called it "civility"—that both parties practiced in the effort to conceal their own members' mistakes. "The system was always political," recalled Stan Brand, former chief counsel to the Democratic majority of the House of Representatives and a critic of Gingrich's use of ethics as a partisan tool. "It was always a political weapon."

What changed all that was the advent of Republican rule in 1994, and especially the advent of Newt Gingrich as Speaker. "Until Wright," added Brand, "ethics was not an offensive weapon. Gingrich changed all that. It is not for the better. In the pre-1994 period, the Ethics Committees reported most actions on a bipartisan basis. The vote to condemn lawmakers involved in Abscam, a scandal involving House members as well as one senator, was bipartisan. They [the committee members] were mostly responsive to newspaper exposés, and to avoid embarrassment to the institution."

Brand believes that the process has been trivialized in the 1990s. "There is a Rube Goldberg assortment of rules that trap people unwittingly," he said. "You can't take them [members of Congress] to lunch at the Palm [a pricey restaurant in downtown Washington], but you can take them on a fact-finding trip to Beri-Beri. I'd rather have him [the lawmaker] go to the Palm for lunch than spend four days in Florida. He is less likely to be corrupted by a lunch at the Palm."

Brand cited the vagueness of ethics rules. "I could make a case against any one of you," Brand cautioned Democratic members of the House. "You set the tripwire." Everyone has done something in the course of daily life that could be construed as a breach of ethics; in the Gingrich era and its aftermath, no one was ever safe again. Brand's observation recalls the opening lecture in many criminal law classes, when professors try to shock their students with the observation that everyone occupying a seat in class has committed a felony according to the law in at least one of the nation's fifty states. Adultery and homosexuality remain illegal in some states, for example, although the laws against them are rarely enforced.

But Gingrich hardly invented partisanship. The "Keating Five," senators accused of intervening with government regulators, should have been the "Keating Three," according to almost everyone—even many Democrats—involved in the scandal. Sen. John McCain (R-Ariz.) was brought to the ethics dock solely because Democratic leaders wanted at least one Republican to balance the four accused Democrats, and Sen. John Glenn (D-Ohio) was added because the Republicans were angry at the unwarranted inclusion of McCain.

RECENT BATTLES

Many hoped that Abscam, the "House bank," and the "Keating Five" scandals would have served as permanent deterrents to lawmakers still susceptible to temptation. Not so. The ethics wars continue to plague Congress to this day, with many battles bearing an uncanny resemblance to the past: All of them revolve around sex, money, conflicts-of-interest, and deep philosophical divisions over the issue of "constituent service." Three examples:

Representative Jay Kim, a Korean-American Republican from California, attended House sessions tethered by an electronic ankle bracelet hidden beneath the cuff of his trousers. As he raced to his office from the Capitol, Phil Jones of CBS-TV trotted alongside and asked him to reveal the device to millions of viewers—a suggestion Kim politely declined. The reason for this indignity? A plea agreement that Kim had just entered into with the Justice Department. In exchange for his guilty plea of having accepted more than $230,000 in illegal campaign contributions, primarily from Korean multinationals, Kim received a sentence of two months' home detention during which he would be hooked to an escape-proof electronic monitoring device.

California Republicans found themselves in an embarrassing position: What to do about the fact that the plea agreement allowed Kim to run for reelection? To prevent his victory, fellow Republican members of Congress jumped in to expand their own investigation to encompass additional violations, including excessive earnings, false statements, and improprieties in financial disclosure statements. Kim eventually lost the Republican primary to Gary G. Miller, who went on to win the contested seat.

Kim's defense embraced the "constituent service" argument, one that would be echoed by almost every member of Congress charged with ethical problems: Foreign multinationals had factories in his district, and he was representing them in Congress as he would any business. That relationship included hefty campaign contributions.

In another example, Rep. Earl F. Hilliard, an Alabama Democrat, was charged with using campaign funds to pay rent on space in his business office and with making improper payments and loans to other businesses in which he had a financial interest. He was later reprimanded by the Ethics Committee.[9]

Finally, Rep. Enid Waldholtz also found herself in trouble over campaign contributions but luckily escaped prosecution although she also lost her congressional seat. The newly elected Republican from Utah, who later reverted to her family name, Enid Greene, initially defeated her opponent, a Democratic incumbent, thanks to a large infusion of illegal funds from her millionaire father. Defeated in a later Republican primary after the disclosure of these funds, she didn't go to prison. Not as fortunate was her ex-husband, campaign manager, and chief-of-staff Joe Waldholtz, who was sentenced to thirty-seven months in federal prison for mishandling campaign contributions.

CHANGING MORES

Lawmakers today are confused. Polls reveal increased public anger at Congress, anger that spikes with each scandal. Even though the scandals involve only a small number of their colleagues, members of Congress say they don't need polls to confirm what they experience every time they go home: widespread wrath at ethical and moral lapses. But they object vigorously to being tarred by the same brush as their scandal-ridden colleagues, especially when they regard themselves as innocent.

Ironically, at the same time public scrutiny over the personal lives and finances of lawmakers has accelerated, public opinion of Congress continues to decline. In 1966 a Harris survey revealed 42 percent of the public expressing "a great deal of confidence in Congress," whereas by 1980 the figure had dropped significantly to 18 percent, and had plummeted even further by 2000.[10]

No tycoon, TV pundit, professor, investigative reporter, or book editor is forced to reveal as much about his or her personal assets or private life as are members of Congress. Increased financial disclosure, intended to improve the public perception of Congress, only made the voters more critical. No ethical Eden emerged from remedies that revealed government secrets to the public; quite the contrary, public accountability on moral issues virtually worked in reverse, and like the emperor's new clothes, government shorn of vestments produced more calls for reform, not less.

As it happened, Watergate and a host of other scandals were followed by the enactment of a strengthened Freedom of Information Act; Ethics in government legislation for the executive branch; and sunshine laws, which required independent regulatory agencies to open up their meetings to the public. Regulations quickly followed in the wake of those ground-breaking laws that eliminated many loopholes and forced agencies to operate more publicly than ever before. During the same period, a more vigorous media pursued government scandals armed with an array of sunshine laws that supported their right to know. Clearly, "disclosure" and "transparency" weren't all they were cracked up to be; judging from the polls, the public didn't really want to know as much as these laws revealed about the seamier details of political life.

In the case of Congress, one striking and totally unanticipated consequence was that the scandals, such as Keating, Abscam, and Koreagate, created the overwhelming impression among the public that members of Congress were more corrupt than the rest of society and more corrupt than ever before. Add to that the intense partisanship and absence of trust that has infected the Ethics Committees, and it is no wonder public confidence in Congress continues to decline precipitously. An interesting sidelight of this phenomenon is that other self-governing groups also find themselves held in relatively low regard by the public, such as the media, academe, and the legal profession.

Where will it end? Congressional leaders wonder if they are living in witch-hunting Salem or sinful Gomorrah. Issues like foreign contributions to political campaigns, which voters and the media ignored a decade ago, could send members to jail today. Members never know what the *issue du jour* will be, what the voters will tolerate, and whether the voters will ever know the difference between what is trivial and what is important to the future of the nation. And given the inequity of enforcement, they also have no idea who will be forced to face the embarrassment of ethics charges and who will remain free to conduct business as usual.

DISCRETIONARY JUSTICE
AND THE ETHICS COMMITTEES

Inconsistencies abound in congressional ethics, especially compared with the stricter rules affecting the executive branch. The chairman[11] of the House Armed Services Committee, wrote ethics theorist Andrew Stark, can take an all-expenses-paid trip from a foreign policy association funded by anyone and not have it "considered private gain from public office. When the secretary of defense does the same thing, it is."[12] Another example of inconsistency cited by Brand involved Rep. Dan Daniel (R-Va.) "who took 240 trips on a corporate plane. Even though he was entitled to the funds to pay his way home, he was attacked. After a press inquiry he made full disclosure, reimbursed the company, and there was never a criminal case [lodged] against him. Another guy would have had the book thrown at him." Congress deliberately left many of its rules vague for purposes of maximizing flexibility, but public reaction to recent incidents may force lawmakers to change or refine their ethics procedures.

Unlike judges and presidents, who can be removed from office after being impeached by the House and convicted by the Senate, the Constitution gives both the House and the Senate ultimate responsibility for disciplining their own members. Thus, the Senate can expel a member without the prerequisite of a House impeachment, and the House can expel a member without requiring a Senate conviction. But the ultimate punishment of expulsion has been used sparingly. In all of its history, the Senate has expelled only fifteen members, all for disloyalty to the United States, and all but one for supporting the South during the Civil War. The House has expelled four members, three for disloyalty and one for corruption.[13] Lesser punishments are censure, rebuke, and reprimand, although these sanctions, along with expulsion, have been used rarely and very reluctantly throughout the nation's history.[14]

Today, the House and Senate Ethics Committees have been given the task of evaluating the misconduct of their colleagues. The Ethics Committees are evenly balanced between Democrats and Republicans so that any action requires a bipartisan consensus. Typically, only intense public pressure can spur these committees into action, and only after a lawmaker has publicly embarrassed the institution.

The Ethics Committees nevertheless saw an explosion of cases in the 1980s and 1990s. These included the first case in more than a hundred years in which a House member, Rep. Michael J. "Ozzie" Myers (D-Pa.) was expelled. During the same period, three senators were formally disciplined for misconduct involving personal or campaign funds, and six House members were censured or reprimanded for sexual or financial offenses. Many others were admonished by the Ethics Committees, defeated for reelection, or escaped punishment by resigning—such as Speakers Gingrich and Wright.

Today, lawmakers also grapple with the question of what merits expulsion, censure, reprimand, or a private chat in the corridor, but the customs have changed considerably, along with the kinds of issues that generate public ire. Although today no one would consider physical violence—at least not openly—an acceptable way of settling differences, public outrage is still the key: Ethics Committees in both Houses vastly prefer to settle scandals quietly and enter the fray only when forced by the media and by public anger to intercede.

The inconsistency that lurks around ethics issues discomfits many legislators, who wonder when and if they will be next victim. Rep. Kim took a huge amount of foreign money, which his colleagues from both parties have pocketed with impunity for years without public disclosure or disapproval. In 1998, President Clinton and the Democratic National Committee were given the chance to return hundreds of thousands of dollars to foreign donors without sporting electronic ankle bracelets. So far, thanks to public indifference and a cooperative Justice Department, they emerged with little more than public opprobrium over the issue—and very little of that.

Inconsistency is all too often the rule rather than the exception, leading observers to use the term "revolving ethics" to describe the vagaries of the process. In 1976, the House shouted down an attempt to expel Andrew J. Hinshaw, a California Republican who had been convicted of accepting a bribe, although scarcely four years later it voted unanimously to expel Rep. "Ozzie" Myers, who had been caught taking bribes in the Abscam investigation. Both men were convicted of the same crime, bribery, but the House treated them very differently.[15]

More often than not, however, the Ethics Committees are sought out for advisory opinions by lawmakers contemplating activities that could put them at risk of violating congressional rules. But some lawmakers push the envelope and find themselves face to face with the Ethics Committees. Some, envious of their wealthy friends, seek to translate their power into riches.

Some lawmakers are betrayed by their libidos. Others take short-cuts to finance their campaigns or to reward campaign contributors. Older lawmakers like former Rep. Dan Rostenkowski (D-Ill.), chairman of the powerful Ways and Means Committee, winked at the new ethics rules only to discover that the Ethics Committee, under intense public pressure, did not wink back. In Rostenkowski's case, the Ethics Committee bowed to the U.S. Attorney's office, and the lawmaker found himself serving a prison sentence. Sometimes a lawmaker will flout congressional rules in order to serve what he or she considers a higher purpose. Rep. (now Senator) Robert Torricelli (D-N.J.) divulged classified intelligence information to call attention to the CIA's involvement in two murders in Guatemala.

Many believe that the proliferation of ethics cases bespeaks a more corrupt national legislature. On the contrary, it is due, instead, to more intense scrutiny by the media, increased financial disclosure by members of Congress, and increased restrictions on their activities. It is also due to the ever-changing congressional culture, with which some veteran lawmakers find it hard to keep up. Whatever their political convictions, today's lawmakers are more honest, better educated, less bigoted, and more socially conscious than their predecessors. But power does indeed corrupt, and the intense public scrutiny, financial restrictions, and increased temptations inevitably bring some into the maws of the congressional ethics process.

THE FUTURE OF ETHICS

Partisan politics still prevails as the most important criterion for predicting the future of ethics cases, despite the efforts of congressional leaders to portray ethics as quasi-judicial. Too many coincidences mar that image: ethics investigations that emerge just before elections; leaks that can be traced to political enemies, even within the same party; and publicity that determines the contours of an issue.

Today, you not only have to do good, you have to be good, say many political leaders. You can reform the system, you can write tighter ethics laws, but there will always be unanticipated consequences that may make the situation worse. The only consistent theme is partisanship, and with both parties in power, the competition in the "gotcha" game has become excruciatingly intense.

Lawmakers are often surprised by what disturbs people and what does not. And what disturbs voters drives the investigations and sparks the controversies. Ethics charges, for example, can often result in a public turn-off from all forms of politics, even when sex is involved—a lesson that was not lost on Congress during the impeachment of President Clinton. Everyone seemed to be fascinated by President Clinton's sex life, as evidenced by the rise in television ratings and newspaper readership during the Monica Lewinsky episode. But public opinion polls revealed more anger at the media for revealing the bad tidings, and at Congress for impeaching Clinton, than at the President's behavior. Even though the public's prurient interest in the sex lives of politicians remains insatiable, the target of their fury continues to startle the experts.

There is still no question that an ethics investigation, like an SEC inquiry into a stock, can have an enormous impact on the political career of a lawmaker, and those who have suffered from it bear the stigma forever. "I wish I could go back and undo it," Rep. Frank told the House Judiciary Committee after his reprimand in 1990 for improperly using his office to help a male prostitute. "It was no triviality."[16] Since the Gingrich era, ethics has suddenly become everyone's business and the subject of great fear ever since the issue has reached the public consciousness. The fact is that an ethics charge remains the most unpleasant highlight of a targeted lawmaker's career, no matter what record he or she has amassed before the scandal hit the front pages of the newspaper. The public will remember the sexual harassment charges against Sen. Bob Packwood long after they forget his role in reforming the tax code.

In the last analysis, morality reflects both the temper of the times and the voting patterns of the last election. A few short years before its widespread tolerance of President Clinton's sexual lapses, the public threw the book at Senator Packwood for breaches that had mostly occurred twenty years earlier. Today, conflicts of interest involving campaign finance clearly bother the public, although voters all too often fail to differentiate between trivial issues and those more endemic to the system. Like generals fighting the battles of the past, ethics wars are reactive.

Take congressional junkets. For years, newspapers have publicized junkets and how lawmakers take advantage of the privilege of foreign travel by taking along their wives, staffs, and occasionally their paramours, with all expenses paid by the taxpayers. The Paris Air Show remains a popular excursion with members of the House Armed Services Committee, even though annual news stories never fail to arouse public ire over these trips. But for every lawmaker caught sipping chardonnay on the Champs Elysée, there are dozens trekking through drought-stricken regions of Africa or risking their lives in trouble spots elsewhere.

Similarly confusing are the growing accusations of conflicts of interest, an issue that will surely dominate congressional ethics for years to come. Sen. William Frist (R-Tenn.) is a former heart and lung transplant surgeon whose family founded one of the nation's largest for-profit hospital chains, the Hospital Corporation of America. Many of his critics believe that his family ties should preclude him from voting on managed care reform or from bringing the first managed-care bill to the Senate floor, and they brought their concerns to the Senate Ethics Committee. Ruling in his favor, the committee said he did not have to recuse himself from votes on issues of health care. Rep. Harold Ford (D-Tenn.) disagreed and barnstormed the state in 1999, charging Frist with "protecting his family's company at the expense of his constituents."[17]

Frist's experience with the Ethics Committee could either be considered a heavily partisan issue, because his accuser is a Democrat and he is a Republican, or a serious question of legislative ethics. Frist defended his actions. He put his stock in a blind trust before the Senate considered managed care legislation, he argued, and made it a practice of not discussing pending legislation with his family. For-profit hospitals did not particularly benefit from the legislation that Frist pushed. His record, he said, spoke for itself and included ten thousand medical procedures and missionary work in Africa. His defenders argued that he was an ideal citizen legislator, a specialist in a complex field, and that the Senate should take full advantage of his expertise.

In the future, Congress will have to struggle with the vagaries of political money because that is so often the root of ethical troubles. Soft money, hard money, and full disclosure: All involve members' increasing involvement in fund-raising, which occupied more of the public agenda in the 1980s and 1990s than ever before. So far, Congress has failed to do very much to support any of the reform efforts that have surfaced in recent years, preferring instead to stick with the Founding Fathers' constitutional proviso guaranteeing the institution the right to govern itself.

Perceptions of corruption, however, are all too often rooted in money, as Jim Wright and Newt Gingrich showed, and until Congress deals with that problem with real solutions, efforts like the rule against accepting a lunch costing more than $50 will be as ineffective as they seem. Too bad the public remains generally unconcerned about the roots of corruption, which originate with the onerous burden of raising money for campaigns that begin the day after election. When McCain-Feingold, a bill that addressed the issue of campaign finance reform, came up for a vote in the spring of 1999, members of the House and Senate reported an average of only two phone calls a week from their constituents. They argued that scant response hardly justified their sticking their necks out on such an unpopular issue. But public support has a funny way of surfacing. McCain's bid for the Republican presidential nomination went further than anyone predicted, largely because of his dogged pursuit of campaign finance reform. And by the 107th Congress, which was seated in 2001, the bill's future looked much brighter.[18]

Charges of corruption ultimately depend on who stokes the fires of controversy and how well the issue is orchestrated. Yesterday's corrupt act is political grist for another ambitious politician's mill today. Corruption in Congress, as elsewhere, reflects public mores rather than anything endemic in the American psyche and often leads to more confusion than enlightenment. We have seen the end of the Cold War, the fall of Communism, the triumph of capitalism, and the implosion of many of our enemies in the former Soviet Union. But Congress continues to concentrate on cleaning out its own stable, with little evidence that it is addressing some of the real issues that muck it up in the first place.

BOOKENDS TO AN ERA

The Gingrich and Wright cases, bookends to each other and to an era, demonstrated the extent to which ethics had become a partisan tool by the late twentieth century. Divided government, such as the split between Republican Presidents and Democratic Congresses or vice versa and the no longer exactly 50–50 split in the Senate in the 107th Congress, continues to encourage the use of ethics as a political tool in a harshly competitive environment, often crippling both branches and both parties in the process.

Ethics was a surefire way to zap the other party while continuing to attract enormous publicity in the process. Predictably, this will continue as long as the two parties share power between the White House and Congress. Divided government encourages the "gotcha" mentality, as well as the "bipolar [issue] syndrome" that has prevailed in Congress for most of the last decade.[19]

"Now that Newt's gone, [many thought] the politics of venom wouldn't work," said Rep. Frank. "It has become depoliticized. How often did anyone ask to increase penalties before Gingrich? He asked to toughen the penalties twice, starting with Crane and Studds. This was not in our interest. Gingrich was like a bad tooth. Having been pulled, the infection is over."

Frank analyzed the Gingrich effort as part of a larger partisan strategy, with Republicans seizing on the ethics issue as a way out of their forty years in the political desert. "They were also acting," explained Frank, "against the excesses of some autocratic chairmen, like Brooks and Dingell [John Dingell, D-Mich., chairman of the powerful House Committee on Energy and Commerce from 1980–1994, and Jack Brooks, D-Tex., who chaired the Joint Committee on Congressional Operations, the Committee on Government Operations, and the Committee on the Judiciary at various times from the 1970s to the Republican takeover in 1994]. This is the reason the Republican revolution started in the House. Newt was smart. He went after Republicans, too."

In a sense, Gingrich and Wright were made for each other and for the era. Wright was as partisan as Gingrich, according to a fellow Democrat, who hinted that he and his fellow Democrats might have defended Wright more enthusiastically if the Speaker had not exacerbated conflicts just as readily as his leading foe. "The Wright case was all political," the Democrat said. "Wright would try to find the line and cross it. He ended up doing things that were stupid. While he made mistakes, the Republicans decided they would 'get that son of a bitch.' He took Republicans on. His attitude was, 'you're the opposition, and you're going to lose.' It was an 'in-your-face' attitude. There was one famous vote that Wright kept open for an hour [presumably until Democrats could get there]. The Republicans were screaming. There was almost a fist fight on the floor. The Republicans never forgave him and said, 'We're going to get him.' Normally, his indiscretions would have been forgotten. It was awful to have a Speaker resign."

With the end of the Gingrich era, the poison seemed to have gone out of the politics of venom. "Things are better now," Gingrich said. "It's partly exhaustion."

But Tony Blankley disagreed. "I don't happen to think the venom is exhausted."

2

The Apple and
Other Temptations

The Evolution of Congressional Ethics

"For if we would judge ourselves, we should not be judged."
—Corinthians 11:31
(English, King James Version)

IN THE BEGINNING

The venom that Tony Blankley decried existed well before Newt Gingrich's arrival on the national scene. Congress just masked it better. Known as the Ghengis Khan of politics, Gingrich brought Congress's ethical problems out into the open, used them to advance his career, and made sure that things would never be the same. The Gingrich era, with its emphasis on ethics, recalled the famed investigative journalist Lincoln Steffens. An Episcopal Bishop once introduced Steffens to a group of New York City politicians early in the twentieth century by asking: Who started corruption "way back in the beginning?" Who was to blame?

"You want me to fix the fault at the very start of things," Steffens answered. "Maybe we can, Bishop. Most people . . . say it was Adam. But Adam . . . said it was Eve. . . . And Eve said no, no, it wasn't she, it was the serpent. And that's where you clergy have stuck ever since. You blame that serpent, Satan. Now I come and I am trying to show you that it was, it is, the apple."

"The bishop sat down," wrote Steffens. "You could hear him sit down. For there was silence, a long moment, and in that silence the meeting adjourned."[1]

On Capitol Hill, the apple remains a symbol of the extraordinary power that resides in the lawmakers. That power brings temptations—monetary, sexual, professional. Notions of corruption have changed over time and have expanded well beyond simple bribe-taking, land speculation, and violence. Modern views of propriety demand much more of today's Congress than simply keeping lawmakers' hands out of the till. Sexual scandals, for example, have occupied center stage for a good part of the late twentieth century, although they were traditionally considered off-limits by the media until recently.

For most of its history, Congress ignored the ethical lapses of its members until rare outbursts of public outrage or media attention forced it to act. It defined the apple and always stuck to its original stance: that only Congress could define right and wrong, could decide which temptations were to be tolerated and which would not and could bear the ultimate responsibility for the discipline and punishment of the transgressors in its midst.

The first scoundrel to test Congress's stomach for punishing one of its own was Sen. William Blount, Independent of Tennessee. Congress's reluctance to act in Blount's case set the tone of congressional indifference to ethics that prevailed for the next two centuries. Blount, a swashbuckling privateer with a penchant for risk-taking, was finally impeached by the House in 1797 but his colleagues in the Senate refused to convict him. Evidently, Blount wasn't troubled by the literal or figurative symbols of corruption. At that time, the apples were plentiful, and he grabbed them; the appearance of impropriety didn't bother him at all.

The charges against Blount involved his excessive activities in land speculation, a popular but dangerous hobby in the early days of the nation's life. At the time he was supposed to be representing his state in the U.S. Senate, Blount was busy buying huge tracts of acreage in the Louisiana Territory. Anticipating fat profits from his investment, Blount tried to sell the land at greatly inflated prices to settlers moving westward, caring little that his scheme threatened to defraud thousands of Americans of their life savings. No doubt, he also enjoyed inside knowledge of where the best parcels of land were located and took full advantage of his position in the Senate to scout out potential trouble spots.

Inconveniently for Blount, the territory happened to be owned at the time by Spain, whose leaders flatly refused to relinquish their holdings to a man they regarded as just another greedy land speculator. Because the land wasn't for sale, Blount had negotiated one-sided deals with a nonexistent seller that also happened to be a sovereign nation. In other words, he stole the land, operating under a "squatters' rights" law of his own invention, which went unrecognized by the land's legitimate owners.

Undaunted by the Spaniards's rebuff, Blount decided to fight to get his land back. He proceeded to organize, "conspire[d] and contrive[d] to promote a hostile military expedition against the Spanish possessions of Louisiana and Florida" for the purpose of wresting the land away from Spain and giving it to England, a nation he presumably viewed as a more tractable business partner.[2] Still smarting from its loss of the colonies, England was only too happy to support Blount's campaign of land-grabbing, however unorthodox.

Blount regarded the Spaniards's resistance as only a temporary setback, and he forged ahead, actively recruiting troops from the Cherokee and Creek Indian tribes for his military campaign. Insensitive to either laws or appearances, he hired a trader appointed by the President to act as his interpreter with the tribal chiefs.

Congress found it hard to continue to ignore Blount and eventually made moves to stop him. His allies in the legislature initially fought the charges against him, which accused him of conspiring with the British to expel Spain, and privately tried to persuade him to cease his subversive activities. He foolishly ignored them and was forced to confront the criticism against him for conducting his own private foreign policy, independent of his own country, and in direct violation of the existing treaties of neutrality between the United States and Spain and between the United States and the Cherokee Nation. In view of the new nation's policy to remain steadfastly neutral in the ongoing war between Spain and England, Blount's efforts on behalf of the British were at the very least, subversive. Two hundred years later, when President Ronald Reagan's administration presided over the Iran-Contra scandal, the same questions were raised about the legitimacy of conducting foreign policy outside the interests of the nation; in contrast to Blount, however, in the Iran-Contra case, it was the White House operating against the express wishes of Congress.

Blount adamantly refused to back off his private war, despite his colleagues' best efforts at quiet persuasion. Unfortunately for him, however, he misjudged the power of his enemies. Frustrated with Blount's independence and embarrassed by his ongoing recalcitrance, Congress was finally forced to act more decisively. The House impeached Blount on July 7, 1797, and one day later, on July 8, 1797, by a vote of 25 to 1, the Senate expelled him on the grounds that he had been "guilty of a high misdemeanor, entirely inconsistent with his public trust and duty as a Senator."[3]

Although Blount didn't take Congress's actions seriously until it was too late, the Founding Fathers must have foreseen situations like this, as well as knaves like Blount. Article I, Section 5, of the U.S. Constitution allows "Each House [to] determine the Rules of its Proceedings, punish its members for disorderly Behavior and, with the Concurrence of two thirds, expel a Member." Blount was a member of the Senate, not the House, but only the House can bring articles of impeachment against a public official; the Senate can then follow through by trying and convicting the impeached official or declaring him innocent by acquitting him. In view of the seriousness of the charges and the punishment, the framers of the Constitution deliberately made conviction of public officials very difficult by requiring a two-thirds majority in the Senate.

Blount defended himself at his Senate trial five months later, on December 11, 1798, on the grounds that the House did not have the power to impeach a fellow legislator. Among other things, Blount argued that:

1. he [Blount] was not a "civil officer," as defined in the Constitution, and was therefore not subject to impeachment;
2. the Senate could not convict him because it had already expelled him;
3. since the House could not prove any high crime or misdemeanor—the Constitutional requirement for impeachment—that he had committed in the execution of his office, it did not have the authority to impeach him; and
4. the proceedings themselves violated his right to a trial by jury.

The Senate agreed with Blount that it did not have the jurisdiction to convict him, and the case was dropped on January 11, 1799, eighteen months after the chamber had expelled him. The view that Blount was not a civil officer, and therefore not subject to impeachment, was shared early in the proceedings by then Vice President Thomas Jefferson. It is ironic that Jefferson was willing to let Blount off the hook, considering his later involvement with the purchase of the Louisiana Territory—deemed by historians as one of his greatest achievements as President. If Blount had prevailed and remained the owner of the land, the territory might not have been so readily available when Jefferson bought it, and the contours of the country would be very different today.

Blount retains the dubious distinction of being the only member of Congress to have been impeached. Since that time, the impeachment power has been used sparingly toward the other two branches: Fewer than ten federal officers have been impeached, including two presidents; the rest were members of the judiciary.

Although Blount was a scoundrel, he was absolved of wrongdoing by a jury of his peers in the Senate, who were well aware that they were setting a precedent that would affect the legislature for years to come. Congress could impeach members of the executive branch as well as judges, but the Blount decision has held fast for more than two hundred years. Senators (and by extension, Representatives) were not civil officers and therefore could not be impeached, regardless of their crimes. Instead, Congress opted for self-discipline, on the grounds that expulsion or disqualification from office—which effectively removed offenders from office—was a much more serious penalty than impeachment.

Since the Blount decision, lawmakers from both Houses were always considered exempt from impeachment. A noted dissenter from that view was Raoul Berger, the constitutional scholar, who argued in 1973 that the founders intended for members of Congress to be subject to impeachment, just as members of Parliament were:

> They had access to the records of English impeachments; they made frequent references to impeachments of the King's ministers; as assiduous students of English history and government they cannot have been unaware of the fact that ministers were members of either Lords or Commons and that such status did not insulate them from impeachment.[4]

The decision to exempt Blount and all his successors from impeachment was not meant to render members of Congress immune from the law. The Justice Department can still bring cases against members of Congress it believes are engaging in criminal behavior, as the agency did in Abscam and other cases.

The truth is that James Madison and the Founding Fathers trusted the legislature more than they trusted the President and certainly more than they trusted other members of the executive branch. They had just fought a revolution to jettison George III, and they identified executive power in any form with the tyranny of kings.

"In revolutionary ideology, corruption of the legislature by the executive was the way in which the people were deprived of liberty," wrote John Noonan, a renowned legal scholar who specializes in corruption. "For much of the eighteenth century, English critics of English administration . . . had focused on the way the ministry ruled by corrupting Parliament with [patronage] jobs and appointments. These partisan outpourings had been devoured in America and formed part of the ideology of those who made the Revolution." Madison also regarded Congress as less corruptible than the executive branch, following Aristotle's maxim that it was harder to corrupt a multitude than it was to corrupt one person.[5]

The Constitution reflected the founders' antiauthoritarian views of the executive branch and gave Congress the power to punish its own members for "disorderly Behavior and, with the Concurrence of two thirds [the power to] expel a Member." Madison insisted on inserting the two-thirds requirement on the grounds that expulsion was "too important to be exercised by a bare majority" and would invariably be abused in times of national emergency.[6]

EXPULSION

In the category of dubious achievements, Blount was also the first senator to be expelled as well as impeached. In the period between his impeachment and trial, senators concluded that the Senate need not adhere to the impeachment process applicable to the other two branches of government because it had the constitutional authority to act on its own. The reason: Under the Constitution, the House and Senate have responsibility for disciplining their own members, including the ultimate punishment of expulsion.[7]

Since the Civil War, the Senate considered expelling seventeen other senators for various reasons, including corruption, disloyalty, or abuse of their official positions. In several of these cases, the Senate waited for the courts either to acquit or to convict the indicted senator; in others, they chose lesser sanctions. What generally occurs is that a senator on the brink of expulsion resigns to avoid facing the disgrace of being turned out of office, as in the cases of Sens. Harrison Williams, Democrat of New Jersey, in 1982, and Bob Packwood, Republican of Oregon, in 1995.

Publicity forces Congress's hand in cases like sex or corruption scandals that lawmakers would rather ignore. When public anger reaches a boiling point, or when the "appearance of impropriety" becomes all too apparent, then Congress metes out a variety of punishments—ranging from the mildest, a private tongue-lashing, to a reprimand, censure, and finally, to the most serious of all: expulsion. There is little difference between the House and the Senate, except that in the House, the member must stand before his or her colleagues while the Speaker reads the censure resolution. The House has displayed an even greater reluctance than the Senate to censure or expel fellow lawmakers: The House has expelled only four members, three in the heat of the Civil War in 1861, and one—Rep. "Ozzie" Myers (D-Pa.)—in 1980, after he was convicted in the Abscam dragnet.

AN EYE FOR AN EYE

After Blount, Congress moved warily on ethics cases, despite enormous provocations. In fact, those who hark back to the good old days find no comfort in nostalgia; even a glance at what was tolerated in the early days of the Republic shows that political life, even and especially in Congress, has improved considerably.

Dueling, for example, was not only acceptable in 1838, many considered it the only honorable means of conflict resolution. As a method of settling political arguments it was "not infrequent," as witness the case of the hapless Rep. Jonathan Cilley, Democrat of Maine, who was "fatally wounded" on February 24, 1838, by another congressman, Rep. William J. Graves, a Whig from Kentucky. Graves was not expelled, censured, or even reprimanded by his fellow lawmakers for killing his colleague.[8]

The duel occurred in response to critical remarks made on the floor of the House by Cilley that were interpreted as an attack on the character of James W. Webb, an editor of a newspaper known at that time to advocate the views of the Whig Party. In response to Cilley's remarks, Graves challenged Cilley to a duel to settle the argument once and for all. The event, complete with rifles and seconds, took place on the Marlboro Pike, in nearby Maryland, and ended with the third volley, which landed in Cilley's stomach and killed him.

The House promptly appointed a committee to look into the affair, which recommended that Graves be expelled from the legislature, and that the seconds in the duel—two members who accompanied the two antagonists—be censured.

Despite the forcefulness of the committee's recommendations, nothing happened—as expected. Then, as now, committees can be relied upon to stall a decision in the hope that the controversy will disappear while the issue and its protagonists cool off. The report was tabled, and none of the surviving participants, Graves and the two seconds, were either expelled, censured, or reprimanded. After the gruesome fact of the killing, and under considerable public pressure, Congress finally bestirred itself to act. Almost a year to the day after Cilley was slain, the House passed a law prohibiting the "giving or accepting, within the District of Columbia, of challenges to a duel."[9] Maryland, where the duel actually took place, was so far away at that time, that lawmakers mistakenly expected the hot-tempered parties to calm down between the period they issued these deadly challenges to each other on the floor of the House and the time it took to travel to the prearranged site.

Although violent crime didn't rate so much as a slap on the wrist, our forefathers in Congress were way ahead of their time in clamping down on hate language. Rep. William Stanberry, a Democrat from Ohio, was censured by the House in 1832, six years before the Cilley-Graves duel, for "insulting" the Speaker during a floor debate. Evidently breaches of decorum were treated with greater severity than murder.

Fortunately, dueling was soon replaced by verbal combat, with ethics cases relegated for the rest of the century to bribery and personal corruption. Regardless of the crime, however, both houses of Congress always insisted on the right, guaranteed by the Constitution, to investigate as well as discipline their own members.

Physical violence at last drew the attention of Congress in 1902, when the Senate censured Sens. John L. McLaurin and Benjamin Tillman, two Democrats from South Carolina, for engaging in a fist fight on the Senate floor over a debate on the Philippines. Offensive as they were, fisticuffs seemed minor to those who recalled the days when weapons or harmful objects were used by hot-tempered lawmakers. In fact, canes were banned from both chambers in mid-century to prevent a repetition of the brutal 1856 caning by Rep. Preston S. Brooks (SRD-S.C.) of Charles Sumner (R-Mass.), whose injuries were so severe they kept him away from the Senate for three years.

Gone, also, are the days when senators represented interest groups for a fee, then unabashedly voted their interests. One of the most famous icons of American statesmanship, Sen. Daniel Webster, was a paid lobbyist for the Second Bank of the United States. At the same time he served in Congress, he was a director of the bank as well as its legal counsel. Webster took "loans" from the Bank, which he neglected to repay, as well as "retainers" from wealthy bankers and tycoons, whose causes he supported in the Senate. In a letter Webster wrote in 1833, he sharply reminded Nicolas Biddle, president of the bank, that his retainer (his fee) wasn't "renewed" or "refreshed, as usual," and to send it forthwith if "it be wished that my relation to the Bank should be continued."

Webster must have sensed that something was not quite right with this arrangement even then because he also reminded Biddle to "burn all his letters."[10] Still, Webster's relationship with the Bank of the United States was perfectly acceptable at the time; bribing a member of Congress was not illegal until 1853, although bribing judges was forbidden as early as 1790.[11] To put in perspective how things have improved since Webster's time, today Webster's "loans" would be comparable to a senator receiving money for his personal use, no questions asked, from a governor of the

Federal Reserve Board in exchange for lobbying for the Fed—seeing that its budget requests were met and voting according to the dictates of its officers.

Verbal incivility has recently become a hot issue on the ethics agenda. Members of Congress are regularly hauled off to seminars that teach them good manners: specifically, how to express themselves in a "civil" fashion and how to deflect their personal anger constructively. In their zeal to conform to current standards of publicly acceptable behavior, congressional leaders have consulted Judith Martin of *The Washington Post* who writes the popular "Miss Manners" column on contemporary etiquette.

What the language police don't understand is that verbal expressions of anger have replaced dueling, with far less disastrous consequences for the loser and far greater political penalties for the aggressor. In 1995, "House Majority Leader Dick Armey (R-Tex.) referred on the House floor to Rep. Barney Frank (D-Mass.), an openly homosexual member of Congress, as 'Barney fag.' A slip of the tongue, Armey averred. . . . This Freudian slip, responded Frank, revealed 'Armey's homophobia.'"[12] The widespread public criticism of hate language that followed in the wake of Armey's "slip" was much more powerful than a congressional slap on the wrist.

The nostalgia buffs also forget what congressional life was really like in the old days, when senators would address their enemies with perfect manners (the "esteemed gentleman from Indiana") before launching into vicious tirades against targeted colleagues. To many, the new "incivility" is far superior to the time when members chafed "under the thumb of autocratic barons who routinely suppressed initiative and creativity." Even though "not every member knows how to handle himself," editorialized *The Hill* newspaper, "it is better for lawmakers to have a voice, even a contrarian, in-your-face voice." After all, "sometimes, even the newest, most contrarian, lawmaker comes up with a genuine contribution to the body politic."[13]

In the past, surface civility often masked ugly prejudices, inflicted by a small group of reactionary southerners who wielded control over the institution. A half-century ago, southerners controlled the Congress by gaining seniority that awarded committee chairmanships in perpetuity to the Russells, McClellans, Bilbos, and Rankins. That persisted into the 1970s, when a floor debate between Senators John McClellan, Arkansas Democrat and chairman of the Appropriations Committee, and Jacob Javits, New York Republican, recalled what was so commonplace in the past. Javits had angered McClellan with his mastery of education formulas. Finally, a frustrated McClellan pointed an angry finger at Javits, a Jew, and said, "We don't need your kind in the United States Senate."

Republican inroads, reapportionment, and the emergence of a two-party system in the South destroyed the power of the southern "barons," as the chairmen were then called. The civil rights laws, which the barons had bitterly opposed, also shortened their tenure, as did the Supreme Court reapportionment decisions of the 1960s. The servility of lawmakers toward their chairmen finally came to a halt with the arrival of television, which finally overthrew the conventional wisdom that junior members should be seen but not heard.

Not only are they less violent, but today's lawmakers are also more honest in their financial dealings than were their forebears. Inherently, they are probably not much different from their predecessors, but the apples of temptation have been removed, just as canes were banned to avoid violence. Gone, for example, are the days when lobbyists would make cash contributions to congressional leaders, who would put the money in their desk drawers for a rainy day. That practice ended with the enactment of post-Watergate financial disclosure laws, which require lawmakers to list their campaign contributors as well as detail their personal financial assets and those of their spouses.

Congress also eliminated "slush funds" from leftover campaign contributions from past elections, which members could legally squirrel away for their retirement or for their own private nest egg. The practice ended in 1992 with a House vote abolishing multimillion-dollar "no-year" financing. Claiming victory were the "Gang of Seven," seven media-savvy freshmen Republicans who led the fight. Republicans also objected to the Democratic leadership's use of the funds: One such expenditure of $314,000 came at the request of Heather Foley, the wife and unpaid chief of staff of the former Speaker of the House, Tom Foley (D-Wash.), to remodel an office for the Democratic Policy and Steering Committee.[14]

LET THOSE WITHOUT SIN . . .

Essentially, for most of the nation's history, Congress left itself virtually immune from prosecution by its own members and with considerable independence from the executive branch, if not the judiciary. Article I, Section 6, clause 1 of the Constitution, for example, gave lawmakers total immunity for speech: "for any Speech or Debate in either House, they [the legislators] shall not be questioned in any other Place." That meant that lawmakers could say anything they wanted on the floor of the House or Senate and not be prosecuted. Presidents and cabinet secretaries have complained ever since about the disproportionate strength of the Congress vis-à-vis the White House, but the truth is that the balance of power depends more often on the personalities, the needs of the times, and the political strength of the leaders in power than it does on constitutional arguments.

Other immunities flowed from these constitutional guarantees, which were loosely interpreted by some members of Congress to mean immunity from many of the laws they passed for the rest of society. Exemption from equal employment and antidiscrimination legislation was another flagrant example of Congress's hubris toward the rest of the nation. For many years, lawmakers rationalized their constitutional immunity as the right to discriminate against women or minorities in their individual congressional offices, while expecting the rest of the country to abide by rules that outlawed discrimination. Congress blithely claimed special privilege, and pointed to Article I, Section 5 of the Constitution, which guarantees Congress's right to self-government, a right the Founding Fathers pointedly did not grant to the executive branch or to the judiciary.

But the Founding Fathers never envisioned the steady stream of privileges lawmakers awarded to themselves, such as subsidized meals and even haircuts, or the right to speed on the nation's highways. Members could claim immunity from traffic violations on the grounds that they were hurrying to a roll-call vote or to an important congressional session, even if they were racing north toward Canada on a road in northern Vermont. When Senate Minority Leader Robert C. Byrd (D-W.Va.) insisted on personally paying the fine for a traffic violation in Virginia, his act made headlines: not for getting caught, but for the act of owning up to a transgression traditionally ignored by local police.

Rationales for not adhering to the laws were transparent and offensive to many Americans. When accused of not adhering to the principles of equal employment laws, for example, Congress reasoned that its members were required to reflect only their constituencies, not the diversity of the nation. A lawmaker from Alaska, for example, could be expected to have a preponderance of Native Americans on his staff who would be more attuned to the district's problems and to its voting blocs. In addition, Congress reasoned that if constituents were unhappy with the conduct of a member's office, they possessed the ultimate weapon: They could vote the offending lawmaker out of office. Although various groups found many of these practices unethical and offensive, they failed to organize around this issue, and nothing happened. Nothing, at least, until the 104th Congress was elected in 1994, and the new Republican leadership forced Congress to adhere to most of its own laws.

LEAVING THE GARDEN OF EDEN

Most lawmakers come to Congress to make a difference—liberals and conservatives, Democrats, Republicans, and independents. Many served on
school boards, county councils, and state legislatures, but now they find
themselves in the major leagues. Assuredly, a few are on power trips or view
Capitol Hill as an avenue for personal enrichment. Centers of power are,
indeed, magnets for rogues and scoundrels. But most lawmakers arrive in
Washington full of idealism and ideology, determined to make a better
world for themselves, their children, and their grandchildren. They want to
end poverty and hunger, homelessness and despair. They want to strengthen
individual liberties and make government a force for decency and progress.
It is too hard to get there, to Congress—the constant fund–raising, hand-
shaking, and speechifying—not to have a purpose. And they carry the
hopes of supporters and constituents who placed their trust in the candidate's ability, integrity, and vision.

Then the socialization process begins. They learn they have to give a
little to get a little. And they begin to compromise because compromise is
the heart of democracy. In time, some lawmakers compromise so much
that they forget why they came to Washington in the first place. Their priorities change. For many, their initial idealism is replaced by a desire to be
reelected, at all costs. Highly competitive to begin with, they use all the
tools in their arsenal to advance their careers. This includes, in some cases,
an accelerating use of ethics charges to destroy political opponents.

Gradually, members amass power in order to control others and to influence the agenda. The Capitol's marble columns inspire a sense of entitlement and shield legislators from unwelcome eyes. Like Fortune 500
CEOs, much is done for them. They use aides as drivers; they use them to
make airline reservations, to pick up laundry, and to perform other every-
day tasks. And they begin to take short-cuts, born of the arrogance of
power. Initially highly dependent on the media to give them name recog-
nition and give their campaigns impetus, some soon turn their backs on
the media and avoid public scrutiny altogether. Surrounded by sycophants,
they interpret all criticism as personal and regard those who oppose them
for reelection as would-be usurpers of power.

They go back home to town meetings and weddings, Rotary lunches
and company picnics, and they socialize with corporate executives
whose wealth makes them feel poor and somehow cheated by the system. After all, their friends' good fortune often owes a great deal to their
timely intervention with federal bureaucrats: getting pesky regulators off

their backs; funneling a lucrative government contract their way; or twisting a highway in the direction of their factory, warehouse, or farm.

Their lives are further complicated by Congress's money culture and the need to raise campaign funds from the day they are elected. In a single California House race in 2000 between Rep. Jim Rogan, a conservative Republican, and his liberal Democratic challenger, Adam Schiff, the candidates spent $10 million. Lawmakers soon find themselves leading a double life, torn between the lowly job of begging for campaign funds and the job of ruling America.

Lawmakers also feel poor, especially in contrast to their friends. They find themselves victims of an affliction that David Brooks of *The Weekly Standard* termed "Status-Income Disequilibrium" (SID), which he defined as a "condition of frustration on behalf of the 'titled class' (such as members of Congress, journalists, editors and other high-status, powerful but lower-paying professions) who must mingle on an equal par with investment bankers, lawyers and other members of the 'Monied Class.'" The pressures caused by SID explain the aberrant behavior revealed by the Abscam scandal as well as other ethical lapses, for even though a congressional salary of $136,700 a year looks high to the average citizen, it pales next to the annual take of an investment banker, sports champion, or movie star.[15]

And when spouses don't work outside the home, legislative salaries must support two households that are often located at opposite ends of the country. In fact, to make ends meet, more than twenty members of Congress live in their Capitol Hill offices during the week to save the high cost of renting an apartment in Washington. SID must kick in hard when lawmakers dine downtown with wealthy contributors, only to return to a sofa bed in the deserted Rayburn building. More often than not, the monied classes are supplicants in this relationship, which makes it even more frustrating to those who rely on their financial largesse.

To add to their problems, lawmakers also claim that unlike their corporate friends, their lives are an open book. The law requires them to divulge financial information that business executives carefully conceal. Their sources of income, investments, and every financial aspect of the operation of their offices are a matter of public record. In 1995, the Republicans initiated draconian restrictions on their fellow lawmakers that would not be tolerated by most CEOs. House members were barred from accepting all gifts, meals, and trips except those from personal friends and family. They were explicitly barred from accepting free travel, even for charity golf and ski trips. They could, however, accept travel associated with official duties, called "junkets" by some. Senators had slightly more latitude. They could accept meals, entertainment, and privately financed trips up to a value of $50, with an annual total of $100 on gifts from any one source, not counting gifts valued at less than $10.

The tightening of ethics rules put congressional leaders in the position of removing the apples and the serpent, in case members of their flock proved unequal to the task of resisting temptation. Power does, indeed, corrupt, and despite Congress's best efforts to remove temptation, lawmakers still find themselves embroiled in scandal, thanks to heightened public scrutiny, tougher restrictions, and swiftly changing public mores.

3

Joe McCarthy
and the Ethics Process

*"I don't like Clay, he is a bad man, an impostor, a cre-
ator of wicked schemes. I wouldn't speak to him, but by
God, I love him."*
—John C. Calhoun on Henry Clay

THE RELUCTANT SENATE

Congress has tolerated a wide range of misbehavior on the part of its
members. Like an overindulgent parent who hides the escapades of the
children and prays they won't misbehave again, Congress tends to act only
when publicity forces its hand or when all the neighbors can finally see the
miscreant standing, baseball bat in hand, in front of the broken window.
Congress tolerated Senator William Blount until his activities became too
embarrassing to hide.

Members of Congress also develop a sense of solidarity with each other,
a natural consequence of spending so much time together. John Calhoun
couldn't abide Henry Clay but still regarded him with affection. That is
why lawmakers tend to protect each other, even sweeping incidents involving violence and corruption under the rug until public reaction prompts
them to act. Over time, both chambers of Congress have become more
transparent, thanks to the increased scrutiny of journalists and the growing
competitiveness of the two-party system. The major shift in ethics over
time showed Congress gradually relinquishing its sense of entitlement over
self-discipline on ethical questions to a more formal set of codes designed
to quell public dissatisfaction. It simply became too difficult to draw the
curtains as the glass houses became more transparent to the outside world.

When it comes to congressional action on ethics, two factors, partisanship and publicity, usually determine the outcome. Partisanship offers the

opportunity for party leaders to go after opponents who have been harmful to the nation to retaliate for an injustice to their own party or to engage in just plain party mischief. Back-bencher Newt Gingrich's attack on Speaker Jim Wright for ethics violations was later followed by a plethora of Democratic counterpunches, destroying the careers of both men in the process.

The case against Sen. Joseph R. McCarthy (R-Wis.), the bullying, alcoholic lawmaker whose very name stands for baseless charges flung with indiscriminate recklessness, reflects both themes: It began as a partisan campaign, then expanded well beyond the Senate as McCarthy's activities enveloped American society. In retrospect, it seems as if the Senate took an awfully long time—four years—to stop McCarthy; certainly, the victims of McCarthy's anti-Communist vendettas considered the chamber's efforts sluggish. But if viewed in the context of Congress's aversion to prosecuting its own members for breaches of ethics, the time lag was more understandable.

What the McCarthy case showed was a Senate in transition from a nineteenth-century code of silence to a more modern stance: Ethics no longer meant merely keeping lawmakers from shooting each other or from stealing from the public till. McCarthy showed the Senate that ethics also meant the institution had to act to protect its own members as well as the rest of society from verbal attacks, from infringements on personal liberty, and from the excessive exercise of power.

The first volleys against McCarthy came from Democrats, but when his behavior became sufficiently aberrant to disgrace the Senate, his colleagues finally joined forces across party lines to condemn him. Initially he attacked only Democrats, but as opposition to him began to grow, he expanded his forays against members of his own party, including President Eisenhower.

McCarthy's behavior did more than disgrace the Senate. It disgraced the nation, so much so that his name became a word in the national lexicon, *McCarthyism*, standing for "the use of unsubstantiated accusations or unfair investigative techniques in an attempt to expose disloyalty or subversion."[1]

The Senator launched his four-year vendetta against people he regarded as subversives in the State Department, the Voice of America, the Army, in universities, and in private life, with a speech before a women's Republican Club in Wheeling, West Virginia, on February 9, 1950. Waving a paper in the air—soon to become his trademark gesture—he charged that listed on the paper were the names of 205 active Communists then working in the State Department. His speech foreshadowed a notorious period in American history, known as "The McCarthy Era," during which the Senator chaired several highly publicized congressional investigations that ruined the lives and careers of many Americans caught in the ensuing public hysteria. At last, the McCarthy era and McCarthy's career finally came to an end after he extended his investigations to the U.S. Army in the Army-McCarthy hearings in 1954. By that time his behavior was so aberrant that even some of his most ardent supporters in the Senate decided that he had to be stopped.

Before 1954, however, strict partisanship prevailed: McCarthy enjoyed a two-year uninterrupted run, thanks to Republican leaders who used McCarthy to destroy Democrats. Because McCarthy terrified most politicians, those leaders didn't have to look far for evidence of McCarthy's electoral power: The two Democrats who initially tried to halt McCarthy's investigative activities were soundly defeated for reelection, thanks to the active role on the hustings of McCarthy and his supporters. The first was Millard E. Tydings (D-Md.), chairman of the special subcommittee created by the Foreign Relations Committee in early 1950 to investigate McCarthy's charges against the State Department. The subcommittee sat for thirty-one days of contentious and highly-publicized hearings. When he ran for reelection later that fall, Tydings was accused of being soft on Communism, and he was defeated by the voters in Maryland. At the time it was alleged and later proven that McCarthy loyalists campaigned against Tydings with a photograph that showed Tydings "listening attentively" to Earl Browder, then head of the U.S. Communist Party. The photo was later shown to have been doctored—Tydings never appeared with or supported Earl Browder—but the final proof of his opponent's successful use of dirty tricks came too late to save Tydings's career.[2]

The following year, William Benton (D-Conn.), another Democratic senator, attempted to expel McCarthy after a Senate report had criticized McCarthy's active role in defeating Tydings in the Maryland election. The upshot was that both Benton and McCarthy were investigated by an elections subcommittee, but before the committee reported its findings, in 1952, Benton was also defeated for reelection. The reason for Benton's defeat was blamed on his feud with McCarthy.[3]

No wonder so few profiles in courage emerged to take on the vocal senator from Wisconsin. Senators respected votes and feared McCarthy and his supporters' speedy retaliation at the ballot box. Both parties feared voter wrath, which was as important then as it is now to members of Congress. McCarthy's minions grew daily, and a call to action from him to his national constituents would draw thousands of pieces of mail from all over the country. Sen. Arthur V. Watkins (R-Utah) wrote that he received thirty thousand letters during the time he chaired the committee that investigated McCarthy, as well as enormous pressure, even from members of his own family. One phone call he vividly recalled came from his sister in California, who wept openly and begged him to withdraw from the issue, citing threats she had received that were intended to be conveyed to him from pro-McCarthy forces in her state.[4]

Partisan politics also played a pivotal role in allowing McCarthy to continue his nefarious investigations. In 1953, his fellow Republicans took over the Senate and not only tolerated his continued activities, but also rewarded him with the chairmanship of the Permanent Investigations Subcommittee of the Government Operations Committee. The Senate Democrats by then were so frightened by McCarthy's power over the electorate that for the most part they acquiesced to his activities as well.

McCarthy finally overplayed his hand in 1954 by extending his investigations of Communists in government to the Army in the person of Dr. Irving Peeress, a dentist who had been promoted despite what McCarthy claimed was a left-leaning past. The senator even smeared George C. Marshall, who as Army chief-of-staff had been Dwight Eisenhower's mentor and who later served as Secretary of State in the Truman administration.

Charges and countercharges were filed in the Senate, one against McCarthy himself for seeking through the subcommittee counsel, Roy M. Cohn, preferential treatment for a former subcommittee consultant, G. David Schine. After thirty-five days of widely televised hearings, the Republican majority report exonerated McCarthy but accused Cohn of bringing "disrepute to the committee." Attempting to appear evenhanded, the report also criticized the Eisenhower administration by charging Army Secretary Robert T. Stevens and his counsel, John G. Adams, with trying to "terminate or influence" the hearings.[5]

As a result of the Army-McCarthy hearings, McCarthy's reputation among his fellow senators shifted from ambivalence to abhorrence; embarrassed for their own party, his fellow Republicans finally stopped him— however tentatively. Sen. Ralph E. Flanders (R-Vt.) introduced a resolution to remove McCarthy from his committee chairmanships and to prevent him from being appointed to any other posts until he answered questions pertaining to his role in the defeat of Sen. Tydings. McCarthy had refused to answer questions about the Tydings defeat that had been submitted to him in 1952 by the Senate elections subcommittee investigating the incident.

Flanders's resolution was opposed by Senate Majority Leader William Knowland, indicating that the Republicans were still protecting McCarthy.

Flanders then substituted his resolution with one charging McCarthy with personal contempt of the Senate. Another resolution recommended that McCarthy be censured for his "conduct in the Benton-McCarthy hearing in 1952" and for his insulting behavior toward Army Brig. Gen. Ralph W. Zwicker, whom he accused during a hearing of not being fit to wear the uniform of the armed forces.

McCarthy was ultimately condemned. Considering his flagrant behavior, shouldn't McCarthy have been expelled? Not if political factors drove the compromise. Even McCarthy's strongest foes in the Senate knew that a two-thirds vote (required by the Constitution for expulsion) would be difficult, if not impossible. And although the committee assigned to report on the censure charges unanimously recommended censure, the Senate regarded censure as too strong a punishment and recommended the compromise of condemnation instead. Unlike expulsion, which required a two-thirds vote, censure required only a simple majority. Still, Senate leaders didn't want to risk a censure vote, which they privately feared might have been defeated, whereas reprimand was considered too mild a punishment. Condemnation was considered a compromise, crafted for McCarthy and used only once before, and it has not been used since.

Finally, on December 2, 1954, the Senate ultimately approved by a two-thirds vote of 67–22 a resolution to condemn McCarthy. Republican votes were split down the middle, with twenty-three Senators voting for condemnation and twenty-two against; all forty-four Democrats present voted for the compromise, as did the Senate's lone independent, Wayne Morse of Oregon. Six senators were recorded as not voting. They were John Bricker (R-Ohio), Homer Capehart (R-Ind.), Albert Gore Sr. (D-Tenn.), John F. Kennedy (D-Mass.), George Smathers (D-Fla.), and his fellow Wisconsin Republican Alexander Wiley. McCarthy himself was listed as "not present." Sen. Kennedy was absent from both the debate and the vote because he was recuperating from back surgery.[6]

The resolution condemned McCarthy for failing "to cooperate"; for charging fellow Senators with "deliberate deception" and "fraud"; for "stating to the press . . . that the special Senate session was a 'lynch party'"; and for acting "contrary to Senatorial ethics and . . . [bringing] the Senate into dishonor and disrepute, to obstruct the constitutional processes of the Senate, and to impair its dignity."[7]

One unsung hero of the resolution against McCarthy was minority leader Lyndon B. Johnson (D-Tex.), later president, who finally entered the fray in late 1954. Johnson was instrumental in creating the Watkins Committee and ensuring its report would be filed before Congress adjourned.

He was also credited with keeping the debate on the narrow issue of Senate traditions, with restraining Democratic liberals, and with crafting the parliamentary maneuvers that would "insure a final showdown."[8] Another courageous senator was Margaret Chase Smith (R-Maine), whose famous "Declaration of Conscience" was actually proclaimed four years before, in 1950.

It is still hard today to figure out why the Senate was so craven in its dealings with McCarthy, stopping him relatively late in the game, and reluctantly at that. Excuses are legion. Fear of McCarthy was widespread. Those who attacked him were smeared as soft on communism. Another excuse, which several members termed "the curse of partisanship," leveled the blame at Republicans as well as Democrats, none of whom would attack a colleague, however odious his behavior. In the current era of intense party competition, it is hard to recall an era in which comity ruled the day, when there was more cooperation than competition, and the concept of gridlock applied only to traffic delays. The flip side of this outwardly congenial legislature was that McCarthy was allowed to flourish for so long given the spirit of bipartisan camaraderie, which resulted in the reluctance to rein him in. Finally, two senators, both Republicans (Flanders and Watkins), lifted the curse and forced the Senate to restrain McCarthy, who they argued was an extreme case. Both Flanders and Watkins were "practically ostracized" by their fellow Republicans, but "these two men, the whimsical New Englander and the narrow, ascetic Mormon, demanded no less of the United States Senate than that it come to terms with Joe McCarthy."[9]

The Senate condemned McCarthy for disgracing the institution of the Senate—not for ruining lives, depriving individuals of their civil liberties, and disrupting society and government for more than five years. Although later writings on McCarthy refer to the Senate's censure vote, it is important to remember the Senate voted for this jerry-rigged condemnation because censure was regarded at that time as too strong a punishment. Still, it was better than nothing; it is still doubtful that a clear-cut expulsion vote would have passed the Senate with a two-thirds majority in that period of anti-Communist fervor, a stalemate in Korea, and widespread distress over the Cold War. To this day, few would speculate on whether a censure vote would have passed.

However it looks in retrospect, condemnation remains a "distinction without a difference," according to Richard Baker, the official historian of the Senate. Since that time, he argues, everyone regards the Senate's action against McCarthy as a full-fledged censure, the precedent being the case against Sen. Hiram Bingham (R-Conn.) in 1929, the only other time in

Senate history that the term "condemnation" was used instead of "censure." In that case, also viewed as a censure, the language of the resolution meant that the Senator was censured. "In voting to censure a member," said the authoritative history on these cases published by the Senate, "the Senate sometimes has varied the specific words employed, using 'condemn' or 'denounce,' but the meaning and impact is essentially the same, the common factor being that the full Senate votes to censure the member. Most of those chastised in this manner have either failed to be reelected or declined to run for reelection."[10]

More recently, the Senate also proved reluctant to use the word "censure" against one of its own, the influential and popular Herman Talmadge (D-Ga.). Instead, the Senate voted to denounce him, following the Ethics Committee's recommendation and explanation that it considered censure and condemnation too strong a punishment to be used against him. Answering to the will of the Senate, the Ethics Committee considered the nature of Talmadge's transgressions, which fell in the category of financial carelessness, not sufficiently damaging to warrant its severest sanctions. But despite the language, the voters of Georgia considered the motion a censure, proving once again that ethics was a potent issue at the polls. It was used by Talmadge's opponents in the primary as well as in the general election, and Talmadge was defeated for reelection in 1980 by the Republican candidate, Mack Mattingly.[11]

There is also no doubt that McCarthy considered the condemnation a censure vote, admitting to reporters afterward that "it wasn't exactly a vote of confidence." Although he said he couldn't wait to get back to the "real work of digging out communism, crime, and corruption," McCarthy's career and health went into a tailspin after the vote; his alcoholism grew worse, and he died several years later, in 1957.

POWELL, BAKER, AND THE
EVOLUTION OF THE ETHICS PROCESS

For the greater part of the first two centuries, Congress overlooked most individual acts of wrongdoing, unless they resulted in murder or scandals too flagrant to ignore. Self-regulation was accepted as the most common form of discipline, and no written codes of conduct existed to guide lawmakers. Scandals in the late nineteenth century, such as Crédit Mobilier, and in the early twentieth century led to a series of federal statutes regulating campaign practices in 1907, but these laws left loopholes large enough for lawmakers to circumvent their intent, just as they continue to do today.

As the century progressed, however, Congress faced successive scandals that forced it to adopt more general codes of conduct for its members. In adopting these codes, Congress was also protecting itself against public wrath: Not only did it systematize the ethics process, but Congress also tried to counter the intensifying criticism over its many privileges. Transparency became the ruling principle. Congress learned that with ethical codes written down for all to see, it was easier to stop erring lawmakers before their lapses became too public. The rule's the rule, the graybeards would say. They (the rules) protect us, and they protect you.

In the process of developing more uniform standards of conduct, Congress had to revisit and eventually revise its longtime pattern of self-discipline. Two cases in particular finally forced lawmakers out of the ethical isolation afforded by the Constitution's early guarantees of legislative independence. The case in the House involved Rep. Adam Clayton Powell (D-N.Y.); in the Senate, charges were raised against the Secretary to the Senate, Bobby Baker, and the case eventually led to the creation of the Senate Ethics Committee. Neither man committed any sins that dozens of their compatriots before, since, and after them had not committed; the problem was that they engaged in those activities to excess. True, they flouted the law, but their violations were so flagrant and so public that they forced Congress to pay attention and act.

Adam Clayton Powell, a black minister, was elected to Congress in 1944 from Harlem and was reelected with huge majorities for more than a quarter of a century afterward. He also served as pastor of the Abyssinian Baptist Church, a large and influential black congregation in his district. The church was his primary political base and remained loyal to him throughout his later troubles with congressional colleagues. Considered the most powerful black representative in Congress, Powell probably remained in power too long; his defenders argued that the fight against him smacked of racism.

Powell defied the law too publicly and too often for his fellow lawmakers to fail to take notice. Early in his career, in 1952, he was accused by the Internal Revenue Service of underestimating his 1945 income tax by $2,749. After a trial in 1960 for tax evasion resulted in a hung jury, Powell finally paid $27,833 in back taxes and penalties. During the same period, he lost two lawsuits filed against him by a widow in his district, Esther James, who sued him for calling her a "bag woman" for the police in a television interview. When he repeatedly failed to pay the judgments from those lawsuits, the court held him in contempt four times.[12]

Powell also displayed a marked contempt for congressional traditions. He took expensive junkets in the 1950s and in the early 1960s; he was accompanied by a staff member, named Corinne Huff, who was not his wife. His wife lived in Puerto Rico but was paid as a clerk from government funds. Powell wasn't the first member of Congress to take advantage of tax-funded travel or to take a lady friend on a travel junket, nor was he the first to hire a relative for a no-show job. But like Blount, he persisted in flaunting his activities and drew constant public attention to his legal and ethical problems.

The initial moves against Powell came from members of his own party: On January 9, 1967, the House Democratic Caucus removed him from the chairmanship of the Education and Labor Committee, a post he had held for six years. His fellow committee members, angered by his frequent absences and by the subsequent delay of an important antipoverty bill, had already stripped him of his powers as chairman the year before by passing a rule that allowed any subcommittee chairman to bring a bill to the floor. Powell called the Caucus action a "lynching, northern style."[13]

The Republicans then moved in, sealing Powell's doom with an alliance with Southern Democrats. A day after the Caucus took away his chairmanship, the House of Representatives adopted a resolution introduced by Rep. Gerald R. Ford (R-Mich.)—a no-nonsense conservative from Grand Rapids who later became minority leader and then President—denying Powell his seat pending an investigation of his activities. Because the Democrats controlled the House, the committee investigating Powell was headed by a fellow Democrat, Rep. Emanuel Celler (D-N.Y.). Celler's committee recommended that:

- Powell be sworn in;
- his seniority be based on the current date of his swearing in (which would insure his exclusion from a committee chairmanship based on seniority);
- he be censured for not cooperating with the House;
- he be censured for his refusal to pay the judgment against him;
- he be censured for misusing public funds;
- he be fined $40,000 to offset his civil liabilities.

The House rejected the Celler committee's recommendations and voted instead to exclude—not expel—Powell from the 90th Congress: 307 voted in favor of exclusion, 116 against. Southern Democrats voted in a bloc with the Republicans to form the majority against Powell. Celler, who admitted in a later television interview and on the House floor that he perceived "an element of racism" in the vote to exclude Powell, might have had a point: Powell was the first lawmaker in the House to be excluded since 1919 and 1920, when the House barred the seating of Victor Berger, a Socialist from Wisconsin, because he had been found guilty of sedition for publishing antiwar literature.

Powell's exclusion was reversed by the U.S. Supreme Court, which ruled that the House had improperly excluded Powell because he had met the constitutional requirements of age, citizenship, and residence. Significantly, Powell knew this, and refused to answer any questions before the Celler committee, except those pertaining to his age, citizenship, and residence. Berger's exclusion was also reversed by the Supreme Court. Berger was reelected and served three more terms.

Powell was reelected by his district in 1968 and served—although he almost never attended congressional sessions—until he was unseated by Charles Rangel in 1970. He died two years later, in 1972.

Bobby Baker, the protégé of then–Senate Majority Leader Lyndon B. Johnson, also got into ethics trouble for wielding his power to excess. Baker became one of the most influential aides in history, although he never held high office. In the course of his career in the Senate, he accrued a fortune of $2 million from, it was alleged, combining the practice of law with influence peddling.

In the initial civil suit against him, in 1963, Baker was charged with using his influence to win contracts for a vending machine company in which he had invested. That was the tip of the iceberg, as a Senate investigating committee found out in two years of subsequent hearings. Baker was then prosecuted and convicted for income tax evasion, theft, and conspiracy to defraud the government, and he was found guilty in 1967. The principal charge against him was that he had collected vast sums of money from savings and loan executives as campaign contributions but had kept much of it for himself. One member of the House and a senator testified that they had never received any of the money he was supposed to have given to them.

THE BIRTH AND POLITICAL
BAPTISM OF THE ETHICS COMMITTEES

Baker was just an aide but was widely regarded as more powerful than most Senators. Because of Baker and the widespread knowledge that aides can wield so much power, they are now included in the codes of ethics for both Houses of Congress, especially because their behavior reflects on the institution as strongly as that of the lawmakers themselves. Baker's activities also had an element of "there but for the grace of God, go I"; it was not so much what he did but the "appearance of impropriety" and his excesses that led the Senate to conclude that it needed more protection than the Constitution's guarantees of privacy and immunity from impeachment afforded them.

The revelations in the Baker case finally forced the Senate to form a bipartisan ethics committee in 1964: the Select Committee on Standards and Conduct. Three years later, the House followed suit in response to the Powell case and created its own bipartisan ethics committee, called the Committee on Standards of Official Conduct. The House made its committee permanent and gave it enforcement as well as investigative power. House rules—especially with regard to disclosure—are stricter in general than are the Senate's.

Today, the House and Senate Ethics Committees serve as the initial arbiters of lawmakers' misconduct, but both are usually loath to take action against their colleagues. Lawmakers consider membership on these committees something to be avoided at all costs, and leaders customarily have to dragoon people to serve by promising them a variety of blandishments, such as better future committee assignments. "If you are ever asked [to serve on the ethics committee] don't," Rep. Marcy Kaptur (D-Ohio) was cautioned by her colleagues after her election to Congress in 1982.

No one wants to be in the position of investigating friends and colleagues; there is no political payoff. Members fear criticism, if not outright retribution, from fellow members, and lawmakers simply dislike assuming the role of prosecutor in an environment that prides itself on collegiality.

Getting members to serve has always been a problem, with the possible exception of Rep. Charles Bennett (D-Fla.), who actually volunteered to become the chairman of the Ethics Committee in January 1979. Fearing his enthusiasm, his colleagues initially rejected his offer, but Bennett eventually prevailed and ascended to the chairmanship. Curiously, he never identified his Ethics Committee position on his stationery.

Since Bennett's tenure, the pressure on ethics committees to act has accelerated, and those who avoid the issue can catch hell from the voters. When she chaired the House ethics panel in 1996, Rep. Nancy Johnson (R-Conn.) came within 1,500 votes of losing her seat in the 6th District of Connecticut, following accusations that she had dragged her feet during the two-year investigation of the charges against her mentor, Speaker Newt Gingrich. The drumbeat against Johnson began with the local newspapers in Hartford, which handed her major opponent, attorney and former professor Charlotte Koskoff, a potent issue in the congressional campaign.

"[T]he committee, chaired by Rep. Nancy Johnson of New Britain, dragged its feet for two years," editorialized the *Hartford Courant*. "Not until Dec. 21, well after the election, did the investigatory subcommittee make public its conclusion that Mr. Gingrich had brought discredit to the House." The consequences of Johnson and the committee's inaction had the "unfortunate result [of] . . . a speaker's being elected to a second term while the committee still debates the charges against him. Choosing a leader under an ethics cloud is unwise."[14]

Other newspapers also joined the pack in attacking Johnson's reluctance to proceed against Gingrich. The *Boston Globe* accused her of keeping the Ethics Committee report "secret until after the election." Her reluctance to proceed, said the *Globe*, was clearly related to the fact that she was an "early ally in Gingrich's climb to the speakership," as well as the beneficiary of his patronage—although her appointment to the Ethics Committee could hardly be called a favor.[15] *The New York Times* called Gingrich's reelection as Speaker "tainted," pointing the blame at Johnson for a "breathtaking display of political servility . . . [and] a shameful parliamentary maneuver aimed at burying two years of work by her own committee."[16]

Democrats soon joined the editorial chorus with charges of their own, culled from the Federal Election Commission: that Johnson had received a request from GOPAC to develop a list of candidates running for Congress, even though the group was prohibited from taking part in a federal election. They also demanded that she step down from the chairmanship of the Ethics Committee, as well as from taking part in any decision involving Gingrich.[17]

Johnson resigned from the Ethics Committee as soon as she was reelected in 1996. As a reward for her struggles, the Republican leadership appointed her to the powerful tax-writing Ways and Means Committee, where she has lived happily ever after. Her new assignment has enabled her to raise a war chest of $622,324 for her next campaign, over $400,000 more than her most serious Democratic challenger.[18]

Not surprisingly, one of Gingrich's first actions after reelection in 1997 was to close down the House Ethics Committee for all practical purposes before it could get into further political mischief. His strategy was simple: limit the powers of the committee. To slow the flow of ethics complaints, for example, the House voted in 1997 to bar outside groups from lodging ethics charges against House members.[19] The change required that only a

House member was permitted to initiate charges, based on personal knowledge of unethical activity. This represented a marked reversal from past practice, which allowed the Ethics Committee to initiate its own investigations based on newspaper articles or citizens' complaints. Paradoxically, at the same time Congress increased the restrictions on members' activities, as well as tightening disclosure requirements, the House made it more difficult to file charges against errant lawmakers.

The Johnson experience shows why issues involving ethics are so unpopular among members of Congress. Few recall the heretical views for which Girolamo Savonarola was burned at the stake, whereas many remember his punishment. Not that lawmakers look to a fifteenth-century Florentine monk for career advice, but there are many cases—Gingrich's among others—that pinpoint the exploitation of ethics as a serious impediment to political ambition. Even though it carried Gingrich from the back benches of power to the seat of power, it also destroyed him. The same was true of Baker, Powell, and McCarthy, all of whom achieved easy fame, which quickly turned to notoriety.

The lesson is that in politics, loyalty is a more closely held value than ethical conduct. Johnson risked her career rather than bear the mark of disloyalty. The truth is that most lawmakers have to be pushed hard before they will go after a colleague, however low those colleagues may have fallen. They are still reluctant to discipline themselves, as they have always been. But when a lawmaker gets truly out of line—like McCarthy or Powell—and public pressure bears down on Congress, then the ethics process finally kicks in to rectify the situation, and the voters are appeased, at least temporarily. In the interim, there still remains a great deal of discretion and partisan politics to fill in the gaps.

4

Abscam and the "Keating Five"

"If everyone abstained from voting on grounds of personal interest, I doubt if you could get a quorum in the United States Senate on any subject."
—Senator Robert Kerr, Democrat of Oklahoma

ABSCAM

Were members of Congress always afflicted with ethical lapses? Or, are people just noticing more? Actually, things were probably worse in the nineteenth century, before communications technologies enhanced public scrutiny. The harsh glare of television cameras would probably have ended duels, fisticuffs, and caning much sooner, but even without all the physical violence of the past, fights over ethics still retain their early passion. Only now, the battles include a much wider range of issues, some real, some phony, and all of them more partisan than ever before.

The sharpest conflicts today revolve around the meaning of constituent service. Lawmakers charged with ethics violations frequently take the "constituent defense": What the average citizen may view as unethical or even illegal behavior is merely the act of lending a helping hand to a needy constituent. Constituent service is engraved into the job description of a member of Congress, and politicians who forget it often find themselves voted out of office: "out of touch," their opponents charge. What this involves is simple: Lawmakers regard themselves as ombudsmen; they act as intermediaries between the voters and arbitrary government bureaucrats. The subject of great debate is whether lawmakers should be penalized by the Ethics Committees, by their colleagues in the Congress, and by the Justice Department, merely for intervening with government officials on behalf of their constituents.

Debates over this issue occurred regularly during the Abscam and "Keating Five" scandals, when the accused lawmakers argued that they were rendering genuine constituent service and not engaging in illegal activity. They were simply doing their job, they argued. Helping constituents came with the franchise: Monetary gain, outright bribery, and seeking campaign contributions were accusations often based on the public's misunderstanding of the real role of a conscientious lawmaker.

The Abscam investigation was initiated by the Justice Department and not by Congress. The case involved six representatives as well as one senator, Harrison Williams, an accomplished liberal Democrat from New Jersey. Acting on tips that it had received over the years, Federal Bureau of Investigation (FBI) agents, some costumed as Arab sheiks, enticed selected congressmen to accept hefty bribes in exchange for introducing special immigration bills, building casinos in Atlantic City, and dispensing assorted political favors.

The FBI argued that Abscam amounted to clear-cut bribery and not constituent service because monetary gain was clearly the goal of legislators who agreed to introduce private immigration bills for a fee. The way it worked was that members of Congress would receive about $50,000 in untraceable cash, which was the going rate at that time, in exchange for submitting a "private immigration bill" that would allow a foreign national to enter the United States. The bill circumvented the long list of applicants waiting to enter the U.S. legally and represented quite a substantial favor. It worked well for everyone because it was also a relatively painless way to fatten the lawmaker's piggy bank at the same time it gave new meaning to the Statue of Liberty's message of welcome. It is hard to say why private immigration bills were allowed to continue for such a long time, especially because it would have been so easy to remove the "apple" to protect lawmakers from temptation.

The FBI investigation took place between 1978 and 1980 and ensnared some influential lawmakers in the stings, which were videotaped on grainy film clips and televised repeatedly on the major networks' prime time evening news shows. The FBI's efforts resulted in the conviction of seven members of Congress and five other public officials on assorted charges, including conspiracy and bribery. In addition to Williams, other legislators included Reps. John Jenrette (D-S.C.), Richard Kelly (R-Fla.), Raymond Lederer (D-Pa.), John Murphy (D-N.Y.), Michael J. "Ozzie" Myers (D-Pa.), and Frank Thompson (D-N.J.). All the representatives except for Lederer, who later resigned, were defeated for reelection.[1]

Embarrassed by all the negative publicity, both houses of Congress finally stepped in: Myers was expelled from the House—the first expulsion since 1861. Williams resigned in 1982 to avoid the imminent probability that he would be expelled from the Senate.

The major difference between the Abscam and Keating scandals was money: In Abscam (a contraction of Abdul—the FBI's cliché for an Arab name—and Scam), the accused legislators lined their own pockets in the interest of personal gain, whereas in the Keating case, senators intervened on behalf of constituents in exchange for campaign contributions or donations to their favorite charities. Both scandals drew extensive media coverage, contributed significantly to the declining reputation of Congress, and assured the longevity of congressional ethics as a political issue.

THE "KEATING FIVE"

The Keating case involved five senators accused of trading favors in exchange for campaign contributions. The case more rightfully should have been called the "Keating Three." Sen. John McCain, the maverick Arizona Republican, was added because Democrats wanted at least one Republican in the dock. McCain had walked out of a key meeting as soon as he realized what was involved. Sen. John Glenn, the former astronaut from Ohio, was added because Republicans were angered by the inclusion of McCain and wanted another Democratic scalp. His involvement was also peripheral. The charges were serious—intervening with a federal regulator on behalf of a wealthy campaign contributor. Those contributions, many argued, fell into a different category than personal enrichment and could, therefore, legitimately be considered genuine constituent service.

The money came from Charles Keating, then-owner of Lincoln Savings and Loan, a failed savings and loan institution based in Irvine, California. Keating's business failures would have gone undetected except for the fact that his organization defaulted on the life savings of thousands of investors, many of them elderly, who were left penniless after the loss of an estimated $288.7 million in fraudulent securities and junk bonds. The bonds and securities were sold to the hapless purchasers as federally insured bank certificates of deposit. When the dust settled, taxpayers were left with a bill of an estimated $2.6 billion. Keating was eventually convicted of securities fraud in 1991 and was sentenced to ten years in state prison. (The conviction was later reversed.) The following year, a federal jury in Tucson, Arizona, awarded $3.3 billion in damage claims against Keating on behalf of the swindled investors.[2]

Keating, a notorious high-flyer and bon vivant, had investment ventures that ranged far beyond the banking world. One such venture in Scottsdale, Arizona, a 250-acre resort hotel and golf course, continues to flourish. Called the Phoenician, it nestles in the shadow of Camelback Mountain, a lavish monument to Keating's excesses. "He spared no expense," say the locals, who still talk about Keating and his investment adventures. The hotel's guest rooms, according to its brochure, boast "Imported Italian linen. Rich Berber carpeting . . . Signed original art . . . [and] Oversized bathrooms with Italian marble." The vast lobby follows the same theme: marble floors, crystal chandeliers, and bellhops costumed in the garb of Phoenician nobility swarming around the entrance to the hotel.

Keating's savings and loan venture failed from poor banking practices; the virtual absence of regulation; and investments like the Phoenician, with balance sheets that bore no relation to future earnings. But many investments fail: Businesses quietly fold, some companies relocate or change their names following a product disaster, and market forces determine which stocks rise and which ones fall. The real question was why the savings and loan was allowed to operate for so long without regulators closing it down. Banks and savings and loans have been considered public utilities since the Depression, when people came to expect government protection against the ravages of the marketplace. But the watchdogs, the banking regulators who were keepers of the public trust, virtually disappeared when it came to Keating's business ventures.

CORRUPTION OR CONSTITUENT SERVICE

Enter congressional ethics. As hearings later revealed, both state and federal regulators turned a blind eye to Lincoln Savings and Loan, thanks to the alleged timely intervention of five U.S. Senators: Alan Cranston (D-Calif.), Dennis DeConcini (D-Ariz.), Don Riegle (D-Mich.), John McCain (R-Ariz.), and John Glenn (D-Ohio). Despite clear violations of standard banking practice, Keating's Senate pals prevailed on the state and federal banking agencies to keep their regulators far away from his banks. Fearful of Senate retribution, particularly at budget time, the agencies' leaders duly complied. The senators later argued that they were merely protecting a constituent from intrusive and heavy-handed regulators; then, as now, regulators were popular whipping boys. At the same time, however, it was very clear that Keating was a very special constituent whose campaign contributions more than compensated for the senators' special services and protection.

Of the charges against the five senators, the most egregious involved Sen. Cranston, a California Democrat, who was ultimately reprimanded by the full Senate in an unprecedented and humiliating action on the Senate floor. It was the first time the Senate had ever used the sanction of "reprimand"; before Cranston, it had either censured or expelled senators, even though other terms like "condemn" or "denounce" may have been substituted for "censure." Before that time, the device of reprimand was used only in the House.

Cranston disputed the reprimand on the grounds that he had done nothing worse than had most of his colleagues in the Senate, admitting to "perhaps bad judgment and an appearance of impropriety—but nothing more."[3] Cranston defended himself with the argument that "without clear and convincing evidence of actual impropriety," there was no justification for disciplinary action, especially because "the Senate has never determined that it is an ethics violation for a Senator to engage in legitimate constituent service on behalf of a contributor."[4] He also emphasized that he didn't profit from his association with Charles Keating: "Neither any member of my family nor I received any compensation or personally benefited in any way from these charitable contributions. I had no financial interest in Lincoln Savings, its parent, or affiliates. I received no income from it."[5]

Cranston emphasized the point that he was just conscientiously doing his job, as he would for any citizen of his state: lending a helping hand to an ordinary California constituent plagued by pesky banking regulations. After all, senators and representatives intervene on behalf of constituents every day to speed tardy Social Security checks to recipients who can't buy groceries without them, request speedier decisions from the Immigration and Naturalization Service, and push otherwise unfeeling bureaucrats toward acting more responsively toward the citizens they serve. It is all a routine part of the job. After years of congressional ethics scandals, no one knows for certain what marks the difference between an innocent call to an official in the Department of the Interior and a similar call that can trigger an ethics investigation.

"Everybody does *not* do it," responded Ethics Committee chair Sen. Warren Rudman, (R-N.H.) in a stinging rebuke to Cranston. Rudman considered the Senate's reprimand too lenient and Cranston's "final defiance . . . a double cross . . . [and] an appropriately nasty, partisan ending to a nasty, partisan affair." In his view, Cranston's statement was "arrogant, unrepentant, and a smear on this institution." Senators, he continued, "by word and deed publicly and privately . . . take great care with their personal conduct as it might be perceived by the American people[;] [It is wrong] to blame it on campaign finance and everybody does it, and you should all be in fear of your lives from the Ethics Committee, is poppycock."[6]

The Constitution says nothing about constituent service, yet members of Congress and their staffs spend much of their time acting as ombudsmen on behalf of voters who are experiencing difficulties with executive branch agencies. The Constitution also says nothing about campaign contributions, yet in return for keeping regulators away from Keating's banks, the five senators netted a total of about $1.3 million for their campaign coffers. No wonder the system has become so stacked in favor of incumbents over challengers.

Keating's contributions to members of the House of Representatives were paltry in comparison to his Senate largesse: The Federal Election Commission reported only $16,000 in contributions from Keating to House members over three election cycles, 1987–1988, 1989–1990, and 1991–1992.

In contrast to Abscam, the only money changing hands in the Keating case involved campaign contributions or charitable contributions and not cash intended for private pocket-lining. Campaign contributions technically do not amount to personal enrichment because the money ostensibly goes to an organization and not to an individual. But because a campaign organization's major objective is the election of a specific individual, the money is still being spent for the candidate's benefit. In other words, although the Senators didn't take a dime of Keating's money for their personal use, the cash went directly toward their reelection, so in that sense they were clearly benefiting from the banker's financial generosity. Cranston tried to separate himself from his colleagues, arguing disloyally that he took Keating's money only for charitable purposes, whereas DeConcini, Glenn, and Riegle raised the money "for their own political use."[7]

The Keating case enveloped the entire Congress, even though only a few lawmakers were involved. Clearly, Cranston would not have intervened with such a heavy hand for just any citizen who asked for regulatory relief. The public correctly perceived that the process was unfair and that it was not intended to be unfair. If this kind of institutional corruption were permitted to continue, wrote ethics scholar Dennis Thompson, it would inevitably lead to long-term damage to the political process: "A fair system of democratic representation does not grant more representation to some citizens just because they have more financial resources."[8]

In the real world, unfortunately, that kind of preferential treatment occurs all too frequently. The exigencies of raising campaign funds often lead lawmakers to intervene for wealthy contributors or otherwise to conduct themselves in ways that would not be considered ethical. It is hard to say what makes the public angrier: the fact that ordinary people cannot get the same level of service as their richer brethren, or that this kind of preferential treatment exists at all in a democratic society. Voters may be cynical about politics, but they still believe strongly that the process and its symbols should remain above reproach. The public was outraged, for example, by revelations that President and Mrs. Clinton had rewarded political contributors with a night's stay in the Lincoln bedroom. After all, the White House was a monument, the people's house, owned by the taxpayers, a historical icon that the President and First Lady sullied with crass political patronage.

Congress wouldn't touch the real issue brought up by the Keating case: political money. Feelings of entitlement, of self-discipline, came strongly into play here. "The committee didn't dare to suggest that campaign contributions could be bribes," and held back from finding Cranston guilty of "corrupt intent," added Dennis Thompson.[9] Instead, Cranston, who received $1 million in contributions from Keating, remained the only senator who was reprimanded; the others were merely rebuked, with Sens. DeConcini and Riegle receiving more severe warnings than Glenn and McCain. During the height of the scandal, DeConcini justified his connection with Keating by arguing that he was in good company: "Mother Teresa was also a beneficiary of Keating's contributions," he said.

Cranston's reasoning followed a similar course: "Mr. Keating was an acknowledged big giver," he testified, as if that absolved Keating from cheating depositors. "He gave and loaned more than $44 million to Mother Teresa, Covenant House, the St. Vincent De Paul Society and anti-pornography drives. He gave and raised huge sums for political campaigns and candidates such as the $200,000 he gave to Senator Glenn's P.A.C. [political action committee] and $100,000 he contributed to George Bush's Team 100."[10]

Cranston, DeConcini, and Riegle all retired from the Senate, most likely before the voters "retired" them; only Glenn and McCain remained in office. "Perhaps there was some rough justice," wrote Rudman. "[T]he two senators who deserved no punishment continued to serve, and the three who deserved punishment chose not to seek reelection. To that extent, the system worked."[11]

Partly as a result of his searing experience in the Keating investigation, Sen. McCain became a vigorous proponent of campaign finance reform and the coauthor of the McCain-Feingold bill, which failed to pass when it was brought up in 1998, 1999, and 2000. He was often quoted as saying that his experience in the Keating scandal was worse than his five years of torture and confinement as a prisoner of war in Hanoi. Campaign finance became his signature issue during his run for the Republican presidential nomination in 1999 and 2000, and it has slowly gathered steam from that time on.

McCain's efforts on behalf of campaign finance reform finally bore fruit in 2001, with a 59–41 Senate vote, despite tremendous resistance, particularly from members of his own party who bitterly resented the implication that they had been corrupted by the system. In fact, discussions of the nature of corruption have occupied Congress since the Abscam and Keating incidents, with lawmakers repeatedly taking umbrage at the accusation that they are propelled by corrupt motives. When campaign finance reached the Senate floor on October 14, 1999, Sen. Mitch McConnell (R-Ky.) challenged McCain to name specific senators who had been corrupted by political contributions. McCain responded with statements about sticking to the issue (barring unregulated soft money from special interests), and "not identifying . . . or attacking individuals. . . . I am attacking a system that has to be fixed," he argued.

One particularly heated exchange drew a challenge from Sen. Robert F. Bennett (R-Utah), who asked McCain to identify the contributions that led him to sponsor a $2.2 million sewer project for the 2002 Winter Olympics in Utah. McCain had identified the project on his Web page as an example of pork barrel legislation that resulted from Bennett's debt to special interests. "Who gave the soft money?" Bennett queried. "How much was it and where did it go?" Only the people of Utah would benefit from this project, he argued, not the special interests.[12]

To the dismay of many of his fellow senators and party members, McCain stuck with campaign finance as the primary issue in his 1999–2000 quest for the Republican nomination. His success in the New Hampshire primary led his opponent, then Texas Governor George W. Bush, to recall McCain's role in the "Keating Five." His strategy, a ruse known as "push-polling," involved a telephone survey of hundreds of thousands of voters that asked them if they were aware that the Senate Ethics Committee had rebuked McCain.[13]

The fault can be spread around: to Congress; to the legislators who won't change or tighten the laws; and to the system of campaign finance, which necessitates the constant money-raising that inevitably leads to the kind of conflicts of interest raised by the Keating case. The statutes still do not define the boundaries between what constitutes bribery and what is legitimate constituent service, and the Keating case failed even to address that issue. The statutes involving conflicts of interest are similarly weak, often leaving legislators in the dark. "If everyone abstained from voting on grounds of personal interest, I doubt if you could get a quorum in the United States Senate on any subject," said the late Sen. Robert Kerr, Democrat of Oklahoma.[14] "Just don't make them retroactive," the late Sen. Abe Ribicoff, Democrat of Connecticut, warned an aide drafting the post-Watergate ethics laws.

Yet at the height of the Keating Five investigation when maverick Sen. William Proxmire, Democrat of Wisconsin, suggested that members of Congress simply refuse to accept campaign contributions from the special interests over which their committees had jurisdiction, Proxmire said, "you would think I had just insulted their mothers."[15] His colleagues conveniently forgot about how both the apple *and* the serpent could get them in trouble.

"Ethics rules are vague," concluded former Sen. Howell Heflin, Democrat of Alabama, who chaired the Senate Ethics Committee during the Abscam and Keating Five investigations. "They ought to be specific. Is it 'conduct unbecoming?' This is the same issue in the military. The courts have said this is too vague a standard. It calls for a subjective evaluation as to what is 'conduct unbecoming.' We need to be more specific than just a 'prohibition on gifts.' To the religious right, right and wrong may differ from what they would be to a religious Jew."

If the personal tragedies of the lost savings of widows, retirees, and orphans hadn't galvanized the Senate, the Keating case most probably would never have seen the light of day. Until the statutes are tightened up, political leaders are left with the famous "I know it when I see it" test, first applied by the Supreme Court to the question of how to determine pornography. In other words, common sense.[16] "How would it look on the front page of *The Washington Post?*" is another informal standard many members use, although they can still be blindsided by the mercurial ethics process. Ask members of Congress like Mary Rose Oakar, Democrat of Ohio, who was turned out of office in 1992 following a scandal involving House members who routinely bounced checks drawn on the House bank.

Ironically, Cranston argued that the "appearance standard" that applies to federal judges and civil servants was "never adopted" by the Senate; moreover, he added, "Federal judges and civil servants do not have to raise funds to stay in office."[17] Heflin advises senators that, in the absence of more specificity, lawmakers should "exercise judgment and reasonable restraint." They should also ask themselves, he advised, "what sort of precedent [their actions would] set for the future."

"There should never have been a Keating Five," wrote Warren Rudman, who argued that the real crime in the Keating case was banking deregulation, and that the burden for that crime should have been shared by the entire Congress for allowing the unraveling of banking laws to proceed unabated. Relaxing congressional oversight allowed scoundrels like Keating to flourish because deregulation encouraged the savings and loan institutions to engage in high-risk behavior at the same time Congress insured deposits against loss. Congress combined—in fact, expedited—the worst practices of capitalism and socialism, said critics of deregulation. "Perhaps there should have been a Keating Five Hundred, since most of us in Congress supported the S & L deregulation and did little while the disaster unfolded," concluded Rudman.[18]

HOW POLITICS PREVAILED

To the cognoscenti, the political fallout from Abscam also showed the President's ability to target an enemy without resorting to the ballot box. An unscrupulous president could use law enforcement officers to ensnare a political enemy by appealing to his or her weakness—alcohol, women, drugs—and then lowering the boom. However, there was no evidence this was the case in Abscam.

To avoid the appearance of partisan politics, the Ethics Committees in both Houses remain evenly divided among Republicans and Democrats; they are the only committees that remain unaffected by who wins the majority. The Ethics Committee in the Senate, for example, has three members from each party. It is the only committee purposely constructed without a majority, the hope being that the group will reach its decisions with both parties in perfect harmony. Occasionally, the committee finds itself deadlocked, as it did between 1989 and 1991 during the Keating case. If the committee can't reach a consensus, it must report back to the full Senate, which will then take up the case. (In the House, the ten-member committee [officially called the Committee on Standards of Official Conduct] is also equally divided between both parties.)

"The Democrats wanted the least possible punishment . . . and were stalling, hoping we would give in," explained Warren Rudman. "The Democrats were trying to save their party. We [the Republicans] were trying to save the Senate, which would be disgraced if the actions of three of the five went unpunished."[19] Scarred by the polarizing fights of the past decade, both committees have recently reverted to Congress's old traditions of bipartisanship and secrecy. Today, Committee members "fight about housekeeping chores," remarked former committee counsel Bob Bennett. "Should they issue a report or not; should they hold a hearing, or not."

Heflin also observed that the ethics process—as currently configured— "created the opportunity for the executive branch to go after its enemies through the FBI," which he felt was the case in Abscam. At the same time, had his colleagues heeded his warning to exercise good judgment, they might have been spared what some observers considered a case of entrapment—enticing members of Congress to commit crimes that under ordinary circumstances would not have occurred.[20] "The FBI went after Pressler (former Senator Larry Pressler, Democrat of South Dakota), who said, 'I don't do things like that.'" Stung by public criticism, the FBI lay low after Abscam and has not involved itself since in any major legislative ethics issue. In 1982, a Senate panel criticized the FBI's management of the Abscam investigation, but it concluded that no one's civil rights had been violated. Since the incidents and subsequent hearings on Waco and Ruby Ridge, Presidents have similarly distanced themselves from the agency. Even though Congress officially absolved the FBI, many considered the unusually long hearings on the incidents at Waco and Ruby Ridge payback for the agency's role in Abscam.

Rudman also argued strenuously all along that the "Keating Five" should have been a "Keating Three" because McCain's and Glenn's "offenses simply did not warrant a full Senate investigation." That, he continued, was "where politics came in. McCain was the only Republican among the Five, and the Democrats would never agree to drop him. . . . As long as the Democrats would not exclude McCain, the Republicans would not release Glenn. Both men were political hostages throughout the entire two-year ordeal."[21]

"I question why he [Rudman] went along [if he felt so strongly]," observed Sen. Carl Levin, Democrat of Michigan, who added that Rudman was one of the most ethical members of the Senate. "You don't have to [go along]." Levin implied that if Rudman had felt so strongly about Glenn and McCain, he should have dug in his heels for as long as it took his colleagues to come to their senses. But the vote would then have gone to the entire Senate, and the delicate consensus maintained by the Ethics Committee would have been destroyed.

5

The New Rules
of the Ethics Wars

Rick: *"How can you close me down? On what grounds?*
Captain Renault: *"I'm shocked, shocked to find that
gambling is going on here.*
Croupier: *"Your winnings, sir."*

—*Casablanca* (1943)

"MR. SAM"

A new member of Congress from Albany, New York, was contacted by his political mentor, who feared a federal criminal indictment for income tax evasion. The investigation had gone on for years and was driving the party boss crazy. All he wanted was to know if the IRS was going to pursue a criminal or civil case against him. The congressman obtained a meeting with the legendary Speaker of the House, Sam Rayburn, Democrat of Texas, to ask for a decision in the matter.

"Come back at five o'clock," Rayburn told the congressman.

Rayburn quickly summoned the head of the IRS to his office and told him he didn't care whether the agency brought a criminal or civil case, but he wanted a decision by 5:00 p.m. that day. The lawmaker returned promptly at 5:00 to learn that the IRS had reduced his friend's charge from a criminal to a civil one.

"I'm forever in your debt," the grateful lawmaker told the Speaker. "If you ever need anything, all you have to do is ask. Whenever you need my vote, you'll have it."

"Funny you should say that," Rayburn replied. "I can use your vote on an off-shore oil bill coming up next week."

"You've got it," the lawmaker answered.

But when the lawmaker returned to his district, he found that the local newspapers had gotten wind of his promise to sell his vote on offshore oil to help his local party boss. He went back to Rayburn and asked to be let off the hook. "You promised me your vote," Rayburn said, "and I expect you to keep your promise. Sit in the front row and keep your eye on the doorkeeper. If I need your vote, he'll nod 'yes.' If I don't, he'll nod 'no,' and you can vote however you want."

The member sat dutifully in the front row, waiting for the signal. Near the end of the vote, the doorkeeper indicated that his vote wasn't needed. As the lawmaker heaved a huge sigh of relief, he noticed a dozen other members in the front row also heaving sighs of relief.[1]

"If you want to know how this place ran, that's the way things used to be," recalled the late Speaker Thomas P. (Tip) O'Neill, comparing his Congress with the era of "Mr. Sam," as he was called. Rayburn also ran his own private campaign finance operation, known as "cash and carry," out of the bottom drawer of his desk. Lobbyists would happily replenish the cash at the slightest hint that the money supply was getting low. When a member in need of campaign funds visited him, Rayburn would ask, "How much do you need?"

"$20,000," was the typical answer, although today that would hardly finance a decent race for dogcatcher.

"Here's $10,000," Rayburn would say, dipping into his drawer. "Go raise the rest yourself."

Mr. Sam's powers of persuasion owed much to this form of financial underwriting, as many legislators prevented from "voting their conscience" could attest. But that was then. And this is now, where instead of basking in the halo of leadership, legislators find they must be more vigilant than ever to avoid the notoriety that has plagued so many of their colleagues. Instead of resting comfortably with the perks of power, today's politicians are always on the alert for new rules of conduct, which change faster than hemlines. Some rules of the ethics game include the following.

"IF YOU GO AFTER A KING, KILL HIM"

After the long reign of Speaker Sam, things started to change, albeit slowly. Challenges to the leadership began to percolate, and the old patterns of self-discipline, congressional entitlement, and privilege started to melt away as voters became more aware of them.

One of the first challenges to party loyalty on an ethics issue emerged from a freshman lawmaker elected in the post–Watergate class of 1974. The

Democrats in that class wrested power from some of the old barons and modernized many of the practices of the Congress. Power no longer guaranteed loyalty, and the following two decades set the stage for the Gingrich revolution of 1994.

The challenges began slowly. Loyalty to the old system was no longer the rule of the day; neither was the practice of giving leaders with a strong power base complete latitude to do whatever they wanted, especially with public money. With one caveat, recounted former Rep. Andrew Maguire (D-N.J.): "If you go after a king," especially on an ethics issue, "you have to kill him."

The monarch in question was Rep. Robert L. F. Sikes, a Democrat from Florida, a thirty-eight–year veteran of the House's First Congressional District and, more important, the chairman of the Military Construction Subcommittee of the House Appropriations Committee. From his power base on the subcommittee, Sikes funneled military pork barrel projects to lawmakers from all regions of the nation. He was also credited with acquiring most of the fourteen military installations in his own district, including Pensacola Naval Air Station and Eglin Air Force Base, which together cover more than seven hundred square miles.

Maguire, a liberal freshman Democrat from Ridgewood, New Jersey, with a boyish shock of red hair, emerged as the dragon-slayer, an unlikely role for such a newcomer. It all started when Maguire was home on a quiet Sunday evening in May 1976, watching CBS's investigative journalism program *60 Minutes.* The program described how Sikes had used his public position for personal gain. Before his election to Congress, Maguire had worked as a political and security affairs specialist at the State Department, was an avid civil rights activist in the South in the early 1960s, and had earned a Ph.D. from Harvard in government.

"Common Cause gave the stuff to *60 Minutes,*" recalled Maguire. "They did a major research job on Sikes. . . . I thought surely somebody is going to do something. Then I said to myself, 'Hey, you're a member of Congress; why don't **you** do something?'" "I went back to Congress," he continued, and "discovered the rules governing the Ethics Committee. The Ethics Committee could seize on an issue only if it was brought to its attention by a member of Congress." (The Ethics Committee has recently reverted to this rule after the partisan fights of the 1980s and 1990s.) "[Because of that rule], the Ethics Committee, established seven years before, had never investigated a case."

Maguire was careful to recruit Democrats and Republicans to his cause. "I talked to Cohen [David Cohen of Common Cause] who agreed to transmit the results of his group's research to the Ethics Committee," said Maguire. "Six other members joined me—Robert Edgar (D-Pa.), Toby Moffett (D-Conn.), Norman Mineta (D-Calif.), Richard Vander Veen (D-Mich.), Don Edwards (D-Calif.), and Stephen Neal (D-N.C.)—the Republican was John Anderson, of Illinois. You can't just have a group of Democrats going after a bad apple fellow Democrat. That's not the way ethics should work." Maguire also consulted regularly with the leadership, including John Brademas (D-Ind.), who was the majority whip, and Richard Bolling (D-Mo.), a senior member of the House who was widely known for his expertise on the workings of Congress. At the end, forty-four members had joined Maguire's six original allies, including two senior members of the House, Anderson and Bolling.

The House was forced to agree with the Ethics Committee that the charges against Sikes had merit—that he had used his subcommittee chairmanship to enrich his holdings not only in Florida real estate but in banking, life insurance, and aircraft companies as well. The opportunities open to Sikes were much more extensive than Senator Blount's, but Congress was just as reluctant to punish him as it was to sanction Blount nearly two centuries before.

The Ethics Committee's recommendation to reprimand Sikes for financial misconduct was finally upheld by a resounding vote of 381–4. The vote also led to Sikes's loss of his subcommittee chairmanship at the start of the Ninety-fifth Congress in 1977. Had Maguire and Common Cause not raised the issue, however, nothing would have happened because the conflicts of interest involving Sikes were routine practices at that time; they shocked only some younger members like Maguire. Maguire was standing at the back of the House chamber with his friend Rep. Paul Tsongas (D-Mass.) when the vote was taken. Maguire says that Tsongas told him, "'You're doing absolutely the right thing, but I wouldn't have the guts to do that.'"

Sikes was no worse than many other members of Congress serving with him at the time. But his profiteering from the public till was just a bit too greedy to continue unnoticed. One investment, for example, turned a $58,000 Florida beachfront property owned by him into a profit of $442,000—as the complaint alleged. Another involved his suspicious vote in 1974 for a $138 million appropriation for the A–10 aircraft produced by Fairchild at the time he owned 1,000 shares of Fairchild stock. Some eyebrows were also raised at his efforts to persuade the Navy to permit an independent bank in which he owned 2,500 shares of stock to operate on the Pensacola Naval Air Station in his district. He argued that his activities were in keeping with normal constituent service; others regarded them strictly in the category of personal enrichment.

Maguire was not satisfied with the reprimand, considered strong punishment because the House had not inflicted such a severe sanction on any of its members for seven years. He called for full censure and removal from office, arguing that precedent dictated such punishment for "serious violations of ethical conduct." Maguire admitted that "even though on the floor I said I was disappointed Sikes wasn't censured, once the Ethics Committee had acted I was delighted. [You'll note] I wasn't pressing the issue."

The size of the House vote was deceptive. The second-term, thirty-eight-year-old Maguire soon learned that his colleagues were not thrilled with his efforts, given that Sikes had dispensed the military construction projects at his disposal to other key congressional districts, many outside his state. Maguire also realized that lawmakers, whatever their views or party affiliation, wanted those military appropriations to continue to flow unabated to their districts.

"The flack I got was never overt," said Maguire. "It was mostly submerged, body language. . . . I think the resentment of me was marginal. There was some grousing among the [New Jersey] delegation—some were friends of Sikes—that we didn't need to do this. But there were many senior members who were happy to have this happen. Sikes was on a short list of congressmen engaging in questionable stuff."

Maguire was proud that his campaign against Sikes set an important precedent: the defeat of a committee chair following ethics charges. "If ever there was a reason not to reelect a committee chair, this was it," argued Maguire. A member of the famous 1974 class that changed congressional rules to provide for the election of committee chairs, Maguire presided over the implementation of one of his group's most important reforms. "At the meeting of the Democratic Caucus at the beginning of the next session, we worked to put this on the agenda," he recalled. "It set a precedent. Sikes was removed from office by a resounding vote, although he [Sikes] wanted to continue."

Maguire's congressional career ended with his defeat by Marge Roukema, a Republican, in the Reagan landslide of 1980. "Ethics had no effect on my defeat," said Maguire, emphatically, nor did the issue "hurt me in terms of committee assignments. It appealed to independent-minded Republican voters in the district . . . which had never been carried by a Democrat. . . . And I lost with over 49 percent of the vote. My defeat was because of the Ayatollah, Carter, and Reagan. I still ran eighteen points ahead of Carter, who only won 31 percent of the district."

"49 percent was still not enough," he added, wistfully.

POWER NO LONGER PROTECTS

From Sikes it was only a short step to the "legendary king of legerdemain," Rep. Dan Rostenkowski (D-Ill.). Chairman of the House Ways and Means Committee since 1981 and one of the most powerful legislators of the century, the Chicago lawmaker was indicted in 1994 for doing what Chicago politicians have always done: using the public till to buy gifts like engraved maple chairs and crystal Capitol domes for friends and for orchestrating such patronage excesses as hiring friends and relatives for "no-show" jobs. Upon his release from prison in 1998 at the age of seventy, Rosty, as he was known, showed little remorse. He still could not understand how the rules had changed and why he went to jail "because I gave chairs away and gave ashtrays away."[2]

"I was there [in Congress] for thirty-three years," Rostenkowski recalled. "They changed the rules thirty times."[3] Elected to Congress in 1961, Rostenkowski served seventeen terms before his indictment. In the course of his illustrious career, he enjoyed a close relationship with his Republican counterparts in the Congress and with the White House, and he claimed to have dined with nine Presidents. The power he was able to amass enabled him to negotiate some of the most important pieces of legislation of the late twentieth century, including the Reagan tax cuts in 1981, Social Security reform, the Tax Reform Act of 1986, and the deficit reduction packages of the early 1990s.

But as influential as he was, Rostenkowski could not stave off the charges against him, nor could he protect his political future from the relentless onslaught of ethics charges. Following his indictment, House ethics rules forced him to relinquish the chairmanship of the Ways and Means Committee; and he was soon ousted from office by a Republican challenger, Michael P. Flanagan, in the November election later that year (1994).[4]

Rostenkowski's attorneys managed to reduce a seventeen-count federal criminal indictment to two counts in a plea bargain negotiated two years later, in 1996. The original indictment accused him of embezzling more than $500,000 from his expense accounts "to benefit himself, his family, and his friends," in addition to witness-tampering, fraud, concealing material facts, and conspiracy. If convicted on all counts, Rostenkowski could have faced a maximum sentence of ten years and a fine of $250,000. Under the plea bargain, the sentence was reduced to seventeen months and the fine to $100,000.[5] Despite the fact that two counts were a vast improvement over seventeen, Rostenkowski must have regretted turning down the first offer negotiated by his original attorney: a plea bargain of one felony charge, his resignation from Congress, and six months in prison. At the time, he wanted to fight the charges; he did not "commit any crimes," he argued, and "truth [was] on his side."[6]

Rostenkowski got caught between Congress and the Justice Department. In contrast to the reign of Mr. Sam, no Speaker today would dare intervene with Justice, the Internal Revenue Service, or any other executive branch agency to fend off an indictment, much less try and influence prosecutorial decision-making. Taking the place of the discreet phone call are open phone logs and transparent negotiations over who investigates whom, with the Justice Department preempting Congress in cases the Attorney General considers the most egregious—such as Abscam and the Rostenkowski case.

Once the Justice Department acted in the case of Rostenkowski, the House leadership—still Democratic in 1994 before the Republican victory later that year—studiously avoided the issue, ostensibly because the Committee on Standards of Official Conduct (the Ethics Committee) had not yet received a formal complaint. The truth was that the Democrats were unwilling to take on a fellow Democrat, especially one as popular and powerful as Rostenkowski, and stalled the congressional investigation for as long as possible. They were also fearful of being embarrassed politically by their association with a Democrat in trouble.

The working principle of bipartisanship on ethics that had prevailed until then was immediately abandoned, perhaps an early signal of the "politics of venom" that accelerated later that year. Christopher Shays, Republican of Connecticut, cooperated with his party leaders and filed a formal complaint, triggering an Ethics Committee investigation that ran simultaneously with Justice's activities.[7] Shays's complaint, which occurred less than four months before the Republicans won majorities in both Houses, showed how restive the Republicans were becoming under Democratic rule.

Rostenkowski was trapped by what we now see as a tectonic shift in congressional mores. The old rules just didn't apply any more, and the lawmaker was so busy with budgets and tax laws that he neglected to pay close attention to the changes taking place around him. To Rostenkowski's regret, he remained wedded to the old tradition of politicians feathering their own nests, with no one the wiser; he trusted those who knew the score to remain quiet and figured the others wouldn't care enough to pursue the issue.

Ultimately, power protected Rostenkowski, but he suffered a great deal of pain in the process. One month before he left office, in December 2000, President Clinton granted Rostenkowski a full pardon, giving no reason for his act. Although a pardon doesn't expunge his criminal record, it restores a citizen's full rights: that means Rostenkowski can vote, run for office again—highly unlikely—and participate in politics.

PAY RAISES COST VOTES

Long before the case against Rostenkowski, Rep. Lyndon B. Johnson prevailed on the Federal Communications Commission (FCC) to double his radio station's wattage, a favor that increased the station's value exponentially. What Johnson did was typical for politicians at that time: Members of Congress traditionally accepted legal fees; franchises; free vacations; contracts; speaking honoraria; and no-show jobs for relatives, lovers, and political cronies. This was the way of the world, epitomized by the colorful Tammany Hall ward boss George Washington Plunkitt, no grammarian, who waved away critics with the phrase he intended for his gravestone: "I seen my opportunities and I took 'em."[8]

The signs of changing times were eminently visible for those who wished to see them. The public now cared a great deal about politicians enriching themselves in office, and it is highly unlikely that LBJ could become a multimillionaire today by leaning on the FCC. No doubt, however, LBJ would have mastered the current art of personal enrichment through politics without submitting to newspaper exposés, General Accounting Office reports, congressional investigations and press leaks from the White House. President Carter, twenty years out of office, was able to command a generous advance for his boyhood memoir; lesser politicians join investment banking houses or law firms that can afford multimillion-dollar salaries for their services—and connections.

One of the most telling indicators of increasing public concern about ethics was Congress's difficulties during the past quarter century in awarding itself pay raises; lawmakers found it politically impossible even to slip small stipends to cover increases in the cost of living into the annual budget. Fearful of voter anger and retribution at the polls, members have regularly withheld pay raises from themselves, knowing from personal experience the public's lack of sympathy with their financial hardships: maintaining two homes, raising money for elections, and keeping up socially with wealthy lobbyists and other high-flying Joneses. Finally, Congress devised a way to give itself a pay raise: by authorizing automatic pay increases in future years, unless their colleagues specifically voted against them. To no one's surprise, such pay raises rarely come to the House floor for a vote.

Lawmakers and the voting public find themselves wide apart on the subject of pay raises. Privately, some members complain about all they have given up to enter public service. But given the average wages and benefits of most Americans, it shouldn't come as a surprise that most people don't consider a salary of $136,700 a sacrifice. Back in 1951, senators were paid $18,000 a year, a salary that pay raise opponents claim kept elected representatives less elitist and more in touch with the people.[9] But today, those who feel they have sacrificed their livelihoods for public service keep their views quiet; in fact, new evidence shows that attitude clearly on the wane. For thirty-eight new members of Congress in 1998, for example, the salary of $136,700 represented quite a substantial boost in pay for them, considering their median income before election was $68,845. Less than half the new members reported assets of more than $200,000.[10]

After years of avoiding pay raises, Congress finally bit the bullet and in 1991 gave itself a whopping hike in salary—from $89,500 to $135,000 in the House, and from $101,900 to $125,100 in the Senate. (Such differentials, when they occur, are short-lived. The two Houses now earn the same salary.) The hefty pay raises did not come free. Leaders predicted that the public would accept these increases only in exchange for a deal on ethics: In exchange for a salary hike, they would impose steep limits on honoraria, speaking fees, and gifts.

They calculated wrong, at least in terms of public reaction. All the public saw was 25 percent increases in pay—far above the cost of living—and it responded forcefully. According to a Gallup survey, 80 percent of Democratic voters opposed the hikes, hand-in-hand with 76 percent of the Republicans. In hindsight, many believe the leadership would have been better off slipping in small raises over the years into the budgets, rather than confronting the issue at one time.[11]

ANGER AND THE
DECLINE IN PUBLIC CONFIDENCE

When the Rostenkowski case broke, several leading Republicans, such as Christopher Shays (R-Conn.), Richard Armey (R-Tex.), and Bill Paxon (R-N.Y.), jumped in to gloat and pursue ethics charges against him. More sophisticated members of both parties realized that when ethical lapses became a partisan issue, they reflected more negatively on the institution of Congress than on individual members. The polls upheld this view: that public opprobrium spread to both parties, regardless of which party was responsible for the current *scandal du jour.*

After Rostenkowski's indictment, a CNN poll found that 49 percent of the American public believed Congress was more corrupt in 1994 than it had been twenty years before, although with much stricter ethics rules in operation and heightened media scrutiny, that was clearly not true.[12] Later polls hovered around the same numbers in recording increasing public distrust of Congress. A Harris poll released in 1998 revealed that 51 percent of the public would not trust members of Congress, both Republican and Democrat, to tell the truth.[13] The Gallup poll, which gave pharmacists and clergy the highest ratings for ethical standards and honesty, noted that U.S. senators (along with policemen—who were also the object of several highly publicized scandals) suffered the most serious decline in image, losing five percentage points in 1997 alone.[14] Accounting for the differences in how questions are asked, the following year Roper reported that 35 percent of the public disapproved of how Congress was handling its job, compared with Gallup, who reported that only 20 percent had "very little" confidence in Congress.[15]

To a certain extent, the polls reflect the public's traditional distrust of public servants, which has been part of American political culture since the first settlers arrived at Jamestown. Some people still retain the image of a congressman from Al Capp's comic strip *Li'l Abner* as a "gross, groggy creature who woke from his nap only at the sound of the gavel and, after voting an invariable 'Nay,' immediately went back to sleep."[16] Together with popular culture, other factors correlate strongly with the public's perception of Congress, including partisan affiliation, socioeconomic status, levels of education, and expectations of what the political system can deliver.[17]

The most curious paradox involves the voters' consistently low perception of Congress as an institution at the same time they give high approval ratings to their individual representatives and senators. Americans have traditionally distrusted government, but the steady stream of scandals from Watergate to Whitewater have done nothing to counter their misgivings; in fact, the opposite has occurred. The continual stream of House and Senate investigations—from Abscam and the "Keating Five" to current scandals—have only accelerated public disapproval, although by the standards of the era of Speaker Sam, members of Congress today are probably less corrupt than at any time in history. One typical poll for Gallup in 1999 showed that 54 percent of the public rated "honesty and ethical standards" of members of Congress "average," whereas 28 percent regarded them as "low."[18]

Congress has become an unwitting partner in boosting its disapproval ratings by focusing on scandals at the expense of its traditional oversight activities. "Committee power," reported Richard E. Cohen of *The National Journal,* "has eroded to the point of collapse. . . . Congress's entire debate on Kosovo . . . occurred largely outside of the committee process. . . . On gun control . . . the key House committee was also circumvented . . . [and] The House Ways and Means Committee and the Senate Finance Committee, though long regarded as two of the most powerful panels on Capitol Hill, recently have been something less than models of legislative effectiveness."[19]

ABSENT PUBLIC WRATH, CONGRESS WILL AVOID ETHICAL TANGLES

At a hearing in 1990, a witness testified in favor of stopping the revolving door that allowed members of Congress, their staffers, State Department negotiators, and just about everyone else to leave government and lobby their former colleagues on behalf of foreign governments and foreign multinationals. Like Captain Renault at the casino in Casablanca, the senators on the Commerce Committee all expressed shock at the case of the chief State Department negotiator who brokered the semiconductor agreement between the United States and Japan and then left to join Fujitsu, a company that no doubt hired him for his government contacts and inside information. But they followed the advice of the State Department Ethics Office, which turned a blind eye and saw nothing illegal or unethical about the negotiator's new position.[20]

Senators amicably agreed privately that the laws on foreign lobbying should be changed to preempt this kind of arrangement—perfectly legal under rules that were current then and remain in force today. But they knew they could count on the old traditions of collusion: Senators privately offered their assurances to each other that expediency would prevail, notwithstanding the conflicts of interest that continued at the expense of the national interest. "We can't change the laws," they explained to one witness. "Our staffers won't let us; they say they have to make a living after they leave Congress." Judging from the lucrative practices that many lawmakers have established with foreign companies and foreign governments after they left Congress, it is now obvious that they were also thinking of their own professional futures. Lawmakers also parroted the popular but spurious argument that has always worked to forestall the enactment of

ethics laws with teeth in them: that good people will not be attracted to
government if they can't look forward to the possibility of leaving public
service for salaries that reward their years of experience.

Purposely, Congress writes its own ethics laws with sufficient vagueness
of language to forestall any serious reforms when the better part of valor
warrants inaction. Rep. Jay Dickey (R-Ark.) escaped an ethics probe, even
though he owned hundreds of thousands of dollars worth of stock in Wal-
Mart at a time when his votes reflected the company's interests. Ultimately,
however, the vaguer the ethics laws, the more trouble awaits lawmakers
who must grapple with these discretionary gaps in the future, gaps that
will undoubtedly be filled in by their political enemies.

The Ethics Committees have managed in the last couple of years to
limit ethics investigations by quietly restricting the right of those who
complain. They have also speeded up existing investigations and dispensed
with frivolous complaints in order to avoid penalizing members at election
time. Sen. Carl Levin (D-Mich.) spoke at length about opponents who
routinely used ethics complaints as political weapons. "If someone has four
pending ethical complaints, [it is easy to] run against that," he concluded.
Levin credited Victor Baird, chief counsel of the Senate Ethics Committee,
for his role in the "quick and early dismissal of frivolous complaints."

Politics also remains the most reliable determinant of punishment
(whether it will be expulsion, reprimand, censure, or a verbal rebuke) as
well as whether an investigation will be triggered at all. In these cases, politics and publicity go hand in hand, leading to such questions as: When are
lawmakers led by public opinion? How do they evaluate public opinion?
And what is the role of their own constituents? The Clinton impeachment
and subsequent trial in the Senate showed lawmakers the public's limited
tolerance for lengthy investigations, as well as its contempt for members
who tried hard to tear down the President over a sex scandal.

The future of congressional ethics turns on how Congress will deal
with its own members' conflicts of interest. Lawmakers will have to decide
whether Rep. Dickey's involvement with Wal-Mart is more troubling than
Rostenkowski's gifts to supporters and no-show jobs. Or whether Gingrich's use of GOPAC as a political tool is comparable to the cost of a trip
to the Paris Air Show, or to giveaways to the health maintenance organization (HMO) industry. Only time and the growing sophistication of the
American voter will determine the future of ethics.

The core question is whether Congress can continue to investigate itself. Can any institution—General Motors, the White House, the police—examine itself to the satisfaction of the public? And once it finds

transgressions, as is inevitable, can it punish its own members? Of course, Congress cannot be compared with other institutions, especially because the Constitution guarantees it the right of "self-government." Also, elections and constant media probes provide the checks on Congress that differentiate it from other groups, if not from other branches of government. General Motors's executives may answer to their stockholders, but they do not face the harsh test of reelection every two to six years, nor must they abide by the mosaic of Freedom of Information and sunshine laws that open public institutions to outside scrutiny. They can lock the media out when it suits them, whereas members of the Ways and Means Committee enjoy no such luxury.

But like General Motors and other organizations, Congress values loyalty above everything else: loyalty to the institution, the party, and, most of the time, even loyalty to members of the opposition. Like the "blue wall of silence" that revealed police officers' reluctance to testify against their colleagues in the horrific Abner Louima case in New York City, Congress responds only when its hand is forced. The police finally testified in New York after the prosecutor forced one of the defendants to turn states' evidence and testify against his fellow officers. Congress also acts only when the newspapers tear down the walls of silence. This explains to some extent the disparity in ethics cases: why some members go to jail for engineering no-show jobs, whereas others go scot-free for selling their votes. It also explains the innate conflicts involved when members of Congress are forced to judge one another. The "distinction between judge and party . . . breaks down," wrote Dennis Thompson, in the name of "collegial interdependence."[21]

The truth is that no institution can investigate itself, and Congress is no exception. Even with the voters in charge of its fate, lawmakers know the public is fickle; it forgets and forgives some of the worst infractions imaginable but can become furious at a relatively minor lapse of judgment. Polls reveal time and again that no matter what scandals have transpired, voters regard Congress with increasing contempt but still reserve great respect for their own individual representatives.

Political realities guarantee that Congress will continue to investigate itself, although the inequities in meting out punishment remain troublesome. Some members get a slap on the wrist; others resign before they have to face expulsion. The only reliable rule of thumb appears to be public reaction to the infraction. Politically that means that the severity of the punishment depends on exactly how much the individual in question has disgraced the institution, for given their druthers, lawmakers would much rather sweep ethics issues under the rug.

Congress is not alone. If anything, inconsistency seems to be the rule rather than the exception. Despite the numerous ethics bills passed by Congress for the executive branch of government—three alone were passed in the autumn of 1978 (Civil Service Reform Act, Ethics in Government, and legislation providing for inspectors-general in agencies)— public confidence in government continues to wane. In the case of Congress, this trend no longer remains a mystery: While relaxing its traditional oversight role over the budgets and enforcement activities of the agencies, both Houses spent endless hours investigating scandals, including a year-long investigation of the sexual liaison between President Clinton and a White House intern.

Observant politicians also know that electoral judgments don't discriminate between Republicans and Democrats or between challengers and incumbents. The House bank scandal, for example, "reduced the reported vote for incumbents [named in the scandal] by about 5 percentage points."[22] In many races that meant the difference between winning and losing or being redistricted out of office—in the case of Rep. Stephen J. Solarz, from Brooklyn, New York—his punishment for embarrassing the party meted out by the New York Democrats.

The scandal, which was originally revealed by the GAO, involved an informal arrangement between House members and a congressional "bank," which allowed members to bounce checks when their accounts failed to balance. Although the House Bank didn't use public funds, the voters were nevertheless outraged by the fact that their elected representatives could "borrow" upwards of $500,000 in some cases, without paying interest or being penalized for overdrafts. To the voters, it was another case of congressional privilege: Lawmakers got off free, when ordinary citizens had to pay high interest fees for home and car loans, as well as hefty penalties for overdrafts of even a few dollars on their personal checking accounts.

Public anger at the voting booth may have taught lawmakers to hide any lingering feelings of entitlement. But not always. At a Washington dinner party, the wife of a New York congressman argued for the inclusion of spouses on congressional fact-finding trips, popularly known as junkets. "The voters owe it to us," she said, forcefully. "We work hard and deserve these trips." Certainly the long-term benefits of exposing members of Congress to the world are immeasurable, but staffs and families don't fall into this category. The public has never bought into this particular perk, and many taxpayers don't agree that they owe even members of Congress, much less their families, free travel in exchange for the sacrifices of public service.

For those who missed the pay raise signals, there were many other indications of increasing public disapproval that prevented the old traditions from returning. Heightened public scrutiny, accompanied by a harsher, more partisan environment, guaranteed that new laws prohibiting honoraria, legal fees, and other forms of retainers would be tightly enforced. Those who ignored the new environment did so at their peril and risked prolonged confrontations with congressional committees, special prosecutors, federal grand juries, and the media.

Since the halcyon days of Speaker Sam, the rules have changed dramatically, with the Speaker and the chairman of the Ways and Means Committee more vulnerable to ethics probes than the lowliest newcomer. In a reversal of roles, the clout that has always accompanied power no longer provides the layers of insulation that it once afforded congressional leaders. In fact, today's leaders' accentuated visibility renders them easier targets than they were before television made them instant celebrities.

Today, even the party in power looks over its shoulder at the vagaries of the ethics process, whose potential has become almost too scary to contemplate. Speakers like Mr. Sam, or leaders like Rostenkowski and Sikes, would never have envisioned, much less tolerated, such threats to their power.

6

Sex–

The Sin of Hypocrisy

*"You were trying Packwood on the mores of the 90s for
conduct that occurred in the 1970s."*
—Senator Howell Heflin, Democrat of Alabama
and former chair of the Senate Ethics Committee

Readers of *The Washington Post* were greeted on a warm Sunday morning in May 1976 by a photo of a young woman in a low-cut black dress splashed across the front page. The mystery woman's name was Elizabeth Ray, a clerk/typist employed for two years by Rep. Wayne Hays, Democrat of Ohio, the chairman of the House Administration Committee and a twenty-eight year veteran of the chamber. Ray cheerfully admitted, "I can't type. I can't file. I can't even answer the phone." Her job description, she continued, included once or twice weekly visits to her bedroom from the sixty-four-year-old, recently married congressman, who heatedly denied her charges when they first appeared in print. "Hell's fire," he said. "I'm a happily married man."[1]

One of the most feared and disliked members of the House, Hays used his position as committee chair to exercise dictatorial control over congressional payroll, travel, staffing, parking, and the Capitol Police. The year before he had barely survived a serious challenge to his chairmanship from House freshmen elected in 1974, the famous class that reformed congressional procedures and chafed under the leadership of powerful chairmen like Hays, whose seniority kept them in power forever. Because he was known as the "meanest man in Congress," a phrase attributed to the late Rep. Phillip Burton (D-Calif.), few lawmakers were sorry to see him embroiled in scandal.[2] Hays eventually admitted a "personal relationship" with Ray and was forced to resign his seat, but he steadfastly "denied her charge that she did no office work."[3]

Why did Ray go public with her story? Was she merely a woman scorned? Was she afraid of losing her job? Did she fear for her personal safety? Judging from her statements, perhaps all of the above reasons made sense. Hays had divorced his wife of twenty-five years and had just married the secretary in his Ohio office five weeks before *The Washington Post* story broke. According to Ray, the congressman assured her that his marriage would not change their relationship or threaten her job "if she behaved herself."[4]

Two years earlier, another venerable powerhouse, Rep. Wilbur Mills (D-Ark.), chairman of the tax-writing Ways and Means Committee, also found himself embroiled in a lurid scandal. Mills was caught by the U.S. Park Police cavorting inebriated in the wee hours of the morning, accompanied by his current inamorata, a strip-tease performer named Fanne Fox (a.k.a., the "Argentine firecracker"). In the midst of this drunken spree, Fox took an indecorous tumble into the Tidal Basin, a Washington landmark best known as the home of the Jefferson Memorial and the capital's cherry trees. The event would have gone unnoticed were it not for several members of the U.S. Park Police, who duly recorded Mills's shenanigans: driving without lights at "unreasonable speed" and engaging in a "scuffle" that sent one policeman to the hospital.[5] When he finally sobered up, Mills faced the consequences of his extracurricular life: He was married; he was drunk; he was driving under the influence; and he was immortalized on a police blotter "socializing" with a stripper from the Junkanoo, a local nightspot of dubious reputation.

The two incidents reflected the media's unspoken policy of ignoring the personal transgressions of public figures as long as they did not affect their work or become particularly flagrant. Local police joined the press conspiracy in burying the misdemeanors of public officials; after all, it was more than coincidence that politicians controlled their budgets. The Park Police probably just didn't understand the unspoken system, or perhaps there were rookies on duty that fateful night.

After Watergate, it was getting more difficult to cover up scandals, and increasingly, members of Congress were forced to defend themselves before the cameras and their constituents for activities that used to be off limits. Of course, nothing helps television ratings and sells newspapers more than a sex scandal, and Congress has been especially cooperative in producing them during the past few decades. This does not mean that more senators and representatives are chasing women than ever before, but rather that today there is a much higher risk of getting caught as more fog is cleared from the glass windows of their two chambers.

Congress never arrived at any consensus about which sins should destroy careers and which should not. As a result, the process involving sexual issues has turned out to be more inequitable, confusing, and hypocritical than any of the other ethics issues. The Ethics Committees have yet to produce standard procedures that protect lawmakers against lies, defamation, or partisan onslaughts. Congressional careers are disrupted with none of the legal protections guaranteed other Americans. Some members survive the scandals, whereas many do not, but all of those involved in sexual imbroglios remember the incidents as the most painful events of their lives, with many still unable to speak about their experiences.

Even their colleagues remember the incidents with pain and embarrassment, as in the case of Gerry Studds (D–Mass.), who was censured by the House in 1983 for engaging in sex with a seventeen-year-old male congressional page in 1973. Studds was reelected after the censure vote.[6] "The gallery was packed in the Studds case," recalled Rep. Marcy Kaptur, Democrat of Ohio. "I was nervous. I didn't even sit down. [In contrast] [o]n the telecommunications bill, no one was even there. I kept thinking, 'is that what I was elected for?' I felt awful."

Women lawmakers have suffered much more than men because the public still expects a higher level of morality from women, who remember all too well that the scarlet letter was pinned on Hester Prynne and not on her lover Arthur Dimmesdale. Times haven't changed all that much. One especially tragic morality tale detailed the destruction of the career of the very promising Rep. Coya Knutson, Democrat of Minnesota. "Coya Come Home" cried the headline atop a public plea from Rep. Knutson's alcoholic husband, Andrew Knutson. In his letter to a local newspaper, Knutson charged his wife with neglecting him and begged her to come home and serve him warm dinners. As if that weren't bad enough in the eyes of the voters, Andrew Knutson in a later statement accused his wife of having an affair with her administrative assistant.

Even back in 1958, negative campaigning worked effectively, and retribution at the polls was swift. Knutson was handily defeated for a third term in Congress, despite her leading roles as the creator of the federal student loan fund in the National Defense Education Act and as the author of the first bill providing research funds for cystic fibrosis, a genetic lung disease. Soon after she lost her seat, a chastened Andrew Knutson admitted to a congressional committee that he had been the tool of a Republican cabal to unseat his wife; even the press release had been drafted, he said, by the campaign manager for the successful GOP candidate.[7] Too late. The voters had spoken, showing that even outright fraud cannot void an election.

Whatever form they take, morality issues are political killers. Mills and Hays lost their chairmanships—that was what the 1974 reforms were intended to do—and both left Congress permanently in 1976: Hays resigned, and Mills "retired." They skulked off not because their fellow lawmakers disapproved of their behavior, but because they brought disgrace upon the institution. It was not the sins of adultery, inebriation, or payroll padding that condemned Mills and Hays, but rather the public nature of their activities that ruined their careers. Simply, they got caught. Falling down drunk at the Tidal Basin in the shadow of the Jefferson Memorial and flaunting mistresses on the public payroll may have raised a few congressional eyebrows, but they were hardly career-breaking incidents until they made the headlines and roiled the voters.

Despite the number of ethics lapses over the years, the Founding Fathers believed they had a good reason for guaranteeing self-government only to Congress and not to either of the other branches. They wanted Congress to retain an independence not enjoyed by the other branches, which surely would have been inhibited by giving the removal power to the President or to the courts. They also trusted Congress to discipline its own members, which has come to mean that Congress can be trusted to punish its own members only when their behavior becomes too embarrassing to hide. Does this mean that lawmakers are naïve? Or that they turn a blind eye to what is going on around them? Hardly. Lawmakers know their colleagues are hardly saints, but they also know it would be a full-time job to weed out all the sinners.

Over time, Congress has been aided and abetted by the media in distinguishing which peccadilloes disgrace the institution and which can languish under wraps. Journalists have long shielded their readers from the salacious side of politics, leaving the public ignorant of facts that were widely known to insiders. The political community, including the press corps, was well aware of President John F. Kennedy's extramarital flings; insiders were also fully cognizant of the hidden sex lives of many members of Congress. None of this was reported because of a self-imposed law of *omerta* (a Sicilian word for silence; in Mafia terms, enforced silence) that protected political leaders from such scrutiny—male leaders, that is. The absence of reporting on sex left society with a sanitized vision of their leaders, which only made revelations about the sex lives of politicians, when they finally came out, all the more shocking. After the Hays and Mills incidents hit the headlines in the mid-1970s, reporters began covering the sex lives of politicians in earnest.

The public's previously idealized vision of politicians has served to increase its cynicism, when a more sober assessment would have viewed lawmakers more accurately as mere mortals or as reflections of society. People also forget how fast things change, particularly with regard to norms involving sexual behavior: What was considered aberrant in the past, for example, may be perfectly acceptable today. President Andrew Jackson's wife, Rachel, suffered grievously from charges that their marriage was not "legitimate," with Jackson blaming her untimely death on the strain of public disapproval. When he was elected, it was alleged that Jackson didn't "officially" marry Rachel Robards née Donelson on January 17, 1794, after they had been living together as man and wife since 1790. Rachel Jackson's former husband, Lewis Robards, had been granted a divorce on grounds of desertion and adultery, although there is some evidence that Robards was abusive and deserted her first. The records from that time are confusing: There was also a question about when the divorce actually came through because between 1790 and 1794, the Jacksons lived in a territory whose civil authority was confusing.[8]

Today, instead of worrying about whether or when the ink on a marriage document was dry, lawmakers struggle with issues like marital fidelity, sexual harassment, homosexual marriage, and whether gay soldiers should be permitted to serve openly in the military. Legislators still avoid issues involving extramarital sex lest they be accused of throwing stones from glass houses. They know all too well that sex scandals suffer from the same political problems as all the other behavioral sins, only the voter retribution is worse. There are no guidelines; sexual lapses are still an easy mark for partisan attacks; and from observing the Anita Hill hearings, members of Congress know they can't count on their fellow lawmakers to defend them. Politicians also know that American voters are unpredictable in their levels of tolerance for sexual scandals: They can't seem to decide exactly what is scandalous or whether a leader should lose power for cheating on his wife.

Cross-cultural barriers abound. For example: Europeans can't understand American "puritanism," whereas Americans find it hard to comprehend continental "tolerance," such as the state funeral of former French President François Mitterand, whose mistress and illegitimate daughter openly accompanied the funeral bier with his wife and sons.

Americans are still conflicted about marital infidelity. "So what if he lied," ran the conventional wisdom in Washington during the year-long congressional investigation of President Clinton's dalliance with White House intern Monica Lewinsky. "Everybody lies about sex." Public ambivalence was reflected in the investigation, which resulted in a House vote impeaching the President, followed by a Senate trial that failed to convict him.

The polls fully reflected the public's cynicism about the affair, which increased substantially as scandals involving marital infidelity encompassed Congress as well as the President. A Roper poll revealed that 64 percent of their sample answered "yes" to the question "Do you think that most members of Congress have lied to someone about having an extramarital affair?" Seventeen percent weren't sure.[9]

In their zeal to pursue the president, many members of Congress never dreamed that the public would so closely identify them with Clinton's troubles. Many lawmakers could never understand how they could be ensnared in the same net as the President. In other words, it's adultery, stupid, to paraphrase Clinton's 1992 campaign slogan about the economy, although the sin of adultery assumes a certain amount of lying. Disapproval ratings in polls reveal that Americans remain conflicted about the extramarital sex lives of their leaders, regardless of how many different ways the questions are asked. Many analysts argued that the public cared more about President's Clinton's lies—about his statement that he "did not have sex with that woman," for example—than about the sexual act itself, although poll data indicated that was not altogether true. Deep down, voters cared about sex: sex outside marriage, sex in the Oval Office, and sex with an employee his daughter's age. Interestingly, Clinton's character ratings remained low, but his performance rankings soared, a dichotomy that indicated that for the first time, the public appeared to be able to separate the president's moral behavior from his other roles. To the surprise and dismay of Republicans in Congress, the public disapproved of the president's behavior but didn't agree with them that his personal mistakes warranted removing him from office.[10]

Clinton's problems bore a painful similarity to congressional scandals involving sex, but that didn't stop lawmakers from pursuing their effort to impeach and try the President. In the process, their own sexual histories were opened to public view, resulting in resignations and several especially nasty partisan battles. In an unprecedented abdication of office, Rep. Robert Livingston, a gregarious and powerful Republican from Louisiana, and the Speaker-designate after Gingrich's resignation, announced that he would not run for Speaker and instead resigned his seat in the House. His confessional speech occurred a few steps ahead of the media, preempting exposés of his long history of extramarital affairs. He was also warned by a small group of House conservatives that they were considering voting against him for Speaker because he had not divulged his adulterous affairs. Livingston used the occasion to call on President Clinton to resign for his own [the President's] "indiscretions."[11]

If any rules have emerged at all on congressional sex, they speak to the importance of not getting caught, of keeping private lives private, however unseemly. Congress may have the power to amend the Constitution and to change the laws, but lawmakers wouldn't dare tackle the Ten Commandments, still honored—at least in the breach—by a nation that still boasts higher attendance at church than at sporting events.[12]

Adultery still counts as one of the deadlier sins, for regardless of what percentage of the American public indulges in extramarital affairs or accepts the practice in others, a majority still registers disapproval of the practice—especially in its political leaders. Accordingly, lawmakers know they live in a glass house and that they have exchanged their right to a private life for the transparent piece of real estate that accompanies their oath of office. No one cared much about Wayne Hays's affair with Elizabeth Ray until it emerged that she was earning $14,000 from the public payroll for nonclerical "services." And Wilbur Mills's dalliance with the stripper, Fanne Fox? Until it became public with Fox's unseemly nocturnal swim, his affairs were strictly personal.

Congressional sex runs the gamut—prostitution, sexual harassment, spousal abuse, and pedophilia. But the rules remain highly discretionary: Charges are still raised primarily on the ability of a partisan group to organize a protest and on the headlines that reveal the scandal. Fortunately, homosexuality is no longer the career-breaker it was when Allen Drury wrote his ground-breaking political novel, *Advise and Consent*.[13]

Under the leadership of Rep. Barney Frank (D-Mass.), homosexual members of Congress have managed to stave off some, if not all, of the more repressive measures that their colleagues have attempted to inflict on those with alternative life styles. And if they have not stamped out all of the prejudices of their peers, at least the mores are changing: In the 1996 edition of *The Almanac of American Politics*, Frank and Gerry E. Studds, another openly gay member of Congress and fellow Democrat from Massachusetts, have listed the names of their companions in their personal biographies.[14] Another positive sign of the times, according to Frank, occurred with the swearing in of his former legislative assistant, Robert Raben, as assistant attorney general for legislative affairs in the late fall of 1999. "Raben had organized the Gay and Lesbian Staff Caucus on the Hill," said Frank. "[Rep.] Charles Canaday [R-Fla.] wrote a letter supporting him, and called me the day after I had open heart surgery to tell me that Henry Hyde would testify for him, and not to worry, that Orrin Hatch [R-Utah] would put the appointment through."

Frank's view is that "no one was ever punished [just for] sex. I lied, fixed parking tickets. In the Studds and the Crane cases, it was age (the age of the pages). There was the perception that the public would be unforgiving." The perception that the public would be unforgiving colored the final decision over Studds and Crane. Newt Gingrich entered the fray during the debate in 1983 over the Ethics Committee's recommendation to reprimand the two lawmakers. Reprimand was too lenient, he said, arguing for the most severe punishment, expulsion. Another Republican, Robert H. Michel (R-Ill.), offered a compromise motion, which was adopted by the House, to censure the two lawmakers. It was the first time House members were censured for sexual conduct.[15]

Although in the Studds and Crane cases an air of bipartisanship prevailed—one member was a Democrat and the other a Republican—a later case involving Barney Frank revealed a decidedly partisan (as well as homophobic) tone to the sexual politics of the case. Frank was investigated by the Ethics Committee for exerting improper political influence on behalf of Steve Gobie, a convicted felon, who was running a male escort service out of Frank's house. The committee found no evidence that Frank knew of the prostitution ring but criticized him for the impropriety of misusing his political influence and writing a misleading memo to Gobie's probation officer. Initially, the committee tried to issue the lighter sanction of a letter of reproval, but faced with the full House's inclination to go with a harsher penalty—as it did with Studds and Crane—the committee preempted its critics and recommended a reprimand.

Frank's allies feared that if the House voted censure, Frank would have to give up his chairmanship of a Judiciary subcommittee because censured lawmakers cannot hold chairmanships for the remainder of the congressional term. Democrats also girded for action against Newt Gingrich, whom they blamed for the resignation earlier that year of Speaker Jim Wright (D-Tex.); coincidentally, it was Gingrich who was lobbying hard for Frank to be censured. In the end, it was the Democrats who prevailed: Only 12 Democrats defected to vote with the 129 Republicans supporting censure, and the motion failed.[16]

THE PACKWOOD CASE

Bob Packwood, the brainy, highly respected chairman of the Senate Finance Committee in the 1980s, was also not targeted just for sex but presumably for other violations that emerged along with the sexual harassment case against him. The Oregon Republican was among the most powerful members of Congress, with jurisdiction over taxes, trade, health care, welfare, and other key issues. His Republican colleagues steadfastly supported him until he politically embarrassed them. Acceding to his request, the Republicans hung together to oppose public hearings, casting a vote that they knew could cost them politically. But forty-eight hours later, Packwood reversed himself and asked for public hearings, leaving his Republican colleagues out on a limb and thoroughly disgusted with him. When they abandoned their support, his fate was all but sealed.

Like the President, Packwood was an easy target for his political enemies. But unlike the President, who escaped removal from office, Packwood was forced to resign a few days before the Senate was about to expel him. He was the fifth senator in two hundred years to resign his seat to avoid expulsion. Before the scandal broke, Packwood enjoyed a reputation as one of the Senate's most accomplished lawmakers. Senators on both sides of the aisle respected him for his expertise. He was one of the major architects of the 1986 Tax Reform Bill and a key fund-raiser for the Republican Party. He is widely credited for his efforts at revising the nation's complex tax code, emerging as one of the heroes of Jeffrey H. Birnbaum's and Alan S. Murray's gripping study of the 1986 Tax Reform Bill, *Showdown at Gucci Gulch*.[17]

Ironically, Packwood was also held in high esteem by women's groups, whose issues he promoted over the course of his twenty-three-year Senate career. He promoted women to the highest positions on his staff and was the only Republican in the Senate to support freedom of choice on the abortion issue, a stance that proved risky politically as well as physically. Assassination threats from extremist pro-life activists were considered serious enough for officers from the Capitol police to move into the basement of his Bethesda home for several weeks in order to protect the Senator and his family.

Despite his earlier support of their issues, none of the leading women's rights groups publicly defended Packwood during his later troubles, although the National Abortion Rights Action League (NARAL), the nation's leading abortion-rights group, refrained from attacking him publicly. Many believed that the refusal of women's groups to come to Packwood's aid meant that they could not be trusted to stand by their allies. Others argued that women's legislative priorities had shifted, with sexual harassment taking precedence over reproductive freedom.[18]

The timing of Packwood's troubles couldn't have been worse. They came on the heels of Anita Hill's charges against Supreme Court nominee Clarence Thomas, and Packwood suffered from the exposure of the issue of sexual harassment in the workplace. Political conflicts build steam from prior crises, and through no choice of their own, Packwood and Anita Hill were joined in the public mind. Both cases reflected the shift in the priorities of the women's movement, and both brought the issue of sexual harassment to the forefront of the public agenda. A year before Packwood drew the attention of the Senate, women's groups, their leaders, and the general public were galvanized by the Anita Hill hearings, the Senate Judiciary Committee's live, televised investigation of allegations of sexual harassment against Supreme Court nominee Clarence Thomas. Thomas ultimately squeaked through the hearings to take his place as an Associate Justice. Ultimately, it was Thomas's word that he did not harass Anita Hill against hers, and senators were reluctant to refuse the President's choice on her charges alone.

In sexual harassment cases, as in rape cases, the evidence of corroborating witnesses is not necessary in courts of law. Similarly, corroborating evidence in virtually all of the charges against Packwood relied heavily on statements from victims' friends, boyfriends, and roommates, who testified on the basis of information they received—often from second-hand sources. In this respect, the Packwood case also echoed the charges against President Clinton during his impeachment hearings: as evidence of her involvement, Monica Lewinsky maintained that she told eleven friends of her liaison with the President, including Linda Tripp, the friend who taped her confessions and turned them over to the Independent Counsel Kenneth Starr. The recollections of friends were regarded as evidence of the President's involvement with Lewinsky.

Clarence Thomas's opponents lost the battle but not the war: The issue of sexual harassment rose to permanent status in the public consciousness, where it has remained ever since. When the Packwood case arose soon after the Clarence Thomas hearings, senators were determined not to be caught off guard again. Quite the reverse: They were fully primed to prove their commitment to the issue. Unlike abortion or gun control, the issue of sexual harassment unified women across the political spectrum. And for politicians, male and female, women's support presented a golden opportunity—the rare "win-win" proposition.

Packwood's troubles began in November 1992, immediately after his election to a fifth six-year term in the Senate. Allegations of sexual harassment against him had surfaced in Oregon, where a reporter for the *Oregonian* was working on a story based on accusations from former aides of the senator. *The Washington Post* held the story, then published it after his election on the grounds that the newspaper did not want to influence the outcome of the election. Because Packwood won by a relatively narrow margin (52 percent–47 percent), the *Post*'s decision to withhold publication drew considerable criticism from those who argued that the voters should have had access to the information about the sexual harassment charges against Packwood before the election so that they could have made a more informed decision.

Under pressure, the Ethics Committee decided to investigate Packwood soon after *The Washington Post* disclosed the allegations of sexual misconduct. Complaints against Packwood stretched back to 1969, totaling seventeen accusations and eighteen formal complaints: Seventeen of the complaints involved incidents that occurred before 1981, the eighteenth in 1990. In civil cases, statutes of limitations would prevent charges from being brought that went back this far in time, but in congressional ethics cases, no such limits apply. (The law provides no time limit in capital crimes.)

The probe continued well into 1993, when the appearance of Packwood's diaries, all 8,200 pages of them, complicated the issue. He introduced the diaries to present exculpatory evidence—evidence that would clear him. Unfortunately for Packwood, the reverse occurred. Why does anyone in public life today keep diaries? For the historical record, as Packwood later testified. Or for future memoirs, which have become a source of considerable revenue—well into the millions of dollars—for high-profile politicians. Packwood introduced the diaries to dispute the harassment charges. When the dust finally settled on the thirty-month investigation, the Ethics Committee had held more than fifty closed-door meetings and had compiled a 10,145-page dossier charging the senator with unwanted sexual advances to at least seventeen women, tampering with evidence, witness intimidation, and abusing his office by trying to pressure lobbyists to find a job for his estranged wife.[19]

It was his diaries that eventually destroyed Packwood and his Senate career. Without them, the evidence would have resembled the Clarence Thomas hearings: his word against theirs. Incredibly, and in his own words, Packwood discussed his sexual life and his political influence, which included soliciting a job for his wife. He fought constantly with the committee over the documents, and withheld 112 of them—many of them memoranda—on the grounds of attorney-client privilege. To the fury of the committee and its staff, he altered entries in the transcripts, "entries which related to the subject of intimidation of witnesses well after his own attorneys had instructed him to collect and forward entries related to the intimidation issue."[20]

Packwood argued that he could alter the diaries because his attorneys had advised him that the committee was not entitled to them; in fact, the first set of attorneys representing him from the Washington law firm of Arnold and Porter resigned after learning that their client had tampered with the evidence. The committee also had to go to court to get the diaries and then fought with Packwood constantly over which entries were "masked" (not allowed as irrelevant to the inquiry) and which were not.

The traditional comity among senators was jettisoned as soon as the Ethics Committee and Packwood sparred over the diaries. At first, Packwood refused to turn over the diaries after promising the committee that he would turn them over; he then balked at the committee's request that entries unrelated to charges of sexual misconduct—such as trying to find employment for his wife—be included. Finally, after what some considered a gross invasion of his privacy rights, the committee voted to subpoena the diaries: The committee was backed by a Senate vote to go to court to enforce the subpoena, which was finally served on Packwood in November 1993. After an appeal to the Supreme Court was rejected the following spring, Packwood finally turned over his diaries to the committee. The committee staff subpoenaed additional documents involving the senator's attempts to gain employment for his wife and spent the remainder of that year reviewing the documents.[21]

While these legal skirmishes were going on, Packwood's political allies maneuvered behind the scenes. At first, it was widely believed that as the ranking Republican on the Senate Finance Committee, Packwood was too powerful for the Senate to force him to resign. It was also widely known that Republican Leader Robert Dole wanted a knowledgeable and politically reliable ally at the helm of the Senate's most important and influential committee. Republicans wanted to solidify their leadership, not weaken it; therefore, pondered the smart money, the leadership could be trusted to protect Packwood against facing lengthy, humiliating hearings that would also embarrass the party.

But conventional wisdom doesn't hold up in extraordinary times. Senators were still chafing from the fallout from angry women constituents that followed the Clarence Thomas hearings. Few could forget the television images of the senators on the all-male Judiciary Committee. They looked foolish, ill-informed, and out of the mainstream. A few shifted uncomfortably throughout the hearings; others behaved inappropriately in front of the klieg lights. Sen. Arlen Specter (R-Pa.) persisted in pursuing an aggressively prosecutorial stance, which may have been effective in a courtroom, but was offensive in the hot medium of television. Some of Specter's more naïve colleagues on the committee and in the Senate openly expressed their surprise at the very notion that women could experience sexual harassment on the job.

Still, anyone betting on the outcome would have wagered on a partisan stalemate because the Ethics Committee was evenly divided between three Democrats and three Republicans. The Republicans were Robert C. Smith of New Hampshire, Mitch McConnell of Kentucky (the chair), and Larry E. Craig of Idaho; the Democrats included Byron L. Dorgan of North Dakota (the previous chair), Barbara A. Mikulski of Maryland, and Richard H. Bryan of Nevada.

What were the precipitating factors that reversed the odds, altered the political chemistry, and sealed Packwood's fate? Two events, actually. The first was a letter to the Ethics Committee from five women senators requesting public hearings. Organized by Barbara Boxer, Democrat of California, the senators emphasized the "reputation of the Senate and the public's interest." Bryan, one of the three Democrats on the committee, publicly supported their request, but his position drew the wrath of McConnell, still loyal to Packwood, who preferred to keep the process secret and the Ethics Committee far away from the tents of the media circus. The bipartisan consensus of the committee then broke down, with the powerful committee chair McConnell suspending deliberations indefinitely. Allegedly, McConnell responded privately to Democratic entreaties to pursue Packwood with threats to retaliate by introducing public ethics investigations of Senate Minority Leader Tom Daschle (D-S.D.) and Senator Edward M. Kennedy (D-Mass.) for his role in the 1969 incident at Chappaquiddick.[22]

Not easily deterred by the Ethics Committee's rebuff, Boxer introduced her motion for public hearings on the Senate floor on August 2, 1995. She narrowly lost, 48–52, but managed to join her cause once and for all as a feminist issue. A highly emotional debate involving all eight female senators resulted in the defection of only one Republican woman, Olympia Snowe of Maine, who crossed party lines and voted for public hearings. The other two Republicans, Nancy Kassebaum of Kansas and Kay Bailey Hutchison of Texas, stuck to their party and opposed public hearings. Only two other male Republican senators voted with Boxer: William Cohen of Maine and Arlen Specter, who was reacting, it was said, to widespread criticism from "women's groups for his attacks on [Anita] Hill during the Thomas confirmation hearings."[23] Senator Daniel Patrick Moynihan, Democrat of New York, voted with the Republicans on the Packwood issue, most likely out of loyalty to Packwood; at that time he served with Packwood as the ranking Democrat on the Finance Committee.

Partisan as they were, Senate Democrats still would have preferred to deal with the Packwood case quietly and resented Boxer's independent action. "She didn't suffer at all," said one Democratic Senator. "The Republicans despised her. She is a very aggressive person."

The second incident occurred later that month—August 1995—when the committee decided to allow two more allegations (one involving a former summer intern) into the Packwood file. The committee's sudden decision threatened to stretch its deliberations into an indefinite future. Angered by this development, Packwood suddenly reversed his earlier position and called for public hearings in order to defend himself and confront his accusers. Republicans who had voted against public hearings felt betrayed. An angry McConnell, who had been an ally and protector of Packwood's up to that point, reversed himself along with many other Republicans who were outraged by Packwood's sudden change-of-heart.

Pressured by Boxer's continued threats to reintroduce public hearings, the committee met on September 6, 1995, and voted unanimously to recommend Packwood's expulsion. The committee dropped its investigation of the two additional allegations and made its decision based on the evidence gathered by its staff. Voting 6–0, they finally reached a bipartisan consensus and found Packwood guilty of all the charges filed against him. Accepting the inevitable, Packwood resigned before the full Senate ratified the committee's decision, just as Harrison Williams had done fourteen years before.

"Packwood should have resigned earlier," said Jake Stein, the attorney who took over the case after attorneys from Arnold and Porter resigned—after Packwood altered the transcripts. "After the Justice Department exonerated him, and before the Ethics Committee investigated and then forced him to resign."

THE CHARGES

What were the charges? And the pattern of proceeding on those charges? Did they warrant expulsion? Were they fair? Were they corroborated? The allegations filled ten volumes of evidence and included excerpts from the diaries as well as the testimonies of women staffers dating back more than twenty years. The committee report concluded that the senator's sexual misconduct reflected a pattern of harassment because the women employees held subordinate positions. The evidence also included a diary entry, written by Packwood, which recorded his effort to solicit employment from a lobbyist from the Mitsubishi Electric Corporation for his estranged wife, Georgie, in order to reduce his alimony payments. Perhaps Packwood could successfully have fought the sexual harassment charges, but he could not rebut the accusation against him of influence-peddling with a foreign corporation, nor could he disprove the most serious legal charge: that he altered his diaries (a possible obstruction of justice) before turning them over to the Ethics Committee.

The balance was finally tipped in Congress by the extent to which disgrace to the institution had occurred, as opposed to operating from a clearly defined list of transgressions. The most damning charges released by the highly graphic committee report involved sex, although senators were more comfortable in the public eye dealing with charges of influence-peddling and obstruction of justice. Before issuing the finding of "inappropriate conduct," the committee staff mailed a letter and questionnaire to "almost 300 women former staff members . . . [then] interviewed . . . or obtained [statements] from 210 witnesses in connection with the allegations relating to sexual misconduct or intimidation [of witnesses]."[24]

The committee's exhaustive review netted more than a dozen allegations by women staffers accusing Packwood of unwanted sexual advances, most of them involving attempted kisses. None of the complainants charged the senator with rape or adultery but focused rather on inappropriate behavior between an employer and his subordinates. Typical of the testimony recorded in the final report was a report submitted by a lobbyist, Mary Heffernan, who was not employed by Packwood but by NARAL. The reported advance occurred between 1981 and 1982, and read:

> Ms. Heffernan set up an appointment with Senator Packwood's staff to meet him . . . to discuss issues relating to abortion legislation. When she arrived at the office, Ms. Heffernan was escorted into Senator Packwood's private office; the Senator sat behind his desk, and she sat in front of the desk. Toward the end of the meeting, when Ms. Heffernan got up from her chair and started to move away, Senator Packwood came around his desk, put his hands on her upper arms and squeezed them, and leaned over and gave her a

sensual, sexual kiss on the mouth. She stepped back, got her coat, opened the door, and quickly left the room.[25]

Other testimony was similar to Heffernan's, except for the fact that other women complainants worked directly for the senator on his personal or committee staffs. Packwood's response was that, "Ms. Heffernan had maintained a warm, close relationship with him after the incident, that she had sought a job with him, and that she had in fact kissed him on a subsequent occasion."[26]

Other charges were similarly damning, although it is doubtful that they would have stood up in a court of law. Packwood apologized at a press conference on December 10, 1992, after *The Washington Post* article appeared and before the committee formally took up his case. He took full responsibility, he said, for "his conduct, that . . . his actions were unwelcomed and offensive to the women involved, and justifiably so; that his past actions were not just inappropriate, that what he had done was not just stupid or boorish, but his actions were just plain wrong." He added that "'he didn't get it [then],' but that he did now." He also admitted that he'd made mistakes and "apologized to the women involved."

Too little and too late, said the committee, which went ahead and conducted a full-scale investigation of the behavior that Packwood had already admitted to at his press conference. It was clear during this period that Packwood was an alcoholic whose clumsy and adolescent lunges at women staffers were driven by his addiction. By reputation and later admission, he was also an adulterer, although that character flaw has never amounted to cause for expulsion in either house of Congress. The committee concluded that regardless of his alcoholism, Packwood was "responsible for his actions."[27]

On the issue of sexual harassment, the committee focused on the inequality of the parties:

Senate Ethics Counsel finds that these incidents . . . reflect a pattern of abuse by Senator Packwood of his position of power over women who were in a subordinate position, either as his employees, as Senate employees, prospective employees, campaign workers, or persons whose livelihood prevented them from effectively protesting or seeking redress for his actions. These women were not on an equal footing with Senator Packwood, and he took advantage of that disparity to visit upon them uninvited and unwelcome sexual advances. . . . All of which constitutes an abuse of his position of power and authority as a United States Senator.[28]

THE PROCESS

The process of Packwood's threatened expulsion raises more questions than it answers, especially against the backdrop of the Clinton impeachment, which occurred three years after Packwood's resignation. Both men were accused of extramarital relationships; they both succumbed regularly to the ever-present temptations of adoring power groupies, with little thought of the political consequences; and they each coped with troubled marriages. Packwood, now a successful lobbyist, remarked during the Clinton impeachment hearings that when he raised the issue of the credibility of the witnesses against him during his congressional investigation, he was pilloried by the same women's groups that supported the White House's efforts to destroy the reputations of the President's accusers, Paula Jones and Kathleen Willey.

The Ethics Committee invoked the rape shield law (which prevents the sexual history of the victim from being entered as evidence in court) in its effort to determine witness credibility. But in the process of investigating Packwood, many questions were left unanswered, leading to some confusion in the process. Were the victims' sexual histories relevant because rape was not involved? Should the same evidence requirements for state and federal courts apply to congressional investigations, which are not trials but rather fact-finding missions? Should other sexual offenses, such as sexual harassment, be treated in the same manner as rape? In the absence of any precedent on the issue of sexual harassment, the committee staff made up its own rules and procedures as it went along. A few include:

The Identification of Witnesses: The committee guaranteed that those who challenged the propriety of Packwood's behavior did not have to be identified if they did not want to be. On the surface, this seems fair to the women who did not want their private lives bared to public view, similar to rape victims who prefer to preserve their anonymity. This is certainly fair to rape victims who no longer have to suffer the double trauma of exposure in addition to the violence they have experienced at the hands of the rapist. It works against the accused, but society has decided to tip the balance in this particular category of felony cases. Is Packwood's case comparable? Packwood was unable to confront witnesses against him. After reading accounts in the media of the incidents, some witnesses came forward in Packwood's defense, but their testimonies were not included in the final committee report.

The Deposition and Subpoena Power: Packwood was not allowed to depose or subpoena witnesses, although the Ethics Committee allowed itself the privilege of issuing subpoenas and forcing witnesses to testify. Only those who volunteered could be deposed by Packwood, and, as expected, none of the hostile witnesses chose that course. Packwood's advocates questioned the fairness of this process. On the one hand, it allowed the committee to prepare its case, but on the other, it prevented Packwood's attorneys from defending him properly. Although their pleas were futile, Packwood's lawyers argued that they could be charged with malpractice if they could not pursue all the evidence, which the Ethics Committee had prevented them from doing. These restrictions do not apply in regular trials, where defendants are given every opportunity available to defend themselves against the state.

Absentee Judges and Jurors: Members of the committee who signed on to the report and its findings of inappropriate conduct never heard the testimony of any of the women making the charges; instead, their depositions were taken by Ethics Committee staffers. In effect, the judges and the jury never heard the witnesses, never heard the defendant, and never interviewed the complainants. Critics argue that it is not possible to judge fairly only on the basis of a written record, without looking witnesses in the eye and evaluating their credibility. At congressional hearings, senators lean over the table and pepper their witnesses with tough questions to get closer to the truth. But not in this case. Were the investigation and final decision staff-driven? Probably not. The senators on the Ethics Committee relied on their staffs to prepare the case but took umbrage at the suggestion that they were prisoners of their staffs. Most likely, they were still smarting from the Anita Hill hearings and wanted to regain the public's confidence by vigorously pursuing the issue of sexual harassment.

No Verification: Witnesses, friendly and unfriendly, were not able to get copies of their depositions; they were not even allowed to tape them or obtain copies for their lawyers. Only the committee had copies of the depositions. The lawyers could be there but were only allowed to take notes. This, too, hampered Packwood's ability to prepare his defense.

The sexual misconduct case involving Laurie Reed, a former staffer, revealed some of the inconsistencies of the process. The evidence introduced included the diary; the statements of Ms. Reed; and the recollections of Packwood staffers, who testified on his behalf. All of the evidence, except for Ms. Reed's statements, weighed heavily in favor of the senator. Senator

Packwood's diaries, taken as primary evidence because they were the "contemporaneous event," reported that Ms. Reed had kissed the senator, not vice versa, as she had alleged.

The statements of male and female staffers described Reed as a "sexual predator," who "dressed inappropriately in the office in low-cut blouses and short skirts." They also testified that she was a pathological liar who lied about her degree from the University of Washington (she didn't have one) on the résumé she used to get a job on Packwood's staff; boasted about her relationships with famous men, including members of Congress; talked about her attraction to older, powerful men; and "got into trouble with her future husband because she lied." Witnesses added that Ms. Reed was the one making the advances toward Senator Packwood, not vice versa, as alleged; that she was not upset by the kissing incident; that she had invited the senator to a concert and to a drinking party at a local bar, called the Irish Times, near the Capitol; and that she was clearly interested in pursuing a personal relationship with Packwood. She failed to heed warnings about her unprofessional dress and her advances to the senator from her superiors on the staff. According to the committee report, Reed was engaged at the time of the reported incident to a man then employed as the legislative director for Rep. Peter DeFazio, Democrat of Oregon, who was considering a contest against Packwood in the forthcoming Senate election.[29]

The Reed case was the only incident concerning the charge of sexual harassment that occurred after 1980. The statements included a deposition from Ginny Worrest, who had worked for Packwood since 1988, attesting to the fact that "C-1 (the way Reed was identified) took every opportunity to have personal contact with the senator . . . in the nature of flirting." Richard Grafmeyer, then-senior counsel to the finance committee, submitted a deposition as a witness to the party at the Irish Times. He left the party because he "found C-1's flirtatious behavior sickening and obvious." Long after the incident at the Irish Times, "C-1 continued to work for Senator Packwood," and tried to move up in the press office, said another staffer, Karen Belding. (Reed was eventually promoted to press secretary). "She was obviously interested in Senator Packwood and would throw herself at him," charged Bobbi Munson, who added, "from my perspective, I think she wanted a sexual relationship with him."[30]

Were these the comments of intimidated witnesses? The Ethics Committee concluded that Packwood's behavior constituted sexual harassment on the basis of evidence that Reed told her roommate about the incident. The gist of the statements on Packwood's behalf from present and former staffers was cited in the final report, but the statements were not included in their entirety. "The incident as alleged by the staff member did in fact occur," said the report, and constituted a "pattern of conduct that reflects an abuse of [Packwood's] position of authority, a pattern of conduct that constitutes improper conduct reflecting upon the Senate."[31]

Fishing Expeditions: The Ethics Committee took the position that its members could use the entire diary, including material relating to any behavior the committee did not consider ethical. Initially, the committee was looking for evidence in the diary of sexual misconduct, which they claimed to find in abundance; in the process, however, they also came across material involving Packwood's efforts to solicit employment for his estranged wife from a lobbyist. The job solicitation was much more damaging than the harassment material because the allegation involved the more serious charge of using public office for private gain. Packwood and his attorneys' efforts to limit the case to relevant material were for naught; so were their efforts to have a third party (a former federal judge, Kenneth Starr, later the Independent Counsel in the Clinton case) determine relevance.

The publicity, along with vague notions of the people's right to know, combined to make the process look fair, but some charged that it undid decades of legal precedent that shored up the protections of the individual against the discretionary power of the state. With respect to ordinary citizens, the Supreme Court has decided that evidence seized in violation of the Constitution (specifically, the Fourth Amendment's protections against "unreasonable search and seizure," as included in the Fourteenth Amendment) is inadmissible in a criminal trial in a state court. [32]

In support of this view, the American Civil Liberties Union (ACLU) filed an *amicus curiae* brief in support of Packwood's fight against the subpoena of his personal diaries, using the words "fishing expedition" to challenge the Ethics Committee's claim that it was entitled to examine the diaries in their entirety. "In our view, this is precisely the sort of fishing expedition that the Fourth Amendment prohibits. Especially when dealing with personal diaries, the Committee should not be allowed to rummage at will." The ACLU brief continued to buttress the claim that there was "substantial legal authority for the proposition that personal diaries should be absolutely immune from disclosure under the Fourth Amendment," concluding that while the Senate had a right to discipline its own members, this did not free the legislature from "abiding by constitutional norms."[33]

An opposing view supporting the right to use the diaries draws on the "plain view doctrine," which justifies the inclusion of incriminating evidence if it falls "within plain view" of the incident being investigated. Used most often by police officers in search and seizure cases, the doctrine specifically says that investigators cannot search "from one object to another until something incriminating at last emerges." The diaries were already introduced by Senator Packwood and could justifiably be regarded as already "within plain view" of investigators.[34]

Rules of Evidence: There is a serious question about whether much of this evidence would stand up in a court of law. To wit: the evidence and corroborating witnesses listed by the report in the Heffernan case, involving the NARAL staffer who accused Packwood of attempting to kiss her. Ms. Heffernan testified that she told no one about this incident. Her former husband contacted the committee and stated that "while he did not think that she would lie about the actual incident that occurred, he would not believe her if she claimed that the incident had a negative effect on her."[35]

Note: Although the word "witnesses" is listed in the plural form, only one witness, Heffernan's husband, was deposed, and his testimony clearly indicated that he was not told about the incident by his wife at the time. Even given that evidence in sexual misconduct cases, from rape to lesser offenses, is very difficult to obtain—and generally involves one person's word against another's—it still represents quite a stretch to arrive at the definitive finding of the Senate Ethics Counsel that "the incident as alleged by Ms. Heffernan in fact occurred. . . . And that Senator Packwood's conduct in this instance fits a pattern of conduct that reflects an abuse of his position of authority, a pattern of conduct that constitutes improper conduct reflecting upon the Senate." The incident in question allegedly occurred in 1984; the finding occurred in 1995.[36]

Another typical case involved a woman who only wanted to be identified as "Packwood Staff Member 100." She also alleged that Packwood inflicted "a sexual kiss" on her, "the type that a boyfriend would give to a girlfriend." After she pushed the Senator away, "the incident did not happen again." The "corroborating witnesses," again plural, in this case were nonexistent. Even the report stated that "The staff member could not recall telling anyone about this incident." Unimpeded by hard evidence, the report nonetheless concluded that "the incident as alleged by the staff member in fact occurred." This incident occurred in 1970, the finding in 1995.[37]

The Ethics Committee report can be opened at random with cases dating back to the 1970s and 1980s, all of them sharing similar troubling evidentiary problems. Whether the allegations are true or not, there is little credible evidence gathered by the committee to bolster its damning conclusions. To call corroborating witnesses "witnesses" when they don't even exist is highly questionable. Is this "I know it when I see it" justice? Ghost justice? Nonexistent justice? Surely, when there are no additional witnesses and little hard evidence, what else is left?

THE COMMITTEE'S POSITION

"They were pretty awful stories," recalled one senator involved in the proceeding who spoke on condition of anonymity. "We didn't need to hear the witnesses; we didn't need the women in front of us. There was a substantial amount of material in the depositions."

"Packwood had a pattern, a history of adultery," the senator continued. "Look at his long affair with his chief of staff, and the degrading circumstances in which she helped him. If you knew everything and had seen the weight of the evidence, you would understand why we had to get him out. He was a very seedy guy."

He also challenged the accusations against committee procedures: "Packwood was invited to have his lawyers provide exculpatory evidence. He had every opportunity to produce evidence."

It was clear from the committee's point of view that "Packwood blew it." Democrats as well as Republicans on the committee did everything in their power to make the case go away. "Packwood became a pathetic figure; it was painful for all of us." If Packwood had acted differently, many agreed that the committee would have meted out a less severe punishment than recommending expulsion; at the very least he would have been allowed to serve out his term. After that, the voters would have decided on whether he could continue in office.

How should he have acted? "When he came before the committee," said one member, "we wouldn't have expelled him if he had said something, like, 'the worst you've heard isn't as bad as what I've done. I'm sorry. I'll go to my grave being sorry. It was alcohol. It was a disease.' If he had said that, the committee wouldn't have expelled him.

"Instead he came before the Ethics Committee with his lawyer, Jake Stein, who looked very severe. Their attitude was, 'you don't know what you're talking about.' Packwood missed an opportunity to have the Ethics

Committee reprimand him, or some kind of lesser punishment. He turned himself into a huge liability. Packwood was the Pete Rose of ethics."

What about the time lag? "This happens with priests who abuse children. All the stories [from the victims] come out later. Those who talk give others confidence to come forward."

Packwood also mishandled the politics of the case at a critical juncture. The key factor for Republicans as well as Democrats was the vote on whether to hold public hearings. All but three Republicans voted no on public hearings, as did many Democrats. Then two days later, Packwood changed his mind, demanded public hearings, and forced a vote on the Senate floor. In other words, Republican and many Democratic senators walked the plank to save Packwood, only to have Packwood pull the plank out from under them. Before that, even many Democrats were loath to throw him overboard.

When McConnell, known as among the most partisan of Republicans, said he'd heard enough, the case was over. With Republicans ready to expel Packwood and risk the loss of a safe Republican seat, it showed that the Ethics Committee regarded the evidence against him as overwhelming. With an even number of Democrats and Republicans, the Ethics Committees in both houses typically act only when there is complete unanimity, especially in controversial cases. They reached that point in the Packwood case after he turned on his protectors after the vote on public hearings.

GRAINS OF TRUTH

"We were trying Packwood on the mores of the 90s for conduct that occurred in the 1970s," said Howell Heflin, former chairman of the Ethics Committee, reflecting on the Packwood case. "There ought to be a statute of limitations. The passage of time dims memories; they are embellished; the embellishment becomes part of the issue. Packwood was a woman's issue."

Packwood's reputation preceded the case against him. The Senate gathered the wagons around and decided he had become an embarrassment to the institution, all the more so in an era in which sexual harassment had become a primary issue for women as well as for many men. Packwood's alcoholism and alleged adultery had never been causes for expulsion in the past. Neither were jobs for friends and relatives, or sexual harassment and intimidating subordinates. Perhaps the Senate would be considerably emptier if its members were screened on these grounds. Hypocritical? Sure. But if Packwood was a sacrificial lamb, others took notice. Deterrence sometimes works, especially in cases involving sexual ethics. Neither house will ever be the same, thanks to Packwood, Hays, and Mills.

The problem also dates back to the nature of representative democracy and to the public's relationship with its leaders. Just as they trusted Congress to discipline itself, the Founding Fathers also made the decision to reject town meeting democracy in favor of a system that was one step removed: representative democracy. This form of government still relies on the public, but it provides for a buffer between the ballot box and the business of governing. Voters cast their ballots for politicians to represent them on important issues, which is why campaign promises have taken on such importance in recent years—as in "Read my lips; no new taxes."

In casting their vote, people also put their trust in those who assured them that they will protect their interests in the legislative arena—or even the White House. Trust for Americans is wrapped up in morality; citizens don't separate sexual character and political performance—although they seemed to make an exception for Clinton. Not yet, however, for members of Congress, who must still abide by a higher standard.

Perhaps a key mistake of Packwood and his attorneys was to regard this case in legal terms, when it was so clearly political. Although they knew full well the case was political, they felt they had to defend it on legal grounds because there was no other option. But, as in all congressional hearings, rules of evidence that took hundreds of years to develop in Anglo-American common law were irrelevant in the face of a political problem as massive as the one confronting the Senate in the wake of the Anita Hill hearings.

Packwood's experience also highlighted the hypocrisy involved in the ethics process on sexual issues. It showed the deficiencies in the process and the inequity in applying standards. But it also showed that the legislature remains a glass house and that a higher standard of behavior is expected of lawmakers than ordinary citizens expect of themselves. The steam keeps getting rubbed off the glass, making lapses of conduct more visible than ever before. What may have been a minor incident in the past—a quick dip in the Tidal Basin or a snatched embrace—is quite literally a federal case in today's transparent environment. For when senators and representatives embarrass themselves, they are also disgracing the institution and exposing their colleagues to overwhelming public criticism. No wonder the retribution has become so severe.

7

Torricelli, the CIA, and the Intelligence Committee

"The Truth Shall Make You Free"
—Gospel of St. John, on the wall of
the CIA lobby in Langley, Virginia

Deep in the Guatemalan jungle in 1990 an innkeeper named Michael DeVine was tortured and killed by soldiers of the Guatemalan army. He and his wife, Carol, operated an inn near some Mayan ruins in the remote village of Poptun, 140 miles northeast of Guatemala City. Two years later, a rebel leader from an insurgent guerrilla movement, Efrain Bamaca Velasquez, was captured, tortured, and murdered, also by the Guatemalan military. Despite years of stonewalling by both the American and Guatemalan governments, evidence mounted that both murders had been ordered by one of the top officials in the Guatemalan army, Colonel Julio Roberto Alpirez, whose salary was supplemented by the U.S. Central Intelligence Agency between 1988 and 1992.

It became clear that Americans were involved in the killings, both as victims and as advisers. DeVine, the innkeeper, was a U.S. citizen; Bamaca was married to an American woman, a Harvard-educated lawyer named Jennifer Harbury. The public did not pay much attention to DeVine's murder until after it was linked to the killing of Bamaca and after Harbury pleaded with the State Department, the Clinton administration, the Congress, and the Guatemalan government to tell her the real story of her husband's murder. Her efforts were to no avail. Ignored by her own government, Harbury finally attracted the attention of the media and eventually the White House only after she conducted two hunger strikes, one in

Lafayette Park, across the street from the White House, and another in Guatemala City. Harbury's first hunger strike in Guatemala City in October 1994 failed: Both the U.S. and the Guatemalan government refused to give her any concrete news of her husband despite her thirty-day vigil.

On November 6, 1994, *60 Minutes,* the CBS News television program, ran a segment that accused the U.S. government of withholding classified data on the case.[1] Five months later, Harbury repeated her ordeal across the street from the White House, losing fourteen pounds in twelve days. Carol DeVine, the wife of Michael DeVine, hired a lawyer and also pressed for information about her husband's torture and mysterious death.

When Harbury had finally captured public attention, the real issue emerged: U.S. policy toward right-wing Latin American governments. If Harbury's allegations were true, the question on many lips was why the United States was still pursuing Cold War policies after the Cold War had ended. In other words, if international communism no longer posed a worldwide threat after the fall of the Berlin Wall, why was the CIA still funding and training foreign military officers to conduct campaigns of terror against their own people as well as against U.S. citizens?

Guatemala has been cited year after year by the United Nations and by human rights groups as one of the worst violators of human rights in the Western Hemisphere: The consensus of these groups was that more than 140 thousand Guatemalan citizens (out of a total population of three million) had been killed by the Guatemalan Army in the three decades prior to the DeVine and Bamaca murders.

The CIA's involvement in Guatemala dates back to 1954, when the agency "led a coup that overthrew the nation's President and helped install a right-wing junta."[2] Many Americans believed that U.S. involvement in the coup in Guatemala came at the behest of United Fruit, a U.S.-based multinational corporation that needed a government that looked more favorably on its needs. Fear of communism during this period propelled U.S. policy in Latin America, where similar interventions in Guyana, Chile, and other countries occurred. Underlying this policy was the widely held assumption that right-wing military dictatorships friendly toward the United States were preferable to leftist governments—like Castro's Cuba—loyal to the Soviet Union. This policy paralleled similar coups in other parts of the world, with the CIA's involvement widely suspected throughout the 1950s and 1960s but documented only recently.[3]

Official U.S. policy finally changed after the fall of the Soviet Union, but it moved very slowly. The murder of DeVine in 1990 drew a strong American protest, followed by a $3 million cut in military aid to Guatemala by

President George Bush. Senator William Cohen (R-Maine), a modest, intellectual lawmaker who wrote poetry and novels and later became Secretary of Defense, charged that the CIA had not kept Congress informed about its role in the DeVine murder. Despite strong signals from Congress and the administration to reverse its policies, the CIA maintained contact with the Guatemalan military, secretly funneling funds to their leaders until President Clinton cut off the money in 1995.

Harbury's hunger strikes most likely would have been relegated to obscurity were it not for the involvement of then-Rep. Robert Torricelli, now a senator (D-NJ), who brought the case to the nation's front pages and nightly news broadcasts. A tightly coiled, highly competitive lawmaker, Torricelli was nicknamed "The Torch" for his incendiary personality—the nickname was also a play on the pronunciation of his name.

Torricelli became deeply involved in the Harbury case and adopted her cause as his own. As a member of the Intelligence Committee, his involvement doubled the stakes and caught everyone's attention much faster than usual. He immediately charged the CIA with covering up the incident and demanded that the White House address the issue. To buttress his campaign, he wrote a strong letter to President Clinton on March 22, 1995, charging that the CIA was an agency "out of control." At the same time he sent his letter, Torricelli also told the story to *The New York Times,* where it appeared on the front page the day after his letter arrived at the White House.[4] "The direct involvement of the Central Intelligence Agency in the murder of these individuals leads me to the extraordinary conclusion that the agency is simply out of control and that it contains what can only be called a criminal element," wrote Torricelli.[5]

Torricelli gave Harbury the information she had long sought unsuccessfully: that her husband had been killed after he was captured in 1992, that the CIA had withheld this information from the White House and from Congress, and that an official of the Guatemalan military linked to the CIA was responsible for his death. After his letter was sent and *The New York Times* article appeared, Torricelli visited the White House, armed with an anonymous fax from the National Security Agency (NSA) warning that documents relating to Bamaca and DeVine were being shredded. He met with Anthony Lake, then-National Security Adviser; Chief of Staff Leon Panetta; and George Stephanopoulos, Senior Adviser to President Clinton on Policy and Strategy. The White House inner circle was reportedly furious with Torricelli for going public with information without contacting them first. But their anger was muted by the public's outraged reaction to Torricelli's revelations, forcing the President and his advisers to react to the charges—and not to Torricelli. They responded in the time-honored way of dealing with controversy: stonewalling, and ordering a study of the situation. The President ordered an investigation of the charges against the CIA that would also include an inquiry into the rape and torture of Sister Diana Ortiz, an American nun, and the deaths of two U.S. journalists in Guatemala.

Torricelli soon found himself embroiled in a battle with the Democratic party, with the Republican leadership, and with his colleagues on the House Intelligence Committee. The charges against him were that he had violated the pledge taken by members of the Intelligence Committee not to disclose classified information and that he had publicly revealed secret information that only he and fellow members of the Intelligence Committee could have known. According to several Democrats who worked with Torricelli, this was not the first time he had revealed classified information from the committee; in fact, it was the third such incident.

Democrats and Republicans in Congress also felt blindsided by Torricelli's whirlwind activities. Like their White House colleagues, they wondered why Torricelli didn't contact any of them before making his story public. Both parties were well aware of the problems of our government's involvement in Central America but resented the independent role Torricelli had assumed, regardless of his reasons. Critics hinted that Torricelli's interest in the region stemmed from his romantic relationship at the time with Bianca Jagger because he had never expressed such a passionate interest in human rights before the Harbury case surfaced. Nicaraguan-born Jagger, the glamorous former wife of rock star Mick Jagger, was known as a charter member of the international jet set, and a human rights activist with a special interest in Central America. Torricelli countered his critics with the argument that he was acting solely out of frustration at his government's inability to escape its Cold War mentality.

In true partisan fashion, Speaker Newt Gingrich led the attack on Torricelli, calling his action "totally unacceptable" and threatening to throw him off the Intelligence Committee for violating his oath to keep "classified material confidential." Torricelli responded by telling fellow Democrats he would hold a special election to see if voters felt he deserved to be punished for revealing criminal activity. He did not get the information from the Intelligence Committee, he said, but from outside sources, which he declined to reveal. Instead of acting alone, as his critics charged, Torricelli claimed that he had kept Minority Leader Richard Gephardt (D-Mo.) informed about what he was doing and had also asked for advice from Lee Hamilton (D-Ind.), former chairman of the International Relations Committee. But some questioned whether he had actually asked Gephardt and Hamilton for advice or had just told them what he was doing.

The central question hasn't been asked, responded Torricelli. What is the U.S. doing spending millions of dollars in Guatemala? There was a conspiracy to hide the truth from the President of the United States and the citizens of the United States, and the CIA has been caught once again operating outside of the law. "No oath imposed by the leadership," said Torricelli, emphatically, "can ask a member of Congress to conceal criminal activity."[6]

The morality question played a large part in the drama. Torricelli argued that he had acted according to a higher morality: a legal and moral imperative to hold the CIA accountable if the agency was involved in the murder of a U.S. citizen. If he violated the secrecy oath, he said, he did so to uphold a higher oath, "the oath of office."[7] "I don't think it was [even] a close call," said Torricelli of the secrecy pledge. "It is what Nixon used for the crimes of Watergate. And Reagan attempted it with Iran-Contra. There's no obligation to hide the crimes of government against its own people."[8]

Five years later, Torricelli still smarted from the experience. "It's a deep scar," he said in an interview after a Senate vote. "It's a festering wound to me. I don't think any decent person would have done anything differently. A person was murdered, and the CIA had information on the murder. The U.S. government cannot classify information to conceal criminal activity. It cost me $100,000 in legal fees, lengthy hearings, internal problems with my colleagues, and public castigation," he continued.

Was it political? Totally, according to Torricelli. "Gingrich came after me bitterly. He led the attack. It was totally partisan."

The warring ultimately reached a stalemate. Many of his fellow Democrats still resented Torricelli for breaking ranks when he supported the Gulf War four years earlier. A fellow member of the Intelligence Committee, Norman Dicks (D-Wash.), argued that he should have come to him first and suggested that the Ethics Committee decide whether Torricelli's duty to "uphold the Constitution superseded his oath of secrecy [to the committee]." Torricelli responded that he would "defend exposing criminal activity if you can defend maintaining a conspiracy."[9]

Minority Leader Gephardt finally persuaded Democrats to stand by Torricelli, arguing that Speaker Gingrich was the greater enemy. Torricelli was charged with an ethics violation, and the House Ethics Committee was asked to investigate the case. Rep. Larry Combest (R-Tex.), chairman of the Intelligence Committee, wrote a strong letter to Nancy Johnson (R-Conn.), then-chairman of the Ethics Committee, asking the Ethics Committee to determine whether Torricelli "violated the Rules of the House."

"[T]his is not the first time that questions have arisen concerning Representative Torricelli's handling of classified information," Combest wrote. "[T]he issue of Representative Torricelli's handling of classified information has made it very difficult for the Permanent Select Committee on Intelligence to operate in its normal fashion. It has unfortunately raised questions about our ability to deal with the highly classified information to which we must have access if we are to perform . . . effective oversight . . . intelligence agencies find it difficult to be forthcoming out of fear of disclosure."[10]

Torricelli argued that he was responding to a higher law in revealing classified information, which paralleled the development of the concept of human rights in U.S. foreign policy. After President Jimmy Carter introduced the concept in relation to Latin America, it became a critical piece of each succeeding President's foreign policy. President George Bush talked about the humanitarian reasons that justified America's entry into the Gulf War, although these concerns were eclipsed by the more compelling need for oil. Human rights also justified the U.S. entry into the conflicts in Bosnia and Kosovo in the late 1990s, accompanied by a surprisingly high level of public support. In three successive public statements on "National Security Strategy for a New Century" from 1997 to 1999, President Bill Clinton linked foreign policy to human rights policy.[11]

In the final analysis, Torricelli's case followed the pattern of most other major ethics cases: It was highly partisan; publicity determined the outcome; and the ultimate test revolved not on national security but on the impact on Congress, or how much "disgrace" to the institution was involved.

Ultimately, Torricelli was saved by the partner who brought him to the dance: public opinion. The public turned decisively against the CIA and against the government for protecting the agency and for misleading Congress. The new CIA director, John M. Deutch, publicly agreed with his congressional accusers. The CIA had not properly informed Congress about its activities, he testified, promising that he would take appropriate action at the agency.

Congress followed suit, and despite widespread animus toward Torricelli, turned its attention outward toward intelligence activities in Latin America. After a closed hearing before the House Ethics Committee in 1995, Torricelli was absolved of any wrongdoing with no final decision on the ethics of his whistleblowing actions. There was no question that Torricelli revealed state secrets, but they were so embarrassing to the U.S. government that attention was diverted instead to the substance of the charges rather than to the process of how that information was received and conveyed to the public.

Torricelli was ultimately cleared because he claimed that he had not received the information about the Harbury case from the CIA's briefings to the committee. Fortunately for him, an ambiguity existed in the rules concerning whether a member could be held accountable only for divulging information gathered in the committee, or whether he or she would be held accountable for revealing secret government data wherever it was obtained. Because of the Torricelli case, the rules were later changed to prohibit disclosure of classified information, regardless of its origin.

THE CIA AND CONGRESSIONAL ETHICS

The role of John Deutch during this period turned out to be highly relevant to subsequent events and to the Torricelli case. In testimony before the Congress, Deutch proposed disciplinary action against CIA personnel for failing to report the Bamaca killing, adding that the agency had violated the law for failing to inform Congress. Two days after *The New York Times* article appeared, the CIA station chief in Guatemala was removed; six months later, on September 30, 1995, Deutch fired two more officers. This was the first time in the agency's history that agents were punished so severely for covert activities.

Critics evoked the Aldrich Ames spy case to condemn Deutch's harsh treatment of agents: Officers involved in the Ames case, the worst in the agency's history, received only letters of reprimand from Deutch's predecessor, James Woolsey. Deutch was trying to separate himself from Woolsey and his policies, from what he considered the agency's pattern of winking at incompetence, and from its culture of "obsessive secrecy." In hindsight, perhaps Deutch was correct in the sense that because Ames's activities led to the loss of so many lives, agents who failed to apprehend the spy should not have escaped with punishment that amounted to mere slaps on the wrist.[12]

Deutch was also criticized for taking actions that were much stronger than the report issued by his own Inspector General, Frederick Hitz, which exonerated the agency but criticized the payment of $44,000 to Colonel Alpirez. No laws were broken, said the report, issued in July 1995, although CIA officials were criticized for not reporting their knowledge of Alpirez's role in the DeVine murder to Congress and for delaying information about Bamaca.[13]

The Inspector General's internal investigation and final report contradicted Torricelli's charges on several counts. First, the CIA Inspector General began his investigation seven months before the report was issued and four months before Torricelli accused the government of ignoring Harbury's case. The report was based on an exhaustive investigation, led by a team of seventeen investigators and support personnel who conducted interviews with more than two hundred participants. The team also had total access to 56,000 pages of agency documents. There is no way of knowing whether the Inspector General's report was a whitewash or an honest piece of reporting, but the report's conclusion that "no evidence [was] found that any employee of the Central Intelligence Agency in any way directed, participated in, or condoned the murder of Michael DeVine . . . or the capture, torture, subsequent disappearance, and possible death of Efrain Bamaca" acquitted the agency of being linked to the notorious human rights abuses inflicted by the Guatemalan military.[14]

With all their access to CIA documents and principals involved in the case, the Inspector General could not find any hard evidence that Colonel Alpirez was even present at the interrogation of DeVine. In the Bamaca case, although Alpirez was present at the interrogation, he had been removed from any control over the outcome of the case by other military personnel. (Hitz, the Inspector General, was among six officials who received written admonitions five years later by a board of inquiry at the CIA that investigated the mishandling of classified information by its former Director, John Deutch.)[15]

Mining the same sources, the President's Intelligence Oversight Board (IOB) came up with similar conclusions one year later in June 1996. The CIA was exonerated of the charges of complicity in the two killings, but the board strongly criticized the management and communications practices of the agency. "Concerning the death, abduction, or torture of other US citizens in Guatemala since 1984, the Board found no evidence that CIA assets or liaison contacts were implicated," said the report, charging the agency with ignorance more than complicity. "[I]ntelligence provides little insight into the circumstances of these cases. Our intelligence agencies are not all-knowing . . . we may never know definitively what happened in these cases."[16]

The IOB took a dim view of CIA operations and recommended in strong terms that the agency improve its communications with the State Department, and vice versa. The board also suggested that the government should inform families of the victims of human rights abuses in a more timely and sensitive way. In an especially interesting section, the report discussed the difficulties of managing "assets," a euphemism for foreign agents—local spies—who provide the agency with information. These agents may not get awards for honesty or credibility, the report admitted; in fact, they may even lie in order to remain on the agency's payroll and may themselves be involved in "serious human rights violations or crimes of violence."[17] The IOB took an even stronger position than the Inspector General on the importance of informing Congress and the ambassador, as well as improving practices of accountability within the agency.

Another important finding of the IOB report emphatically disputed Torricelli's charge that the NSA and the Army were shredding documents on Guatemala. "We found no evidence," said the report, "to support the late March 1995 allegations that the NSA and Army officials altered records on Guatemala to prevent scrutiny in any investigation, and we believe that there is no foundation to this charge." In fact, the IOB came close to accusing the anonymous letter-writer of forgery: "Finally, the anonymous letter, which purported to be on NSA letterhead, does not match any letterhead used by the NSA in at least the last twenty years."[18]

Five years later, Deutch fell under a cloud himself for allegedly removing classified material from the CIA to his unsecured home computer. He faced investigations from the Justice Department as well as from Congress for these breaches of security. On his last day in office, on January 20, 2001, President Clinton pardoned John Deutch.

Were agency officials lying in wait for Deutch? Probably. After Deutch left, in March 2000, Terry Ward, the CIA official fired by Deutch in 1995, was awarded the CIA's highest honor, the Distinguished Career Intelligence Medal, for a performance that was "characterized by overall excellence," a "demonstrated . . . talent in managing operations, resources and people," and success at "recruiting sources who could provide information on the intentions of hostile governments" that were "not available by any other means." The award cited his career, which spanned thirty-five years in nine locations, including East Asia, Latin America, and Europe.[19]

Many believed the Terry Ward award represented the agency's attempt to ensure poetic justice. To be blunt: The clandestine division at the CIA (the Directorate of Operations and the Office of Security) were retaliating against Deutch, who had publicly criticized the agency and handed Congress Ward's head under political pressure to produce a scapegoat. Deutch's critics at the CIA also charged Deutch with leaking Ward's name to the media at a time Ward was serving undercover abroad, thus jeopardizing his life as well as the lives and safety of his family. (Deutch denied leaking Ward's name.) The CIA press release was careful to deny the obvious, stating that the decision to confer the honor upon Ward should "in no way be construed as a nullification of the decision taken by former CIA Director John Deutch in 1995 to ask Mr. Ward to retire as a result of an issue uncovered in the Guatemala review."[20]

TORRICELLI AND NUCCIO

Another ethical issue surfaced during the Guatemala crisis that was not covered by congressional ethics laws and regulations: the protection of the whistleblower, the innocent government employee who puts his or her neck on the block in the interest of integrity in public service. Torricelli would never have received classified data on the Bamaca and DeVine murders in the first place were it not for the real whistleblower, his former aide, Richard Nuccio, then working as a senior foreign policy adviser with the State Department.

In the course of mediating the thirty-five-year-long civil war in Guatemala between the nation's right-wing military officers and left-wing guerrillas, Nuccio came across classified documents implicating Colonel Alpirez in the murders of DeVine and Bamaca. This contradicted what he had originally told members of the House and Senate Intelligence Committees: that the CIA and the State Department knew almost nothing about the killings. After discovering the documents, Nuccio feared that he had lied to Congress by concealing the CIA's role in the murder of American citizens; moreover, he was now convinced that the CIA was engaged in a massive cover-up.

In hindsight, it would have been wiser for Nuccio to testify immediately to the Intelligence Committee about the documents, thereby limiting his own liability. Instead, on March 17, 1995, he told his former boss, Torricelli, "what the headline is here: 'The CIA is involved in the murder of an American citizen.'"[21] Five days later, Torricelli gave the story to *The New York Times* and marched straight to the White House, triggering a five-year-long shake-up of the agency as well as a shift in U.S. foreign policy in Latin America. Nuccio didn't expect Torricelli to go public so quickly, but evidently he didn't know his former boss as well as he thought he did.

At that time, neither Congress, nor the CIA, nor the White House could touch Torricelli, who won a Senate seat in 1996 and briefly considered a run for governor of New Jersey. In contrast, Nuccio's career went straight downhill, the inevitable and unfortunate trajectory of virtually all whistleblowers in government, no matter how powerful their political protectors. Nuccio weathered blows from all the agencies involved in the Harbury case as well as from Congress. The CIA regarded him as a traitor for disclosing the identity of one of its foreign agents—Colonel Alpirez— and expended a great deal of its own resources destroying his credibility. The agency's leaders even accused him of being an agent of the left-wing Guatemalan guerrillas. Nuccio soon found himself under investigation by the State and Justice departments, followed by a request by Rep. Combest to the FBI, the State Department, and the CIA to discipline Nuccio. The State Department eventually put Nuccio on probation for a year, and the federal prosecutor dropped the case against him, but in an unprecedented move, the CIA revoked his security clearance, effectively ending his career. In one of his last official acts before leaving the CIA, John Deutch revoked Nuccio's security clearance, the very week that both sides in the thirty-five-year Guatemalan civil war, which Nuccio had worked so hard to resolve, signed an agreement ending the conflict.[22] When the dust settled, Nuccio found himself facing $55,000 in legal bills and no job or resources to pay them. Today, he lives far away from Washington and is unreachable.

Nuccio's friends argue that Torricelli could have helped. Unfortunately, members of Congress, no matter how powerful, cannot protect whistle-blowers from the wrath of their agencies, other members of Congress, and the White House, no matter how legitimate their cause. They just take their chances and often bear the brunt of the controversy; by now, they know that the whistleblower protections written into the Civil Service Reform Act of 1978 have turned out to be meaningless in the face of powerful opposition from the bureaucrat they have charged with fraud, waste, and abuse. Even Sen. William Proxmire (D-Wisc.), chairman of the Senate Banking Committee, couldn't protect famed whistleblower Ernest Fitzgerald, who first revealed the cost overruns of the C-5A transport aircraft. The Defense Department was never the same—it became far more cost conscious—and Fitzgerald finally won his fourteen-year court battle against the government, but his career at the Pentagon went up in flames the minute he testified before Congress. He held on to his job but spent years at the agency in a back room, with an empty desk.

THE ENDS AND THE MEANS

The CIA was also never the same. The two murders set in motion a five-year shake-up at the agency that had more of an impact on intelligence policy than five years of oversight hearings could ever have had. Under pressure from Congress and the administration, the CIA cleaned house and, in the words of the agency, got many of its "assets"—the "murderers, thieves, character assassins and fingernail-pullers"—off the payroll. There was also a shift away from the agency's Cold War mentality to a view that more closely reflected new international realities, although the fallout from the case remains palpable as evidenced by the strong feelings that still prevail at the agency against Torricelli.

The agency learned that it ignored Congress at its peril. Both internal studies exonerated the CIA of direct involvement in the murders of DeVine and Bamaca but excoriated the agency for acting independently and for neglecting to inform Congress until it was too late. Congress responds first and foremost to public opinion, and it was clear that the public was especially critical of intelligence policies that led to the murder of American citizens. The murders also embarrassed Congress publicly, and that is politically unforgivable.

In fact, the agency's role toward Congress has changed appreciably since the early 1970s. Far from ignoring Congress, the CIA spends an increasing amount of resources on keeping Congress informed, often responding to requests from committees whose mandates range far afield from intelligence. In addition to answering inquiries from committees, agency representatives also brief individual members—and their staffs—who request information. Their role is typical of other executive agencies whose relationship to Congress has also changed appreciably; cabinet secretaries, for example, spend what many of them consider an inordinate amount of time testifying before congressional committees—time they feel would be better spent on agency business.

"Congressional committees elicit a lot of information," recalled one agent. "They get the mother lode. No requests from Congress are turned down. We used to turn down requests routinely. Even when we turn down requests for specific studies, it is easy [for Congress] to get around the refusals and get what they want. [The CIA, for example, turned down requests in August 2000 for information about the agency's role during the Pinochet rule in Chile.] All the member has to do is to ask someone from the executive branch to ask for the study. We brief foreign relations committees, ways and means, defense committees. The notion that they don't have information is incorrect."

As for Torricelli's role, the result was less clear. Do the ends justify the means? Torricelli violated congressional mores and embarrassed the institution, but he claimed to answer to a higher law. The political truth was that Congress couldn't contradict his arguments effectively, especially when public sympathies stood so clearly on his side. True, Torricelli put the CIA, its agents, and the entire intelligence process in jeopardy. But at the same time, he brought to light some appalling intelligence practices that have since been corrected. It is not likely that polite congressional queries or closed hearings would have produced the same results.

Ultimately, many doubt whether Torricelli's actions helped his political career. No doubt the publicity he generated by the Harbury case helped him rise above the pack and win his Senate seat in New Jersey. But in the long run, his character was his fate, and in the process of winning the national spotlight, he lost his political base—the Democratic leaders of his own state. On August 1, 2000, Torricelli withdrew his bid for governor, just three weeks after announcing that he alone had the stature to win the race and unify the party. His self-confidence—some called it arrogance—was also an exercise in self-deception; it led him to neglect the head counting that is so critical to winning before he barreled full steam ahead. In the end, even Torricelli was surprised at his lack of support among the county leaders; at the strength of his opponent, who had been carefully cultivating the grass roots; and at the general lack of enthusiasm for his candidacy. There was also the factor of payback at work, too: Powerful Democrats like Sen. Frank R. Lautenberg and Rep. Robert Menendez had felt slighted by Torricelli during his rise to power and were eager to retaliate by withholding their support.[23] In 2001, Torricelli was under federal investigation for campaign finance irregularities.

Does this mean that national security can be sacrificed in the interest of individual freedom? Did Torricelli have the right to publicize classified material? Can this be addressed by the ethics process?

Not likely. Congressional ethics and national security are an improbable mix. Lawmakers often lack the knowledge and the resources to make informed decisions about national security and find themselves dependent on the executive branch for their information. All too often, the information they do receive can be self-serving, incorrect, or incomplete. How can they balance what they consider the national interest with the organizational and political interests of the intelligence community?

The Torricelli case highlighted these problems, but Congress failed to resolve them. Like other ad hoc ethics decisions, future cases will hinge on public opinion, the skill of the individual leading the fray, and the political environment.

8

Forgery

The Case of the Purloined Stationery

> *"Power does not corrupt men. Fools, however, if they*
> *get into a position of power, corrupt power."*
> —George Bernard Shaw, in
> Stephan Winsten, *Days with Bernard Shaw*

If one regards politics, as many do, as "war by nonviolent means," then ethics do not matter, and we can hand the Republic over to those who will do anything to win. For them, results are the only things that count, and if they have to cut corners in the interest of justice, so be it. At least justice, they rationalize, prevails in the long run. Like the young boy of Sparta who allowed the fox to eat his innards rather than reveal he had stolen the animal, lying is considered acceptable. Getting caught is not.

The problem with this approach to the craft of politics is obvious: Who defines justice? Who decides what is right and what is wrong? The ends rarely justify the means, no matter how virtuous the results seem on the surface. The fox is still stolen; there is a victim (although it is hard to imagine why anyone would own a fox, even in ancient Sparta); and no one bears responsibility for breaking the law.

In Congress, issues like this confront lawmakers every day, with uneven results. Since the Watergate scandal, lawmakers know that it is easier to get caught today than it used to be: Cover-ups, white lies, and other euphemisms for political mistakes look downright sordid under the harsh glare of round-the-clock media coverage. In this era, the threat of public humiliation serves as a much more effective deterrent than ethics laws, virtue, public trust, or "inherent goodness." At the same time it reveals the naked emperors, modern technology can also hide deceptions better than ever before. That goes for lying, forgery, and other petty crimes that are hard to detect, particularly when the criminals are smart.

Take the case of the forged stationery. The perpetrators were not particularly bright, but in the absence of any sanctions, punishment, negative publicity, or electoral retribution, they were able to get away with their transgression. Their experience proves that although they are risky, cover-ups still work—particularly if the Ethics Committees turn a blind eye to what they consider "petty" skullduggery. Is forgery a petty crime? You be the judge.

The incident began with hearings on legislation introduced in 1995 by three Republican members of the House: David M. McIntosh of Indiana, Robert L. Ehrlich Jr. of Maryland, and Ernest J. Istook Jr. of Oklahoma. The bill, known as the Istook Amendment, was designed to curb public advocacy by nonprofit groups by prohibiting the use of federal grant money for lobbying activities. Because federal law already prohibited the use of federal funds for lobbying, the bill duplicated legislation already on the books and in some respects went beyond the law to punish nonprofits. The Istook Amendment, however, strengthened the prohibition against using federal funds for political activities.

All three representatives were strong supporters of Newt Gingrich and the principles behind the Contract with America. Two of them, Ehrlich and McIntosh, were elected in the Republican sweep of 1994; Istook was elected two years before, in 1992. The ringleader, McIntosh, was the most active, and given his background, was probably the best suited to promote the amendment. He had served as one of Gingrich's "key political operatives"; had worked as special assistant to Vice President Dan Quayle; had served in the Justice Department under President Reagan; and was executive director of President Bush's Council on Competitiveness, an antiregulatory group located in the White House. McIntosh was elected to Congress from a traditionally Republican district that had been represented by a Democrat, Philip Sharp, since 1975. He survived a close primary election and finally beat his Democratic opponent by a comfortable margin of 54 to 46 percent. The seat was valuable to the Republican Party, which sent high profile leaders Judge Robert Bork and presidential assistant Boyden Gray out to Indiana to campaign for him. Istook was also no stranger to attaching his name to amendments. In an "intra-party fracas," thirty pro-choice Republicans prevailed on Speaker Gingrich in 1995 to prevent Istook from offering an amendment to a budget bill preventing states from paying for abortions in cases of rape and incest.[1]

The amendment took the form of a rider to a Senate appropriations bill for the departments of Veterans Affairs, Housing and Urban Development, and the Environmental Protection Agency. (When they are attached in this way to appropriations bills, the bills themselves often become hostages to the passage of these riders—which often bear little relation to the task of funding federal agencies. Given its political cast, the Istook Amendment fell comfortably into this category.)

The Istook rider duplicated IRS regulations but added two new requirements: The first would require nonprofit groups to maintain separate bank accounts to differentiate between federal funds and private money used for lobbying and litigation; the second punished nonprofits by prohibiting them from receiving federal money for five years if they violated lobbying rules or neglected to set up separate bank accounts. The clause went further than current regulations, under which nonprofits found guilty of violating prohibitions against using federal funds for lobbying could be ordered to repay the money, lose future grant money, or pay additional penalties and fines.[2]

Under the rubric of "lobbying reform," the Istook Amendment threatened to curb the activities of charities and nonprofit groups that received federal money, including the American Heart Association, the Red Cross, the YMCA, Mothers Against Drunk Driving, and the Girl Scouts, among many others. Defense firms and other contractors that received federal funds were exempted from the amendment, despite the efforts of Rep. Pat Schroeder (D-Colo.) and others to include them. Also exempted were groups that spent less than $25,000 a year.

"It is ironic," noted Sen. Bob Kerrey (D-Neb.) that House Republicans would "decrease government intervention in the affairs of some of America's worst polluters while increasing the Federal Government's intervention and regulation of America's nonprofit organizations."[3] Another senator, Carl Levin (D-Mich.), rose up on the Senate floor to criticize the legislation as a "blatant attempt to muffle the diversity of opinion in the forum of public policy debate." Levin and others regarded the introduction of the amendment as a clearly partisan ploy to cripple the activities of nonprofit groups.[4]

The partisan character of the bill was apparent from the start. Many new Republican members of Congress were still hurting from the political opposition organized against them in their districts by groups that had received federal funds. Rep. James B. Longley Jr. (R-Maine) complained that members of the National Council of Senior Citizens had staged protests against him over his stance on Medicare. Longley implied that the senior citizens were using money that came from the $73 million in grant money their group had received from the federal government. A spokesman from the council countered that the money came from the Department of Labor, was earmarked for a jobs program for poor senior citizens, and was not used to advocate against Rep. Longley.[5]

"[The Istook amendment] would have made it impossible for nonprofits to do advocacy; they were defanging the left," charged Nan Aron, the president of the Alliance for Justice. "Organizations receiving federal funds were already prohibited from lobbying with that money," said Aron. "Groups were lobbying with private funds. The [Republican] members of Congress were feeling their oats; they had already won the 104th Congress." (The Alliance is an umbrella organization of more than sixty public interest groups that support issues involving women's rights, environmental pollution, employment discrimination, and gun control. The group includes such organizations as the Natural Resources Defense Council (NRDC), the Legal Defense and Education Fund associated with the National Organization for Women (NOW), and the Food Research and Action Center.)

On an operational level, the amendment would have crippled the ability of nonprofits to do business of any kind. It could have prevented the "Red Cross . . . from helping local governments prepare emergency-response manuals or drafting guidelines to safeguard blood supplies", or it could have hampered "a community drug counseling center [from asking] city officials to close crack houses."[6]

In one of its more intrusive provisions, the amendment tried to prevent coalitions from forming by restricting nonprofits from associating with other entities that spent more than 15 percent of their budgets on advocacy—wherever that money came from. "[W]hat if a federally funded rape-crisis center wanted to hire a physician to develop a pamphlet on treatment for sexual-assault victims?" wrote Aron. "That center would have to inquire about the physician's advocacy activities to determine whether they exceed[ed] 15 percent of the physician's expenditures."[7]

In the course of debating the issue, the Istook Amendment's advocates never answered the question of whether their amendment violated the First Amendment's guarantees of freedom of speech and freedom of association. Indeed, they were so intent on passage that they forgot the distorting effect of the means/ends conflict and perpetrated a blatant forgery to prove their case: that the nonprofits were spending federal funds to lobby the Congress. Their "proof" was presented on stationery that bore the Alliance for Justice's letterhead, listing nonprofit Alliance members together with the amounts of federal grant money they had received. The implication was clear: The groups listed were spending "$7,025,005 Total in Grants" on lobbying activities. Consumers Union was circled, with the handwritten figure "$300,534 in Grants"; the National Education Association, with "$937,678 in Grants"; and the National Wildlife Federation, with a mere "$16,000 in Grants."

The document was discovered by Aron, who was approached at the hearing by a reporter from the *Legal Times,* who asked, "Is this your document?" Copies of the document were distributed on the press table before the hearing was scheduled to begin and were picked up by members of the press and the audience. No one could recall who distributed the fake document.

"It was a counterfeit document," Aron recalled. "We said we received no federal funds. They [the proponents of the Istook Amendment] were trying to show our members received federal funds. We checked with all the groups. All the figures were inaccurate. It was a counterfeit document; the information was wrong."

"The layout of the stationery was virtually identical to that of the Alliance's letterhead," charged Aron in a complaint to the Ethics Committee against Rep. McIntosh, the chairman of the House Subcommittee on National Economic Growth, Natural Resources, and Regulatory Affairs, who presided over the hearing on "the political advocacy of federal grantees"—the Istook Amendment. "The only differences between the counterfeit and genuine letterhead were that a couple of the member organizations' names were misstated [such as] 'Sierra Club Legal Defense Club' instead of the Sierra Club Legal Defense Fund."[8]

Other errors were revealed by member organizations at the hearing. The executive director of the Arts Alliance, a member group, said the figure of $658,593 was wrong because the group had never received any federal funds. Similarly, the National Education Association (NEA) countered the misinformation involving the NEA in a letter to Chairman McIntosh, informing him that not only had they not received $937,678 in federal funds, they had never received federal funds at all.

The Alliance for Justice also accepted no federal funds—only 6 percent of the group's entire budget came from dues from organizations that received federal money, and those organizations were careful to pay their dues from private grants. "In spite of this," noted a backgrounder from the Alliance, "Congressman McIntosh has told the press repeatedly since the September 28 hearing that the document was accurate . . . .[H]e has consistently referred to the Alliance as a 'front organization,' even though all of its members are listed on its letterhead and all of its financial information has been provided to him." On November 10, 1995, Rep. McIntosh displayed the same document on forged Alliance for Justice stationery that he had distributed at the September 28, 1995, hearing. The *Muncie Star* reported the next day that "McIntosh used a projector to show a copy of a document his staff created." It didn't matter that the "projection was too blurry to read from the back tables, but the red marks appeared to be numbers." The audience in Muncie numbered 180 people—all of them unaware of the tampered visuals.[9]

The unrepentant Rep. McIntosh was still using the faked document six weeks after the hearing, well after the document was declared false before the media and congressional colleagues, and well after he had issued an apology of sorts in a written letter to the Alliance for Justice. Also, his use of the term "front organization" was a coded message of similarly dubious ethics: The phrase was commonly used before, throughout, and immediately after the McCarthy era to denote organizations that were fronts for the Communist Party. McIntosh also took advantage of the high negatives affecting the First Lady, Hillary Rodham Clinton, by calling the Children's Defense Fund "Hillary Clinton's Children's Defense Fund" when referring to one of the Alliance's member groups.

Was this an act of forgery? A strong charge, and if true, a crime serious enough to rate felony status in many jurisdictions. Usually, forgeries involve false signatures on checks or other documents, which could result in the loss of money or property. But the definitions of forgery extend further than monetary losses and include:

- The false making or material altering with intent to defraud, of any writing which, if genuine, might apparently be of legal efficacy or the foundation of a legal liability.
- A fraudulent marking and alteration of writing to prejudice of another man's right, or a false making, a marking *malo animo* [literal translation: "with evil mind"] of any instrument, for the purpose of fraud or deceit.
- The thing itself, so falsely made, imitated or forged; especially a forged writing. A forged signature is frequently said to be 'a forgery.'[10]

Because the actions of the committee and its staff fell squarely within the legal definition of forgery, the services of Sherlock Holmes to seek out the real villains were clearly unnecessary. McIntosh admitted that his staff had fabricated the document, although he said it was distributed prematurely. The villain was identified as Jon Praed, the thirty-one-year-old chief counsel to the committee, who eventually took the rap for the forgery, although none of the other perpetrators admitted they were parties to this particular fraud. Praed eventually resigned and to the best of anyone's knowledge has since disappeared from the public arena as well as from the D.C. area. The committee does not have a forwarding telephone number for him, and there are no listings with his name in any of the telephone directories in the three surrounding states. He defended himself at the time by saying that he didn't think anyone would be "fooled by the reproduction," and the "fake letter . . . was meant merely to make a point." About the poor quality of the forgery, Praed complained that "all he had to work with was a faxed copy of an Alliance letter. After whiting out the text, he sent the letter over to House Information Resources, the in-house computer center for the House of Representatives, with instructions to reproduce the letterhead and circle the names of the offending alliance members."[11]

Justice triumphed in the sense that the Istook Amendment failed, the sponsors were caught red-handed, and the press had a field day. Aron asked the reporter from the *Legal Times* to ask Praed about the document, and Praed admitted he was responsible. "We turned the hearing into a press conference," said Aron. "During the break we organized a spontaneous press conference."

As far as anyone knows, forgeries are relatively rare in congressional politics. They are too easy to detect and too easy to prove false; besides, McIntosh and the committee's chief of staff admitted the wrongdoing. In an unflattering comparison to McIntosh, *New York Times* columnist Anthony Lewis recalled a previous congressional forgery during the Army-McCarthy hearings in 1954, when the infamous Senator Joseph McCarthy produced backdated memoranda to showcase his accusations against the Army. The documents were clearly "forgeries, fabricated and backdated by his committee staff. By McCarthy standards it was trivial stuff. But the purpose was familiar and menacing: to punish citizens whose views the committee chairman dislikes."[12]

Chairman McIntosh admitted that the document "should have had a disclaimer" but stood by his $7 million figure, arguing that the purpose of his hearing was to "examine the details" of "welfare for lobbyists."[13] McIntosh never apologized for the forgery, which he must have known about, but wrote a letter to Aron saying that although "the graphics, unfortunately, appeared to simulate the Alliance's letterhead," the document was not "intended to create the appearance of an Alliance document or mislead the public or the press."[14]

The Istook Amendment lost, thanks to the clumsy efforts of its advocates to sell it by means of false documentation. The press reaction was intense and negative, although it lasted only a few days. Most likely that is why the Alliance's effort to bring the case to the Ethics Committee failed even though they had the facts nailed down in an airtight case. The steady drumbeat of publicity was absent, allowing the ethics process to paper over the case and exonerate the culprits.

Following the hearing, Aron and consumer activist and future presidential candidate, Ralph Nader, brought a complaint against McIntosh to the Ethics Committee. They were backed by several members of Congress, including Louise Slaughter (D-N.Y.) and Luis Gutierrez (D-Ill.), who filed the official complaints under their names. Slaughter was so outraged that five years later she planned to travel to Indiana specifically to campaign against McIntosh when he was running for governor. She was listed as the keynote speaker at a fund-raiser for his opponent, but had to cancel because the House remained in session in late October 2000.

"We make laws against forgery," Slaughter said in an interview. "It's a federal offense. For a guy to come here and say it's all right, I was appalled." Furthermore, she added, "There was anti–Semitism," noting that the committee had ordered the Alliance's counsel, who was Jewish, to produce documents on Rosh Hashanah, one of the most important Jewish holidays. Slaughter also was dismayed by the lack of support of fellow Democrats. "I thought my party would get behind me, but they took the attitude, 'boys will be boys.'"

The Alliance complaint alleged that McIntosh had "violated House rules regarding proper and ethical conduct by creating and distributing a forgery," of the Alliance letterhead, by "continuing to distribute the forgery, and by fabricating a quote by Alliance for Justice President Nan Aron and falsely attributing it to official House records of proceedings." The complaint also charged McIntosh with violating the Lanham Act (42 U.S.C. section 1125(a)), a federal law protecting organizations from "having their trademarks and other proprietary insignia used in such a way as to create a false representation as to the item's origin."[15] Rep. Slaughter introduced a resolution directing the Speaker of the House to "provide an appropriate remedy in response to the use of a forged document at a subcommittee hearing . . . to ensure that the integrity of the legislative process is protected."[16]

McIntosh and his defenders fought back. Rep. William F. Clinger Jr. (R-Pa.) called the ethics complaint "beating a dead horse . . . an incident [that] has been exaggerated and blown way out of proportion." He asked rhetorically, "Was there a crime committed?" on the House floor. "Was there a conscious effort to deceive? Was this a forgery?" Certainly not, he answered. Just a "human error," committed by a "new staffer on the Hill." In point of fact, Clinger added that a tempest in the teapot was triggered by "Our Democrat colleagues [who] want to spend more taxpayer money on trying to pursue an ethics violation."

Rep. McIntosh defended himself by offering the argument that the ends justified the means. The bill, he argued, would have ended the "money laundering scheme in which the taxpayer dollars go out as grants to groups and end up subsidizing the efforts of lobbying by the Alliance for Justice." Because the Alliance declined to answer his questions about the type of subsidies they received, "I asked my staff to illustrate the point to prepare the. . . chart, which is a blowup of the letterhead of that group. . . . Now the purpose for this blowup was to demonstrate how this money laundering scheme operates in this particular group. . . . The plan was that we would demonstrate the poster and then place the flier in the committee room so that anybody who was interested could have a copy. Unfortunately, what happened was that the fliers ended up out on the press table in advance of the poster. And I apologized later that night to Ms. Aron for any confusion with the use of their letterhead," concluded McIntosh. "But nonetheless, the attacks continue because they do not want the American taxpayer to see how their money is being used."[17]

McIntosh's argument was evidently convincing enough for the Ethics Committee, which dismissed the charges. The two ethics complaints against him were dismissed, and the committee issued a statement finding that the lawmaker had not broken any rules. But it was not a total whitewash: The letter to McIntosh from chair Nancy Johnson contained a private rebuke, criticizing the distribution of faked materials at a congressional hearing and the antireligious sentiments attributed to Jon Praed, McIntosh's aide.

It was an unusual solution for the committee, which cleared McIntosh and allowed him to announce its decision but at the same time criticized his actions. The committee also broke with precedent in not releasing its letter to the public on the McIntosh case. Indeed, no one would have known that the committee privately rebuked McIntosh if not for the committee's insistence that the lawmaker include that fact in his news release.[18]

"We lost the battle [the ethics complaint] but won the war," said Aron. "A deal was struck. Praed was fired, and the amendment was buried. The Ethics Committee made a back room deal to get rid of Praed. They knew McIntosh did wrong and was culpable, but they didn't want to hold him accountable. Praed took the responsibility for McIntosh. McIntosh knew about it [the forgery], but he never apologized to us. . . . It was not even a good forgery." She added: "It was another expression of the excesses of the 104th Congress. The Istook amendment showed the axes they had to grind. That was the motive. We were able to turn it to our advantage."

McIntosh and his allies never admitted guilt. Instead, they tried to explain away their behavior: faking a document was merely a way of dramatizing a practice that they believed had gotten out of hand—lobbying the Congress with federal grant money. It was all-out war, where all's fair and only results matter. The problem is that wars and politics are as different now as they were in Sparta. You can still steal a fox, or steal an election, but getting caught is a whole lot riskier today than it was before the Internet and "all the news all the time" became permanently entwined in our lives.

Getting caught is also more devastating politically, especially if the press pursues the case. But exposure is only part of the story, although it still serves as a highly effective deterrent to unethical behavior. When legislators fail to differentiate right from wrong, they often find that their issue loses, even when they pursue the noblest of ends. They can learn from the canny military strategist Carl von Clausewitz, who emphasized the relationship between means and ends in politics and in war. "War," he wrote, "is not a mere act of policy but a true political instrument, a continuation of political activity by other means. The political object is the goal, war is the means of reaching it, and means can never be considered in isolation from their purpose."[19]

In other words, dishonesty perverts the cause, no matter how lofty, for the simple reason that the goal itself gets lost in the process. That goes for war, for politics, and for legislation.

9

The Noble Lie

Modern Ethical Dilemmas

*"Oh! What a tangled web we weave, when
first we practise to deceive."*
—Sir Walter Scott, *Marmion*

Misrepresentation, exaggeration, deception, and downright lying turned out to be a major issue in the 2000 presidential campaign. Most of the criticism was directed at Vice President Al Gore, who exaggerated his career accomplishments, giving himself credit for inventing the Internet and inspiring the novel *Love Story*. During the campaign finance investigations after the 1996 presidential elections, Gore defied credulity by denying that he knew that his visit to a Southern California Buddhist temple was a fund-raising event and by denying that he had made fund-raising calls from the White House, prohibited by federal law. During the presidential debates, Gore mistakenly said that a high school student had to stand during her classes (she had to stand only on the day new computers were being installed), and he also cited as poverty-stricken a woman who had spurned the help of her rich son. Republicans made an issue of Gore's dissembling, which put off many voters.

But Gore was not alone. Texas Governor George W. Bush also told some whoppers, taking credit for a health reform bill that he had initially vetoed and later allowed to become law without his signature because the legislature's vote was veto-proof. Bush also wrongly claimed that the state of Texas spent $4.7 billion a year on health care for children. That amount represented the total, public *and* private funds, spent on health care for children. He also said that the bulk of his proposed tax cuts would go to "the people at the bottom end of the economic ladder." Wrong again.

The last weekend of the presidential campaign, on November 2, 2000, the media broke a story about Bush's 1976 arrest for drunk driving. Wayne Slater, Austin bureau chief of the *Dallas Morning News,* said that he had asked Bush whether he had ever been arrested after 1968, when Bush joined the National Guard and reported his 1966 arrest in New Haven for a college prank at Yale—stealing a Christmas wreath for his fraternity house. Asked whether there were any further arrests, Bush said "no," reported Slater. Bush's press secretary, who had been present during the conversation, disputed Slater's account, but Slater said his notes backed him up.

But somehow Bush's dissembling failed to affect voters. Perhaps they believed that Gore was intelligent and knowledgeable enough to know that he had fabricated, whereas Bush was widely viewed as an amiable lightweight who might not have known fact from fiction. Also, Gore was carrying the weight of that champion dissembler, President Bill Clinton.

Members of Congress are used to verbal combat in committees and on the House and Senate floor. The phrase "the gentleman is mistaken" echoes and reechoes throughout those chambers. During tense debates, each side arrives armed with competing charts and graphs, and the truth often lies somewhere in between. Are the Republicans destroying Social Security, as the Democrats charged, or are the Democrats destroying Medicare, as the Republicans charged? The process is exacerbated during election campaigns, when negative ads seek to destroy opponents with data that is often questionable, at best.

Are lies a necessary evil of political life? The cynical definition of a statesman, "a politician who lies for his country," is quoted so often it virtually qualifies as the truth. And don't forget the ethical dilemmas involved in fraud, "illicit" sex, graft, and broken campaign promises. They all involve a degree of lying: to the public, to families, and to voters.

So many lies have been unleashed in recent political history—from Watergate to the Vietnam War to Iran-Contra—that they seem almost a necessary component of governing. Leaders often use the excuse of "national security" to trump ethical considerations of their acts. They argue that we really don't want the President to answer truthfully when asked about a forthcoming bombing raid on an enemy target. If he did, he would alert the enemy, jeopardize our military operations, further endanger our soldiers, and give aid and comfort to the enemy—all in the interests of honesty in government. Members of Congress hold similar responsibilities, as witness the case of Robert Torricelli, who allegedly revealed state secrets learned from intelligence committee briefings in the interest of improving foreign policy.

Ethical dilemmas always produce more questions than answers. The late James Reston, *The New York Times* Washington bureau chief and columnist, recalled how his newspaper downplayed a story on the planned Bay of Pigs invasion in Cuba by deleting the word "imminent" and by erasing all references to the CIA's part in the Bay of Pigs invasion. The journalists who knew that the invasion really was imminent—it was planned for April 17, 1961—were furious at the distortion of their story. For their part, the editors and top managers who changed the story felt it was not the newspaper's job to inform the enemy, Cuban leader Fidel Castro, of the exact timing of the American invasion. Journalistic ethics were very different in those days, when Presidents, columnists, editors, and reporters often enjoyed close personal relationships with each other; when political leaders played on the patriotic sympathies of journalists; and when editors, publishers, and reporters unquestioningly honored their requests, often making judgments on their own about the national interest—as they did in the Bay of Pigs case. After the invasion, which turned out to be a disaster, President John F. Kennedy confessed privately that he wished *The New York Times* had run the real story after all. If the article had been published, he admitted, perhaps he would have come to his senses, aborted the invasion, and spared the government one of the most colossal embarrassments in its history.[1]

Professional ethics in journalism have since changed, many think for the better: Close friendships between politicians and columnists are now viewed with suspicion. And with the explosion of cable channels and Internet news outlets biting at the heels of the major networks and newspapers, few editors today would think of suppressing a major story—even at the bidding of the President—unless American lives were at stake.

The current dilemma over lying finds the pendulum pointing in the direction of too much information—some of it accurate, some not. Presidents' wishes are rarely honored except by their own loyalists, and their every move is considered fair game by the media. The same goes for congressional leaders and even backbenchers, who now take it for granted that they will give up their private lives and take up residence in glass houses when they arrive on Capitol Hill.

Is there a way to differentiate among the many lies—and charges of lies—that infuse political life? How do lawmakers counter accusations that are patently untrue? The Supreme Court has unwittingly contributed to the negative consequences of this unchecked information flow with its earlier decision in *The New York Times v Sullivan* case, which ruled that a public figure could not be libeled unless "he [the plaintiff] could prove [that the newspaper had acted with] 'actual malice'—that the statement was made with knowledge of its falsity or with reckless disregard of whether it was true or false." Those who would rule us are deemed fair game for strong criticism and personal attacks, provided it is not malicious. That's the American way.[2]

When President Clinton told the American people, "I did not have sex with that woman," polls revealed that the public objected more to the fact that he had lied to them than to his extramarital activities, which were no-body's business but his own. But what was Clinton lying about? A sexual affair, not an affair of state. No matter. Lies are lies, and woe betide the politician from Congress or the White House who gets caught in its web.

With that in mind, political opponents are ready to seize on any untruth in order to capitalize on the new morality in politics. "Read my lips—no new taxes" finished off President George Bush's campaign for reelection in 1992, despite his protestations that his tax hike represented a sincere change of heart about the nation's budgetary needs. Political leaders change their minds all the time; they must in order to be sufficiently flexible to address the nation's needs according to their judgment and the best information available to them. Did Bush's decision to change his mind constitute a lie? It did, once Clinton's pollsters seized control of it, put a name to it, and hammered away at it. It was a brilliant strategy on the part of the Clinton campaign that capitalized on the voters' aversion to both taxes and lying; it proved once again that those who control the language of an issue—a.k.a. "spin control"—also determine its outcome.

THE NETHERCUTT ADS

Even as the presidential candidates in the 2000 campaign traded accusations of lying, similar charges were leveled against congressional candidates. When Rep. George Nethercutt (R-Wash.) abandoned his campaign pledge to serve only three terms, U.S. Term Limits blanketed his district with radio, television, and billboard ads, accusing him of lying to the public. The group announced it planned to spend upwards of $20 million in ads targeting members of Congress who reneged on their term-limits pledges by running for reelection in the year 2000. Nethercutt was first elected in 1994 by a slim margin of 3,983 votes out of 215,000 cast, making him particularly vulnerable in successive elections. His initial victory made national headlines because it was the first time in 134 years that a

Speaker of the House (Rep. Tom Foley, a Democrat) had been defeated. Despite the best efforts of the U.S. Term Limits group, Nethercutt won his election in 2000.[3]

One powerful video ad targeting Nethercutt used the word "lies" four times and evoked famous presidential liars past and present—even though Nethercutt was a member of Congress. Titled "Promise," the first shot featured President Richard Nixon at a press conference declaring, "I am not a crook." A clip of President George Bush followed with "Read my lips—no new taxes." And finally, President Bill Clinton appeared, angrily exclaiming that he "did not have sexual relations. . . ." The parade of Presidents ended with a clip of Nethercutt himself, campaigning six years before, in 1994, with the slogan: "I meant it when I said, 'six years is enough.'" If anyone in the district failed to get the message, the ad clarified it further in its closing passage: "Enough lies. Sadly, Congressman George Nethercutt is talking about breaking his promise and violating our trust. Send a message that we've heard enough lies. Tell George Nethercutt to keep his promise on term limits."[4]

The ads accusing Nethercutt of lies and broken promises dogged his footsteps. A billboard prominently featured on the highway welcomed Nethercutt back to his district with the message: "Congressman George Nethercutt—Thanks for Keeping Your Word!" And the Eastern Action Term Limits Committee also weighed in with signs on fifteen metro buses in Spokane asking Nethercutt to "Keep Your Word George."

"We don't need another truth-bending politician in Washington," ran the text of another ad, which accused the lawmaker of succumbing to the Washington syndrome: "George Nethercutt promised he was different. . . . [H]e said he'd be a citizen legislator, not a career politician. . . . After living in Washington, D.C., with all the perks and privileges, Nethercutt wants to be a career politician."[5] In spite of all this heated rhetoric against the nation's capital, the home office of U.S. Term Limits happens to be located on Fifteenth Street, smack in the middle of Washington, D.C., and at least ten miles "inside the Beltway" that rings the nation's capital.

Paul Jacob, the national director of U.S. Term Limits, was quoted widely on the subject of Nethercutt's lie: "If you say you're going to do something, and it's completely within your power to do it, and you don't do it . . . it's a lie."[6] And on sin city itself: "A few who come to Washington to drain the swamp decide it makes a great hot tub."[7] Since Jacob's organization and its sister organizations poured money into Nethercutt's first campaign and took substantial credit for his slim victory, they felt especially betrayed by his reversal.

Nethercutt vigorously defended his change of heart on the grounds that three terms was simply not enough time to complete his work on such important issues as protecting Social Security, balancing the budget, and overhauling the tax code.[8] "I simply changed my mind," he told a news conference in Spokane in June 1999. "The only people who don't change their minds are in cemeteries and insane asylums."[9] He also argued that he was encouraged to seek a fourth term by the Republican Party State Committee, which had organized a petition drive to urge him to run again. True, his change of heart was an about-face from 1994, when he vowed, "if we break this contract [referring to the Contract with America's pledge on term limits] throw us out." Or, "If I can't effect some change in six years, maybe I'm in the wrong place." During those six years, however, Nethercutt "discovered that Congress is a nice place to work and longevity of service brings rank, which has its privileges and its usefulness. What a revelation. Tell that to Foley," wrote Marianne Means, a columnist for King Features.[10]

Why was Nethercutt's lie worse than other members' (among them, Tillie Fowler [R-Fla.], Scott McInnis [R-Colo.] and Marty Meehan [D-Mass.]), who also changed their minds about running for reelection? Stung by their criticism, Nethercutt finally decided to counterpunch his opponents in the term limits organization. "I'm going to fight fire with fire," he said, and he proceeded to run his own set of ads against his major foe, Paul Jacob, the director of U.S. Term Limits. The Nethercutt campaign ad claimed that Jacob was a convicted criminal who had served time for draft evasion in 1980 and that U.S. Term Limits was funded by rich "secret donors." "So when you see the next U.S. Term Limits ad," continued the Nethercutt ad, "recognize it for what it is—lies from convicted felons."[11]

A forty-year-old college dropout, Jacob did in fact serve five months in federal prison in 1980 for "resisting in the name of principle the Government's attempt to create a roster of men theoretically eligible for future military draft." Jacob identifies himself as a Libertarian, and is not, as many have assumed (because his group supported so many Republicans during the Contract with America campaign in 1994), a conservative Republican.[12]

In contrast to their vigorous support of term limits in their party's platform of 1994, Republicans struggled valiantly to keep the term limits issue from affecting their slim six-seat majority in the House of Representatives in the 2000 elections. Although they enthusiastically promoted term limits when it helped unseat Democrats in 1994, by 2000 they were incumbents, and the picture looked very different. As they quietly began detaching themselves from this issue, Republican leaders also banked on the steadily eroding public support for term limits. The concept of term limits still sounded good on the hustings, but voters tended to grow attached to their individual representatives and did not want to see lawmakers—particularly the good ones—forced from office by such an artificial standard after only three terms. After all, old political habits die hard: Before 1990, more than 90 percent of the Congress was returned to office; ironically, the contempt voters felt for Congress as an institution never affected the esteem they held for individual members. At the same time, many experienced lawmakers themselves opposed term limits, and rather vocally at that, with the best line coming from Judiciary Chairman Henry Hyde (R-Ill.), who asked: "And how about the virtues of experience? When the neurosurgeon has shaved your head and made the pencil line across your skull and he approaches with the electric saw—ask him, won't you, one question: 'Are you a careerist?'"[13]

Changing one's mind should not fall into the category of outright lie. Nor is it fair to link a change of heart about running for public office to "I am not a crook" and "I didn't have sex with that woman." Clinton's lie about his affair with Monica Lewinsky just doesn't compare with the lying involved in the government-sponsored break-in at the Watergate. Nevertheless, the affair resulted in an impeachment; the break-in did not, although Nixon resigned before he could be impeached. Politicians almost always change their minds when confronted with the hard realities of governing. And the same goes for their campaign platforms, which rarely get translated—especially in their entirety—into public policy. There is only one reason to put the Clinton affair and Watergate in the same category, wrote *Los Angeles Times* reporter Robert Shogan in an essay on presidential lying: "What makes the lies that Clinton told about Lewinsky and Nixon told about Watergate rare in the annals of presidential mendacity is that both men were lying mainly to shield themselves rather than protect a policy."[14]

Negative ads, a staple of modern politics, often cross the line and enter the realm of flagrant dishonesty. In fact, the field is littered with politicians who have suffered from blatant lies that linger long after their accusers have admitted their mistakes. The late Rep. Coya Knutson (D-Minn.) lost her election and her career, and never regained her political footing, even though her alcoholic husband subsequently admitted he'd been set up by her Republican opponent and that the charges he had leveled against her were totally untrue. Similarly, accusations of cocaine use and bribery against President Jimmy Carter's Chief of Staff, Hamilton Jordan, were later dismissed as untrue. Alas, the exoneration came too late to protect Jordan's reputation, despite a six-year investigation that cost him thousands of dollars in legal fees and ended with a unanimous grand jury and a strong statement by the Independent Counsel, Arthur Christy, who said, "There is no way he took cocaine."[15]

Lies concocted by political opponents also ruined the presidential ambitions of Sen. Edmund Muskie, Democrat of Maine. The lies started with a phony story about his wife planted in a local newspaper by the notorious team of dirty tricksters from the Republican National Committee during his campaign for the 1972 New Hampshire presidential primary. Muskie was so upset by the story that he cried publicly on national television, thus losing the respect (and votes) of many Americans whose image of men at that time—particularly men who sought the presidency—didn't allow for public weeping. During Watergate, the pranks of the dirty tricksters were finally revealed, but like Coya Knutson, too late to save Muskie's presidential candidacy.

History may have taken quite a different turn if Muskie had won the primary, defeated McGovern, given the Democrats a viable candidate in the 1972 elections, defeated Nixon, and spared the American public from the traumatic experience of Watergate. Unfortunately, much of this is pure conjecture. Dirty tricks and broken campaign promises come with the territory.

Critics faulted Muskie for crying in 1971. Years later, it became acceptable—at times even desirable—for strong men to show emotion publicly. But it was clearly *verboten* back in 1971. Ironically, at the same time they ruin candidates' chances, primaries also test a politician's mettle. However drawn-out and unfair, they give the public a good look at the candidates, often revealing personality characteristics—like Muskie's feisty and emotional temperament—that may not bode well for a future president. If Muskie became so upset by small-time pranks involving insults to his wife, the argument ran, how would he react to all the lies routinely leveled at a president by political opponents, unfriendly foreign leaders, and irate citizens?

"NOBLE LIES"

Scholars find it difficult to decide when, if ever, a lie is acceptable, or at times, even desirable. Lying is a strong word and implies an even greater form of corruption than telling a falsehood or changing your mind. Lying is defined as a deliberate misstatement of an existing fact. But political theorists have admitted through the centuries that there are some situations that force political leaders to tell lies for a variety of purposes, mostly in the interest of saving the state or the lives within it.

Plato's concept of the "noble lie" accepts the necessity of lying thus: "[W]hen is the state so in danger that the ruler is constrained to act against humanity?" Or, when are the demands of public order so compelling that it becomes noble to lie? The argument sounds very much like the national security rationale, offered so often by political leaders in wartime.[16]

When can fraud and other petty crimes, like lies, be rationalized by the argument that they are committed in the interest of arriving at a greater good? But what is the higher good, and who defines it? Can Plato's "noble lie"—a lie told for the good of the state—still be rationalized in the context of the public interest?

Niccolò Machiavelli, author of the political classic *The Prince and The Discourses,* wrote about times when the ruler was impelled to act against humanity—for the sake of humanity. "[A prince] is often obliged, in order to maintain the state, to act against faith, to act against humanity. . . .[He] must not deviate from what is good, if possible, but be able to do evil if constrained [to do so]."[17] Machiavelli's theory will only work when the prince is "wise enough to know when it is noble to lie." Democracies must also put a great deal of faith in their leadership to know when it is noble to lie. History is replete with times when princes, as well as more plebeian leaders, have lied with impunity, rationalizing that even if they acted badly, they were acting to preserve the general good.[18]

Later theorists understand that this is all relative. One prince's idea of the general welfare may range no further than his own minuscule city state and may not include the world or even the region around him. The consequences of victory for one nation mean defeat for others, resulting in widely differing perspectives about what constitutes the public good. This is why leaders often find it politically desirable, when they can, to lie about military defeats and cease-fires. The Vietnam War was called a stalemate by officials; it was really a resounding defeat for the United States. In Egypt, leaders recall the "October 6 victory"—even a boulevard is named after it—in reference to the Yom Kippur War in 1973, when Egypt attacked Israel, Israel counter-attacked, and the dispute ended the same month with a negotiated cease-fire.

Political theorist Theodore Lowi argues that no political figure is capable of judging real corruption—what he terms the "big C"—as opposed to petty corruption because both the Supreme Court and the President have been guilty of so many misinterpretations over the years.[19] One doesn't have to look too far to see corruption in the executive branch. Lowi uses the example of Nixon, whom he accuses of being constitutionally incapable of telling the difference between noble and ignoble lies. But presidents with loftier reputations than Nixon's have also lied with impunity:

> There isn't time enough to explain everything to everyone, to cajole every-one, to persuade everyone, to make everyone see why it has to be done one way rather than another," reflected Thomas Corcoran, one of FDR's top aides. "If a President tried to do this, he would have no time left for anything else. So he must deceive, misrepresent, leave false impressions, even some-times lie—and trust to charm, loyalty and the result to make up for it.

Taking a line from Lord Acton, he concluded, "A great man cannot be a good man."[20]

President Johnson and military leaders involved in the Vietnam War believed it was absolutely critical to lie—about body counts, victories, and enemies—in order to maintain the level of public support they needed to win. There is no doubt they all believed these were noble lies. At the top of the pyramid resided the President who condoned—and perhaps encouraged—lies from his generals, his secretary of defense, and others involved in the war. Johnson was the first President publicly accused of a "credibility gap," the gulf noticed initially by the press between the President's public statements and reality.

Why did Johnson lie? He certainly wasn't the first president to lie to the public about the course of a war, and he won't be the last, although Johnson eventually had to leave the presidency after one term, his administration destroyed by the war issue. He lied for the same reason wartime presidents have always lied: for the greater good, which in Johnson's view amounted to victory over the North Vietnamese. Ultimately, lying didn't help President Johnson: The ten-year-long war ended in defeat, the North Vietnamese Communists took over the country, and Americans to this day have never resolved the deep conflicts inflicted on their society during this period.[21]

No one has ever attained Plato's ideal of the philosopher king. Everyone makes mistakes, and even the best leaders have shown themselves to be prisoners of their cultures, events, and political variables. Lowi also reminds us that it was the Supreme Court that violated the due process clause of the Constitution by allowing the government to force Japanese-Americans into internment camps during World War II in the infamous *Korematsu* decision.[22] Justice Jackson dissented, calling the Court's ratification of the internment order "a far more subtle blow to liberty . . . than the order itself," which "validated the principle of racial discrimination in criminal procedures."[23]

The *Korematsu* decision showed that one of the worst problems of the noble lie remains its timing, namely, the pressures of the moment. One leader's rationale makes sense at the moment of decision: a war, a defensive move, a political victory. Nixon somehow thought it was necessary to condone, if not mastermind, the Watergate break-in to protect the Republic. Stealing documents (specifically: lists of contributors) from the Democratic National Committee in the name of protecting the Republic was a stretch, but shrewd as he was, Nixon's mind often worked in strange ways. The Supreme Court's decision to support the government's misguided policy to imprison Japanese-Americans as security risks was also questionable in terms of national security. Japanese-Americans, some of them third-generation American citizens, posed no security risk at the time; furthermore, no concrete evidence existed that indicated they were not loyal citizens.

No criteria justified the official lies that accompanied the Vietnam War. The American people grew more and more confused and divided throughout the war and for the next quarter of a century—notwithstanding Johnson, McNamara, and Westmoreland's many lies about enemy deaths, victories, and body counts. Even the Gulf of Tonkin incident—involving the alleged North Vietnamese attack on a U.S. ship—and the subsequent resolution that propelled us into the war have recently been revealed as a fraud, almost forty years after the fact. Yet it was used repeatedly by President Johnson to increase the military presence in Southeast Asia and to win congressional approval to escalate the war. Evidence of the attack was spurious, to say the least; even former defense secretary Robert McNamara later admitted after a visit to North Vietnam that the attack probably never occurred.[24]

The noble lie relies on the judgment of one individual, such as a king, a president, one of the nine members of the Supreme Court, or key members of Congress. The range of human nature, as well as the exigencies of democratic government, virtually precludes decision-making that reaches beyond national borders or into the future. Plato's philosopher-king might have encompassed these qualities, but he never really existed; the rest of us are forced to deal with reality.

WHEN LYING FAILS

Lies fall into a range of categories: there are malevolent lies, intentional falsehoods, and "white lies." In *Lying,* the best and most comprehensive study of lying in public life, Sissela Bok traces the concept of lying in all its possible incarnations, from the hard-line secular Kantian view that lying is always morally wrong to the many situations in public life that expose the shades of gray.

One theological view, that all lies are wrong, follows the argument that "by a lie a man throws away and, as it were, annihilates his dignity as a man."[25] But some theologians allow for mitigating circumstances, admitting that in a scale of lies, some are worse than others. If a known murderer, for example, comes to your house seeking vengeance on someone, do you lie or tell the murderer where the person is hiding? The Talmud, the Book of Laws governing the Jewish people, says that if peace demands it, a lie may be told. In public life, examples that call for the necessity of lying abound. Hiding runaway slaves on the Underground Railroad during the Civil War required many people to lie to save the lives and freedom of the slaves. What about the "righteous gentiles"—so honored today by the Israeli government—who lied to the Gestapo and hid Jews from being sent to certain deaths in Nazi concentration camps?

Machiavelli justifies deception and violence on almost any grounds if the object is to defeat an enemy. That goes for engaging in hoaxes to fool the enemy, diversionary maneuvers, and almost anything else that falls under the heading of war. How would Machiavelli have regarded the lies that blanketed the Vietnam War? Were wars always like this, or are wars now just more visible and accessible to the public thanks to television news? Is it easier to discern the truth today than it was when we relied solely on government pronouncements?

The real problem with lying in public life focuses on the effect of lies. Al Gore's fabrications almost derailed his presidential campaign. How long will it be before the public trusts the Central Intelligence Agency again, given all the lies that have since been revealed involving agency-sponsored coups in foreign countries over the last quarter century? Were those lies simply falsehoods, perpetrated in the interest of national security, or were they lies with only a tenuous connection to national security?

One of the worst consequences of lying involves the effect of lying on the liar as well as on the object of the lies. When lies become public, they destroy public confidence, no matter what the excuse. One example Bok cited involved President Eisenhower's public denial about the real mission of Francis Gary Powers, the U-2 pilot who was shot down 1,200 miles inside the Soviet Union, near the city of Sverdlovsk. Powers, a CIA agent, was charged by Soviet officials with gathering aerial intelligence of our Cold War enemy.[26] Eisenhower denied that Powers was on an intelligence-gathering mission, but the President was contradicted at the time by the existence of the captured pilot and by all the evidence copiously presented by a gloating Premier Nikita Krushchev, who used the incident as an excuse to attempt to break up a forthcoming summit meeting.

When the story of the U-2 broke, the government immediately responded with an official statement explaining that the plane, chartered from the Lockheed Aircraft Corporation by the National Aeronautics and Space Administration (NASA), was on a weather-observation mission. The pilot was identified as a Lockheed employee who was forced to land when his oxygen supply failed.[27] "One of NASA's U-2 research airplanes, in use since 1956 in a continuing program to study gust-meteorological conditions, has been missing since 9 o'clock Sunday morning (local time), when its pilot reported he was having oxygen difficulties over the Lake Van, Turkey area," said the statement.[28] In response to the controversy, and to Soviet Premier Nikita Krushchev's charges of U.S. spying, the State Department finally issued its own statement two months later admitting that the U-2 was an "unarmed reconnaissance plane, piloted by Francis Gary Powers who was employed by the Central Intelligence Agency."[29]

Strictly speaking, Eisenhower did lie: He issued an "official statement," known at the time as a cover story, which was and still is standard operating procedure in covert missions. In operational terms, Eisenhower authorized NASA to claim that the agency had sent the airplane on an information-gathering mission. But he knew that he alone was responsible for the lie, and he even considered resigning over the incident.[30] In fact, Eisenhower admitted many years later to British Premier Harold Macmillan that "the only thing he regretted about the U-2 incident was the original cover story."[31]

The U-2 case is used frequently in academic literature to show the extenuating circumstances surrounding official prevarications, the complexity of government actions, and the national security reasons that necessitate lying at the highest levels. Soon after the U-2 incident, few hesitated to use the case for what it was: a perfect example of official lying. Public expectations about honesty in government also changed around that time; it became harder to argue national security to justify intelligence activities. Today, the issue has developed a new dimension, as scholars, citizens, and political leaders continually question government's system of classifying information to hide it from public scrutiny.

If people learn to expect distortions of the truth, they quickly lose their trust in public institutions. Bok argues that although many Americans were "genuinely astonished" when they learned of President Eisenhower's lie in 1960, by 1969, 69 percent agreed that "over the last ten years, this nation's leaders have consistently lied to the people."[32]

Scholars continue to argue that there was a cause and effect relationship between Eisenhower's lie and the continuing slide in public confidence in government. In the 1960s, 76 percent of the public responded affirmatively to the question posed by the pollster Daniel Yankelovich, "How much of the time can you trust the government to do what is right?" compared to 19 percent in the 1990s.[33] Put another way, if a lie is made public, it destroys public confidence in the liar. When columnist William Safire called Hillary Rodham Clinton a "congenital liar" in a 1996 column over her role in the White House travel office firings and her 10,000 percent profit in a 1979 commodity trade, her reaction was volcanic, despite his tongue-in-cheek protestations, which he credited to comedian Mark Russell, that all he really said when he telephoned in his column was "congenial lawyer." Even her husband, the President, became involved, threatening to punch Safire in the nose to defend his wife's honor.[34]

There was a definite correlation between the high negatives that trailed Mrs. Clinton in her race for the New York Senate seat and public mistrust. Four months before Election Day, Mrs. Clinton became embroiled in a flap involving a book that accused her of having used the word "Jew-bastard" twenty-six years earlier. Although she heatedly denied the charges—especially devastating in New York State with its substantial Jewish vote—the issue quickly became a question of her word against her accuser's. Previous charges of lying made it much more difficult to defend herself, regardless of whether or not the accusations were true.

Bok also points out the problem with "discrepant perspectives," or cases in which a lie is not a lie, but merely an honest difference in perspective.[35] What is considered violence in one culture, for example, may be considered honest retribution in another. This happens even in our own culture, when issues divide clearly along religious or cultural lines. Abortion is viewed as murder by some segments of the population, and as a fundamental freedom, the right to choose, by others. Discrepant perspectives occur all the time in negative advertising. Critics cried "lie" when the right-to-life committee in South Carolina sent a mailing before the state's presidential primary in February 2000, alleging that John McCain had voted in the Senate for using body parts of unborn fetuses for medical experiments. It was a distortion, to be sure, but was it a lie?

Then there is the role of information and its relationship to lying. Many consider the withholding of information tantamount to a lie, or at least a deception, because its intention is to mislead. When the editors at *The Washington Post* decided to withhold the *Oregonian's* story of Senator Packwood's sexual history, critics labeled the newspaper's act an intentional deception. To the newspaper's editors, the decision boiled down to a question of journalistic ethics: They held a different perspective from many of their readers, even though they shared the same culture and acted within the same time period. But many readers considered the newspaper's decision to withhold information patronizing because it had the effect of distorting the voters' choices by eliminating information and influencing their ability to make their own decisions on the basis of all the information available to them. How many Oregon voters read *The Washington Post*? Not many, but a Packwood scandal story would have traveled cross-country with the speed of light.

The spigot regulating the information flow isn't always turned on; you have to know where and when to ask. The elliptical former head of the CIA, William Casey, found himself boxed into such a situation when he was grilled by the Senate Committee on Intelligence. Asked why he failed to apprise the senators of the circumstances surrounding a CIA action, he answered: "You didn't ask the right question."

"White lies" really do not fall into the same category as lying about body counts and false victories. They are often told to "preserve the equilibrium and often the humaneness of human relationships" and include lying to children, deceptive propaganda, and misleading advertising.[36] Believability also comes into play here: Do we really think that using a certain toothpaste will land a lucrative job or that drinking a brand of coffee will lead to new and exciting sexual adventures? When children are too young to understand death, what is the harm of using myths or fairy tales to relieve their anxieties and fears? And who expects any country to include its failures in its propaganda materials?

In the case of police practices, lying is considered acceptable if the policy is fully debated by the public before it is implemented; only then can society openly debate and choose whether such practices as unmarked police cars, police officers masquerading as decoys, and entrapment are worth the risks to their civil liberties. "Under case law and general police practices, police are allowed to create the opportunity for crime, but not the intent, which must rest with the wrongdoer," wrote former Drug Enforcement Administration official John Coleman.[37]

The practice of entrapment, alleged by critics of the FBI in the Abscam scandal, can also be justified on the basis of intent: Targeted individuals have to be intent on committing a crime. Entrapment, which is clearly unacceptable as a police practice, occurs when a person is induced "to commit a crime not contemplated by him . . . for the purpose of instituting a criminal prosecution against him."[38]

On a political level, what about false and deceptive advertising? Are negative ads merely benign white lies, or are they deliberate falsehoods intended to sway voters and impugn reputations? When McCain lost the South Carolina primary, what was the impact of all those ads against him, and to what extent did the ads contribute to his loss? No wonder money plays such a huge role in politics: It pays for the barrage of advertisements, true and false, that have become a staple of political victory.

Bok takes a jaundiced view of the noble lie, including the role of lying in public life. She debates the question of whether those "who govern have a right to lie . . . believing that they have [a] greater than ordinary understanding of what is at stake." In other words, she accuses those in power of arrogance because they "regard their dupes as having inadequate judgment, or as likely to respond in the wrong way to truthful information." The noble lie relies too heavily on the perspective of the liar, whose interpretation of the "national interest" requires deception "in order to lead." Indeed, judging from all the deceit for "private gain" that "masquerades as being in the public interest," or all the lies that have promoted "aggressive schemes of national defense," Bok feels eminently justified in questioning the right of those in power to lie in the national interest, for reasons of national security, or for misguided notions of the public good.[39]

Duplicity of all kinds has become so prevalent in public life that people have become almost immune to it. Bok suggests that all lies eventually redound to society's loss and recommends several government measures that will reduce the practice, such as improved enforcement of fraud and perjury laws and streamlining regulations that encourage deception—such as welfare and tax laws. She also agrees that only open debate about where and when deception should take place will check the free rein enjoyed by government leaders who "manipulate and distort the facts and thus escape accountability to the public."[40]

THE FUTURE OF LIES

Ironically, the codes of ethics governing Congress say little about lying among its own members. But members of Congress take a dim view of lying before congressional committees and can cite those who lie with "contempt of Congress." There is a pronounced theme of Congress's reaction to lies, which lawmakers interpret as the "failure to report" information to Congress. Lying is even worse. Even though Congress hates to be kept in the dark about anything, lying knowingly to Congress often seems worse than the actual crime Congress is investigating. In the case of Torricelli, Congress seemed angrier at the CIA for withholding information than it was at the agency's alleged complicity in murder.

After the Koreagate scandal had broken in 1976, the House Ethics Committee recommended that Reps. John J. McFall (D-Calif.) and Charles Wilson (D-Tex.) be reprimanded and that Edward R. Roybal (D-Calif.) be censured because they had all lied to the committee. The committee wasn't concerned that all three were charged with receiving lavish gifts from Korean businessman Tongsun Park, for lobbying their colleagues, for various forms of financial misconduct, for selling their votes, or for any of the highly improper activities conducted on behalf of a foreign government and foreign corporations. It was only lying to Congress that concerned them, and eventually all three lawmakers were mildly reprimanded; the censure move against Roybal was rejected. Similarly, in the Senate, Herman Talmadge's disgrace involved his failure to report personal and campaign contributions to Congress.[41]

People react to lies exactly as the political consultants predicted they would: insisting on the truth from their political leaders, as well as from authority figures in many other areas of their lives. Medical ethics are changing, many believe for the better, as patients insist on the truth—about their condition, their treatment, and their future. Codes of ethics that incorporate strictures against lying have emerged in all the professions as they seek to stem the steady erosion of public confidence. That includes the American Medical Association, which has added "honesty" to the Hippocratic Oath; the American Bar Association; universities—with honor codes; electronic and print media; social and physical scientists; business management; and others.

Lies matter a great deal to the American public, and getting caught brings swift retribution. Woe betide the politician who has lied about his or her record; if the falsehoods are revealed, that politician risks defeat by irate voters at the next election. Lawmakers who invent fictitious war records will soon find their ersatz heroism challenged by political opponents or enterprising journalists. "Negative research" has become increasingly sophisticated at uncovering deception, and as nefarious as it seems, may actually help politicians to ward off specious attacks. The problem is the separation between outright lies, like Coya Knutson's jealous husband, and actions made to look like lies, like George Nethercutt's opponents who distorted his change of heart about running for reelection. Voters should also remain on the lookout for distortions often spun as lies: false promises, phony résumés, and bogus voting records.

10

The Politics of Venom

"I have been surprised by how the ethics rules have changed the culture of [Washington] . . . and . . . how much damage campaign financing has done to policymaking."
—former HHS Secretary Donna Shalala

Sen. Tom Carper (D-Del.), who previously served as a governor and House member, discussed the difference in the civility levels of the three jobs. As a governor, he said, he received advice from other governors without respect to party affiliation or ideology. Other governors had suffered the same sort of problems—difficulties with managing prisons, mental hospitals, and other institutions; and the natural disasters like hurricanes and floods that occasionally afflict every state.

In the House, he said, there was no such collegiality. Republicans and Democrats went off in different directions and savagely attacked each other across the aisle. But in the Senate, Carper found the kind of collegiality he had found as governor, with senators helping each other without regard to party or ideology. That's because in that much smaller chamber, one is always in need of votes from across the aisle. However, even in the Senate, civility isn't what it used to be.

Attempting to achieve more civility on Capitol Hill, some lawmakers have searched for ways to improve the ethics process and remove the partisan infighting that has increasingly characterized ethics cases. But most senators and House members like it just the way it is.

In that respect, the obstacles to reforming congressional ethics are similar to those that have blocked campaign finance reform: Members of the Congress have learned to live and prosper under the existing system and are wary of changing the rules in the middle of the game. Nevertheless, some have offered recommendations for making the process less discretionary and less partisan. In fact, Sen. Richard Lugar (R-Ind.) "surprised some of his colleagues" at a 1995 hearing by suggesting that the Ethics Committees be abandoned in favor of the criminal justice system. "One solution to the ethics committee problem is not to have one," Lugar said. Persons who file ethics complaints, he said, could be told to "see the local court system or State court or the Federal court, and let them try your case."[1] But many congressional transgressions do not rise to the level of felonies or misdemeanors. Nor should they. In fact, the Supreme Court made such prosecutions more difficult by ruling in the case of former agriculture secretary Mike Espy that a gift must be tied to an official action to be illegal.

"The standards for serving in Congress ought to be higher than whether or not you have committed a felony," Rep. Lee Hamilton (D-Ind.) said in response to Lugar. Nor must conclusions be based on evidence beyond a reasonable doubt. Only "substantial credible evidence" is required to impose sanctions or initiate investigations, concluded ethics scholar Dennis Thompson, who nevertheless pointed out that former Sen. Alfonse M. D'Amato (R-N.Y.) was "rightly rebuked for permitting his brother to use his office improperly, even though the committee had no evidence that the Senator knew about his brother's conduct."[2]

Others have suggested that Congress should merely require full disclosure of financial interests and get rid of the elaborate regulations on conflict of interest, acceptance of gifts, and allowable outside income. Another recommendation involved the privatization of ethics cases by empowering a panel of distinguished citizens to supplant the congressional Ethics Committees. Such a panel would be made up of former senators and House members, schooled in the ways of their colleagues. It would certainly relieve lawmakers of the onerous task of judging their colleagues.

But the ethics process, like everything else on Capitol Hill, is inherently political. Members of Congress are rightfully reluctant to cede their authority to nonmembers and point to the Constitution, which regarded sitting members of Congress as the best judges of the actions, motivations and consequences of their colleagues' behavior.

"Passing judgment upon our colleagues is a role for members, not for ambitious outsiders," Jim Wright wrote Rep. Martin Frost (D-Tex.) in December 1989, shortly before Wright's resignation. "Only in extremes should this delicate and important work be turned over to an outside counsel. In those cases where it becomes an absolute necessity, great care should be taken to select a person with a knowledge of Congress, with a reputation for fairness, an even temperament and equable disposition. Never again should any member be subjected to the heavy-handed opportunism of someone with an enormous personal ego and political ambition."

Wright also suggested that when an ethics complaint is filed, the investigation should be confined to the charges in the complaint "and not become an open-ended fishing expedition into the member's entire life." He also urged that the "defendant" should have the same access and opportunity for discussion with members of the investigating committee as the prosecutor has and that a majority of Ethics Committee members be required to hear the testimony of witnesses. Both those proposals would greatly have helped Senator Packwood.

Others would like to reverse restrictions on ethics complaints, imposed by the House in 1997. These obstacles, which were intended to slow the complaints, bar outside groups from lodging ethics charges against House members.[3] Now, only a House member is permitted to initiate charges, based on personal knowledge of unethical activity, whereas previously, the Ethics Committee could self-initiate an investigation on the basis of newspaper reports and citizens' complaints. Paradoxically, at the same time Congress increased the restrictions on a member of Congress's activities, as well as disclosure requirements, the House made it more difficult to file charges against errant lawmakers. Some citizens, particularly those with group backing, can circumvent these barriers by persuading a member of Congress to initiate charges on their behalf—the case with the Alliance for Justice in its forgery charges against Rep. McIntosh.

Although the changes cut back on citizen involvement in congressional ethics, they still did not stem the rancorous partisanship that characterizes the current era. Outraged Democrats initiated an action against Rep. Tom DeLay (R-Tex.), the Majority Whip, who had threatened to retaliate against the Electronics Industry Alliance if the group hired a Democrat as its president. The Ethics Committee wrote an advisory opinion warning that lawmakers and their aides "are prohibited from taking or withholding any official action on the basis of the partisan affiliation or the campaign contributions or support of the involved individuals."[4] Several years earlier, similarly outraged Republicans brought charges against Rep. Jim McDermott (D-Wash.) after he gave *The New York Times* a tape of a 1996 telephone conversation in which House Republican leaders discussed their legislative strategy. The charges were ultimately dismissed.

Others suggest lifting some of the restrictions that Congress has placed on itself. The prohibition on accepting meals, for example, trivializes the ethics process and buttresses those who support lax enforcement. "The ethics laws have [changed] the basic culture and informality of the town where you could have dinner with the press people and lobbyists and sort of mix the people who are a part of the government structure," reflected former Health and Human Services Secretary Donna Shalala, on the eve of her departure from office. "That is, the emphasis has been on not buying people off, but the smaller things that actually made this place work a little more smoothly . . . [like] part of building a bipartisan coalition is building personal relationships. . . . I have been surprised by how the ethics rules have changed the culture of [Washington] . . . and . . . how much damage campaign financing has done to policymaking. . . . You can win the debate and lose the vote because of how the money is spent to influence the system."[5]

Disclosure requirements and limitations on campaign financing are the key to effective and judicious government. "You can't have a democracy without strong ethics rules," said Gary Ruskin, head of the Congressional Accountability Project, a Ralph Nader group. Rules give lawmakers something to cling to in the murky waters of ethics politics, despite their often confusing messages. In spite of the increasing number and more vigorous enforcement of ethics laws, for example, patterns of inconsistency continue to plague members of Congress without regard to status, power, or length of service. Lawmakers look around and watch the sharks devour some of their colleagues while other offenders swim freely away.

Dan Rostenkowski, former chairman of the Ways and Means Committee and one of the most powerful members of the House, found himself serving jail time for ethics violations that at the time seemed relatively minor: no-show jobs, crystal gifts for supporters, and misappropriation of office funds. He never understood how he got caught in the ethics whipsaw: To him, this was the traditional way of doing business on Capitol Hill; to the Justice Department, they were crimes.

The temper of the times, societal customs, and public exposure invariably seem to be the most important factors in deciding the outcomes of ethics scandals. In the infamous duel between Reps. Cilley and Graves in 1838, one member died, but the killer was not so much as mildly rebuked by his colleagues. In contrast, six years earlier, another member was censured for insulting the Speaker. The only conclusion extracted from those incidents is that the prevailing customs of that era regarded insults more harmful than injury! President Clinton escaped conviction by the Senate for cavorting with a White House intern and then publicly lying about it, whereas Senator Packwood was forced to resign shortly before the Senate was about to expel him for incidents that occurred more than two decades before his sexual harassment scandal erupted.

Congress has also found itself in the front lines of profound societal changes, which have been reflected in the way it handles its own ethics problems. The women's movement, the birth control pill, and a host of other factors have drastically altered the nation's sexual habits. But ironically, just as Americans have loosened up their moral codes regarding premarital sex and shown an increased appetite for sex and violence on television, they have gone in the opposite direction with respect to the extramarital lives of their elected leaders, as Packwood, Hays, and Mills can attest.

Even the public tolerance for traffic violations has waned, no doubt the result of the successful campaigns against drunk driving. So has Rostenkowski's Chicago-style politics, as voters pay closer attention to how government spends their tax dollars. And although the public always frowned on no-show jobs, mistresses, check-bouncing, and speeding on the highways, members of Congress always enjoyed a measure of immunity from embarrassment and apprehension. In the old days, the local police in Washington, D.C., were under orders to paper over traffic infractions of members of Congress, and the media could always be trusted to ignore the sex habits of politicians. No more.

"What I encountered as a [new] member was an intensifying ethical concern in Congress itself, which was partly but not entirely a defensive reaction to the willingness of Newt Gingrich and others to wield ethics charges as weapons of partisan warfare," wrote David Price (D-N.C.), a former political science professor from Duke University, who was elected in 1986.[6] For virtually all of Price's congressional career, the government was divided, with either the Democrats in power in the Congress, and the Republicans in the White House, or vice versa. When he came to Congress, Ronald Reagan was President, and the Democrats occupied the majority in both Houses. In 1992, Clinton was elected, but he only enjoyed two years with his own party in power; and in 1994, Newt Gingrich led the Republicans to victory with his famous Contract with America platform, winning GOP majorities in the House and the Senate for the first time in forty years. Clinton was reelected in 1996, but his coattails were too short to bring back a Democratic majority in either chamber.

Some voters pride themselves on casting votes for a President from one party and a Senator and member of the House of Representatives from another. Common rationales include voting "for the person, not the party"; being "independent"; and creating a government closer to the Founding Fathers's ideal of checks and balances. Neither branch can go too far without being checked by the other, and leaders rarely accrue enough power to dominate the process. The traditional American fear of tyranny, dating from the American Revolution, has finally reached its apex with the unprecedented number of divided governments in the last three decades.

Unfortunately, the flip side to this version of checks and balances has also condemned the government to eternal "gridlock"—a term that entered the political vocabulary during the 1990s. The branches may have checked each other, but they also check-mated each other, often bringing the White House into the fray. When Clinton and Gingrich failed to agree on a budget, the government was simply shut down. Several years later, the 106th Congress was called the "do-nothing Congress" for its failure to enact even the most urgently needed laws. A patient's Bill of Rights? The HMO industry had nothing to worry about: Even that watered down legislation was put on hold for the next Congress.

Divided government also changed the landscape of congressional ethics. Far from checking each other into a state of quiescence, the competition between the branches led to an intensely partisan environment: Democrats didn't want Republicans to look good, so they stopped legislation in its tracks and lodged ethics charges against them. Similarly, Republicans shied away from giving Democrats credit for anything, so they, too, held up appointments and legislation and used the ethics process as a political tool. Gingrich enhanced his career by exploiting Wright's ethical problems, then faced a bitter reaction on the part of Democrats retaliating for the loss of their leader. Divided government ensured that both the Democrats and the Republicans were living up to the oft-cited adage that "politics was war by non-violent means."

Ultimately, Congress and the White House are inextricably bound together on ethics issues, as the impeachment of President Clinton demonstrated. In the blizzard of partisan charges and counter-charges, the normally sensitive politicians in Congress ignored voter sentiment. The polls clearly said, "don't," but Republican leaders nevertheless proceeded.

Voters were not receptive to impeachment in a buoyant economy, and although they disapproved of Clinton's private sexual behavior, they didn't regard it as grounds for impeachment. But the Republicans in Congress saw an inviting target. They thought the time was ripe for underscoring moral issues. As a result of their misjudgment, two of the impeachment managers lost their next election; the incoming Speaker resigned; and the outgoing Speaker, Newt Gingrich, retired from office. Rep. James Rogan (R-Calif.), an impeachment manager, lost his bid for reelection in 2000; Rep. Bill McCollum (R-Fla.), another impeachment leader, failed to win a Senate seat from his state.

Taking the high moral ground on White House ethics also left Congress's leadership ranks depleted: Rep. Bob Livingston (R-La.) vacated his seat in early 1999 and declined the Speakership in December 1998 because—as he confessed in a statement televised around the world—he'd engaged in a number of extramarital affairs. Gingrich, also involved in an extracurricular affair and weary of the numerous ethical charges against him (including one that resulted in a $300,000 fine), resigned to pay off his legal bills and contemplate a future outside the glass houses of Congress.

Clearly, partisanship doesn't work effectively unless it is in tune with the times. Ethics may look good in black and white, but most issues cloak themselves in shades of gray, as shown by the Torricelli case. Torricelli revealed intelligence secrets to a reporter from *The New York Times,* bypassing his colleagues on the Intelligence Committee and his fellow Democrats in the Congress and in the White House. He justified his actions by saying that he was following a higher law that superseded House rules, the higher law being that no one could force him to be a party to a government policy that involved a felony—in this case, two murders. Ultimately, the right and wrong of the Torricelli case was never adjudicated: The House majority at that time was Democratic, and the Ethics Committee quietly exonerated Torricelli. Many other ethical dilemmas, like the Torricelli case, also lack clear-cut answers; others haven't appeared in the official House and Senate ethics rules; and still others remain quiescent, waiting to be tested by some hapless lawmaker.

Another side effect of partisan divisions in government has led to increasing conflicts on ethical questions between executive agencies and Congress. In effect, agencies suffer the same fate as whistleblowers when they buck members of Congress or committees. Many lawmakers protested privately that the FBI and the Department of Justice were at fault in their Abscam investigation. To them, it was clearly a question of entrapment: setting up their colleagues to engage in criminal acts that may never have occurred to them under ordinary circumstances. In fact, one Senator, Adlai Stevenson III (D-Ill.), did not keep his reservations private and asked the Judiciary Committee to look into the FBI's practices. Stevenson was chairman of the Senate Ethics Committee at that time. What remains unclear, however, is the ambivalence of Congress toward the Justice Department: Does Congress want to discipline its own members or, preferably, to deal privately with them, or does it want the Justice Department to intervene?

Over the years, the most serious cases involving members of Congress have originated with the Department of Justice. These included criminal conflicts of interest, bribery, exchanging campaign contributions for favors to a defense contractor or business interest, and the diversion of money for personal use. Since World War II, sixty criminal prosecutions have been filed against members of Congress, almost all of them involving money. Rep. Daniel J. Flood (D-Pa.), for example, faced thirteen criminal charges: pay-offs, bribes, and perjury. (Evidently the voters didn't mind; he was re-elected in 1978 after the indictment was returned, although he resigned in 1980, citing poor health.)[7]

One problem that has plagued scholars and members of Congress alike involves the extent to which the politicization of the ethics process can destroy otherwise productive members of Congress. Both Packwood and Rostenkowski were instrumental in bringing about tax reform; does that mean they should be absolved from ethics challenges? Former Senator and Lincoln scholar Paul Simon has written extensively about politics, hunger, Congress, and a range of subjects, including the problem of congressional ethics. Sporting his trademark bow tie, he devoted himself to public service, rising from the state legislature in Illinois, to four years as lieutenant Governor, nine years in the House, and finally his election to the U.S. Senate. His career was marked by his independence, as well as his involvement in humanistic causes—from fighting for money for medical research to student loans and other educational programs.

Simon devotes an entire chapter in one of his fifteen books to the case of Allan Howe, a former Democratic member of the House from Utah. With shades of Abscam, Howe had the unfortunate experience of being arrested in Salt Lake City in 1976 for "soliciting sex acts for hire." According to the arresting officers, Howe propositioned a female police officer who was impersonating a prostitute. The political consequences for Howe were devastating: He was married, a member of the Church of Jesus Christ of Latter-day Saints, and the father of five children. (He charged that he was lured to the scene by his political enemies, who then engineered his "entrapment.") Pressures from the state Democratic organization followed calls from the *Deseret News* (a newspaper owned by the Mormons) to resign "in the best interests of all concerned," whereas church spokesmen hinted that Howe might face excommunication. Howe was convicted by the city court; he lost his appeal to the district court and his bid for reelection.

During his only term in Congress, Howe had voted for the two-year authorization for international development assistance—aid for the overseas poor—but his successor voted against a similar bill. "Which is the greater evil?" asked Simon. "Soliciting a police decoy, or voting against food for hungry people? Who committed the greater immorality, Allan Howe, or the people of his district?"[8]

Absent a public outcry, the Ethics Committees are usually passive. Some examples:

The Senate Ethics Committee ruled that despite the gift ban, the Clinton Legal Expense Fund may continue to accept individual contributions as high as $10,000 to pay the legal expenses incurred by Sen. Hillary Rodham Clinton (D-N.Y.) and former President Bill Clinton before and during their tenure in the White House. This ruling came despite the Senate rule that senators may set up funds for legal expenses incurred "relating to their service in the United States Senate." The Clinton fund relates to legal expenses incurred in the Whitewater, Travelgate, Filegate, and Monica Lewinsky cases that predated Clinton's election to the Senate.[9]

The House Ethics Committee concluded merely that Rep. Corrine Brown (D-Fla.) had exercised "poor judgment" in allowing a West African businessman, Fountanga Dit Babani Sissoko, to provide her with free lodging and to give her adult daughter a car in 1997, in exchange for the congresswoman's help when he faced bribery charges. The committee also cleared her of yet another charge: that she failed to disclose that she received $10,000 from Henry J. Lyons, a former president of the National Baptist Convention.[10]

In 1997, the ethics panel found "credible evidence" that Rep. Barbara Rose-Collins (D-Mich.) committed eleven violations of ethics rules, including using campaign funds for personal items, but it took no action against the retiring lawmaker because voters had already removed her from office. The case resulted from disclosures in *The Hill*.[11] The committee also took no action against Rep. Jay Kim (R-Calif.), another retiring lawmaker, who acknowledged accepting illegal contributions and improper gifts. Kim was found guilty by a federal district court and was placed under house arrest.

After a four-year investigation, the Ethics Committee reprimanded Rep. Earl Hilliard (D-Ala.), who made well over $100,000 in payments from his campaign to businesses and charities he controlled. From 1992 to 1996, his campaign headquarters was located in a two-story brick and stone building owned by a company he controlled, although campaign laws prohibit the conversion of campaign funds for personal use. Shortly after ethical questions were raised about how his business interests benefited from his public office, Hilliard took steps to separate his campaign, congressional, and business offices.[12]

The recipient of the greatest largesse recently dispensed by the Ethics Committee was Rep. Bud Shuster (R-Pa.), chairman of the Committee on Transportation and Infrastructure. He was only mildly chastised for engaging in a long-standing relationship with transportation lobbyist Ann Eppard, who had served as his chief-of-staff for twenty-one years. Most of her clients had business before Shuster's committee, and companies and communities that sought contracts for highways, bridges, and other public works projects regarded Eppard as the person to see to gain Shuster's favors. Eppard served as Shuster's chief campaign consultant and major fund raiser; he was also known to stay often at her townhouse in Washington. In November 2000, Eppard pleaded guilty in federal court to a misdemeanor charge that she had accepted an illegal payment while on the congressional payroll.

The Ethics Committee issued a "letter of reproval" to Shuster that concluded: "By your actions you have brought discredit to the House of Representatives." In contrast to its strong language, however, the Ethics Committee ended a four-year investigation by giving Shuster the mildest punishment possible—a mere letter of reproval, a "rebuke," in which they took him to task for accepting improper gifts and for potentially misusing campaign funds.

The committee not only failed to reprimand or censure Shuster, but it also granted him immunity from federal prosecution. As the Transportation and Infrastructure Committee chairman, Shuster had the ability to determine which legislators brought home the bacon, and few were willing to offend him. The Ethics Committee virtually ignored the impact of his wrongdoing. The Committee found that eighteen months after she left Shuster's staff, Eppard continued to play a key role with the committee, acting as Shuster's doorkeeper by advising his aides whom to see. "Representative Shuster was aware that Ms. Eppard was a registered lobbyist with clients in the transportation industry and knew that she could use her influence over his congressional schedule to benefit her business interests," the committee noted.[13]

The charges against Shuster were lodged by Gary Ruskin, head of the Congressional Accountability Project, a Ralph Nader group. He was outraged by the committee's action. "They call it serious misconduct," he said of the committee's report on Shuster, "but they won't punish it."[14] Ruskin initiated his action before the rules changed to prevent private groups from filing complaints. The voters couldn't have cared less. Shuster was reelected in 2000 but resigned in February 2001, citing poor health.

It is the American public, of course, that determines congressional priorities. Usually, voters passively accept the status quo. Without an aroused public, things seldom change. When voters overwhelmingly agreed that something had to be done to curb the obscene amounts of money that poured into federal campaigns, the Senate, which had previously sidelined the measure, finally approved campaign finance reform.

In the final analysis, the congressional ethics process is unlikely to be strengthened without a public demand for change. Because the process deals with the internal activities of members of Congress, the likelihood of such demands are minimal. Unless, of course, the media and political leaders fulfill their watchdog function and educate the public on the relationship between the inner workings of Congress and the substantive legislation that will affect their lives.

APPENDIX A
Expulsion, Censure, Reprimand, and
Ethics Proceedings in the Senate 1797–2001

Year	Member	Party/State	Charge/Grounds	Action/Sanction
1796	Humphrey Marshall	Fed.-KY	Perjury	None
1797	William Blount	Indep.-TN	Anti-Spanish conspiracy	Expelled
1808	John Smith	D-OH	Disloyalty	None
1811	Timothy Pickering	Fed.-MA	Breach of confidence	Censured
1815	George Poindexter	Anti-Jackson-MS	Allegations of conspiracy	None
1838	John Ruggles	D-ME	Allegations of conspiracy	None
1844	Benjamin Tappan	D-OH	Breach of confidence	Censured
1846	Walter Colquitt	D-GA	Improper influence	None
1846	Spenser Jarnagin	Whig-TN	Improper influence	None
1846	John Clayton	Whig-DE	Improper influence	None
1850	Thomas H. Benton	D-MO	Disorderly conduct	None
1850	Henry S. Foote	Unionist-MI	Disorderly conduct	None
1858	Henry M. Rice	D-MN	Corruption	None
1861	James M. Mason	D-VA	Support of rebellion	Expelled
1861	Robert M. T. Hunter	D-VA	Support of rebellion	Expelled
1861	Thomas L. Clingman	D-NC	Support of rebellion	Expelled
1861	Thomas Bragg	D-NC	Support of rebellion	Expelled
1861	James Chesnut, Jr.	States Rights-SC	Support of rebellion	Expelled
1861	Alfred O. P. Nicholson	D-TN	Support of rebellion	Expelled
1861	William K. Sebastian	D-AR	Support of rebellion	Expelled
1861	Charles B. Mitchel	D-AR	Support of rebellion	Expelled
1861	John Hemphill	States Rights-TX	Support of rebellion	Expelled
1861	Louis T. Wigfall	D-TX	Support of rebellion	Expelled

Year	Member	Party/State	Charge/Grounds	Action/Sanction
1861	John C. Breckinridge	D-KY	Support of rebellion	Expelled
1861	Lazarus W. Powell	D-KY	Support of rebellion	Expelled
1862	Trusten Polk	D-MO	Support of rebellion	Expelled
1862	Jesse D. Bright	D-ID	Support of rebellion	Expelled
1862	Waldo P. Johnson	D-MO	Support of rebellion	Expelled
1862	James F. Simmons	Whig-RI	Corruption	None
1862	Benjamin Stark	D-OR	Alleged disloyalty to the Union	None
1872	Powell Clayton	R-AR	Vote buying/improper influence	None
1873	Samuel C. Pomeroy	R-KA	Bribery/corruption	None
1873	James W. Patterson	R-NH	Corruption	None
1873	Schuyler Colfax	R-IN	Insider trading[1]	None
1873	Roscoe Conkling	R-NY	Insider trading	None
1873	John Logan	D-IL	Insider trading	None
1873	James Patterson	R-NH	Insider trading	Resigned[2]
1873	James Harlan	R-IA	Insider trading	None
1873	Henry Wilson	Amer./R-MA	Insider trading	None
1873	Alexander Caldwell	R-KS	Vote buying/bribery	Resigned[3]
1878	Stanley Matthews	R-OH	Allegations of corruption before Senate term	None
1893	William N. Roach	D-ND	Embezzlement	None
1902	John L. McLaurin	D-SC	Assault	Censured
1902	Benjamin R. Tillman	D-SC	Assault	Censured
1904	Charles Dietrich	R-NE	Bribery/improper influence	None
1905	John H. Mitchell	R-OR	Corruption	None

[1] "Insider trading" refers to the Crédit Mobilier scandal (see Butler pp. 189–195).
[2] Recommended for expulsion, Patterson resigned.
[3] Recommendation to invalidate election prompted Caldwell to resign.

Year	Member	Party/State	Charge/Grounds	Action/Sanction
1906	Joseph Burton	R-KS	Bribery/conflict of interest	Convicted[4]
1907	Reed Smoot	R-UT	Religious disqualification (Mormonism)	None
1919	Robert M. La Follete	R-WI	Disloyalty	None
1921	Truman H. Newberry	R-MI	Election fraud	Resigned
1924	Burton Wheeler	D-MT	Conflict of interest	None
1926	Arthur R. Gould	R-ME	Bribery, right of Senate to exclude a member-elect for actions long before election	None
1929	Hiram Bingham	R-CT	Bringing Senate into disrepute	Condemned
1934	John H. Overton	D-LA	Corruption	None
1934	Huey P. Long	D-LA	Corruption	None
1942	William Langer	R-ND	Corruption	None
1953	William Benton	D-CT	Financial disclosure	None
1954	Joseph R. McCarthy	R-WI	Obstruction of legislative process, insult to Senators	Condemned
1967	Thomas J. Dodd	D-CT	Financial misconduct	Censured
1967	Edward Long	D-MO	Improper intervention/bribery	None
1975	Hugh Scott	R-PA	Illegal campaign contributions/ misuse of funds	None
1977	Mark Hatfield	R-OR	Disclosure	None
1979	Herman E. Talmadge	D-GA	Financial misconduct	Denounced
1979	Edward Brooke	R-MA	Disclosure	None
1980	Howard Cannon	D-NV	Conflict of interest	None
1980	Robert Morgan	D-NC	Conflict of interest/accepting improper campaign contributions	None
1980	Birch Bayh	D-IN	Misuse of frank/misuse of campaign funds	None

---

[4] Criminal conviction prompted Burton to resign.

Year	Member	Party/State	Charge/Grounds	Action/Sanction
1982	Harrison A. Williams, Jr.	D-NJ	Corruption	Resigned[5]
1984	Mark Hatfield	R-OR	Conflict of interest	None
1990	Dave Durenberger	R-MN	Financial misconduct	Denounced
1990	Phil Gramm	R-TX	Conflict of interest	None
1991	Alan Cranston	D-CA	Improper conduct	Reprimanded[6]
1991	Mark Hatfield	R-OR	Disclosure/conflict of interest	Rebuke (disclosure)
1991	Dennis DeConcini	D-AZ	Improper intervention for campaign contributor	Rebuke
1991	Donald Riegle	D-MI	Improper intervention for campaign contributor	Rebuke
1991	John Glenn	D-OH	Improper intervention for campaign contributor	Rebuke
1991	John McCain	R-AZ	Improper intervention for campaign contributor	Rebuke
1991	Alfonse D'Amato	R-NY	Improper use of office/bribery/ improper influence	Rebuke for misuse of office
1995	Robert W. Packwood	R-OR	Sexual misconduct/Attempting to obstruct investigation/Using position to solicit employment for his wife	Resigned[7]

---

[5] Facing probable expulsion, Williams resigned March 11, 1982.

[6] The Senate Ethics Committee reprimanded Cranston on behalf of the full Senate. This was the Senate's first use of reprimand.

[7] Resigned effective October 1, 1995 when Select Committee on Ethics recommended his expulsion.

Sources:
Mary Ann Noyer. *Catalog of Congressional Ethics Cases.* Washington: Brookings Institution, 1993.
Dennis F. Thompson. *Ethics in Congress.* Washington: Brookings Institution, 1995.
Congressional Ethics: History Facts and Controversy. Washington: Congressional Quarterly, 1992) pp.168–1169.
Anne M. Butler & Wendy Wolff. *United States Senate Election, Expulsion and Censure Cases 1793–1990.*
    Washington: GPO, 1995.
For Packwood:
See http://bioguide.congress.gov/scripts/biodisplay.pl?index=P000009.
For a comprehensive history on Senate expulsion and censure:
See: http://www.senate.gov/learning/brief_20.html.

Summary of Expulsion, Censure, Reprimand, and Ethics Procedures in the House of Representatives, 1797–2001

Year	Member	Party/State	Charge/Grounds	Action/Sanction
1798	Matthew Lyon	Anti-Fed-VT	Assault on representative	None
1798	Roger Griswold	Fed-CT	Assault on representative	None
1799	Matthew Lyon	Anti-Fed-VT	Sedition	None
1832	William Stanbery	Anti-Jacksonian-OH	Insult to Speaker	Censured
1836	Sherrod Williams	Whig-KY	Insult to Speaker	None
1838	William J. Graves	Whig-KY	Killing of representative in duel	None
1838	Henry A. Wise	Tyler Dem.-VA	Service as second in a duel	None
1839	Alexander Duncan	Whig-OH	Offensive publication	None
1842	John Q. Adams	Whig-MA	Treasonable petition	None
1842	Joshua R. Giddings	Whig-OH	Offensive paper	Censured
1856	Preston S. Brooks	D-SC	Assault on Senator	None
1856	Henry A. Edmundson	D-VA	Complicity in assault on Senator	None
1856	Laurence M. Keitt	D-SC	Complicity in assault on Senator	Censured
1857	Orsamus B. Matteson	Whig-NY	Corruption	Reprimand[1]
1857	William A. Gilbert	Whig-NY	Corruption	None[2]
1857	William W. Welch	Amer.-CT	Corruption	None
1857	Francis S. Edwards	Amer.- NY	Corruption	None[3]
1860	George S. Houston	D-AL	Insult to representative	None
1861	John B. Clark	D-MO	Support of rebellion	Expelled

---

[1] Expulsion resolution tabled upon member's resignation.
[2] Member resigned upon recommendation of expulsion.
[3] Expulsion resolution tabled upon member's resignation.

Year	Member	Party/State	Charge/Grounds	Action/Sanction
1861	Henry C. Burnett	D-KY	Support of rebellion	Expelled
1861	John W. Reid	D-MO	Support of rebellion	Expelled
1864	Alexander Long	D-OH	Treasonable utterance	Censured
1864	Benjamin G. Harris	D-MD	Treasonable utterance	Censured
1866	Lovell H. Rousseau	R-KY	Assault on representative	Censured
1866	John W. Chanler	D-NY	Insult to House	Censured
1867	John W. Hunter	Indep.-NY	Insult to representative	Censured
1868	Fernando Wood	D-NY	Offensive utterance	Censured
1868	Edward D. Holbrook[4]	D-ID	Offensive utterance	Censured
1870	Benjamin F. Whittmore	R-SC	Corruption	Censured
1870	Roderick R. Butler	R-TN	Corruption	Censured
1870	John T. Deweese	D-NC	Corruption	Censured
1873	Oakes Ames	R-MA	Corruption	Censured
1873	James Brooks	D-NY	Corruption	Censured
1875	John Y. Brown	D-KY	Insult to representative	Censured[5]
1875	William S. King	R-MN	Corruption	None
1875	John G. Schumaker	D-NY	Corruption	None
1876	James G. Blaine	R-ME	Corruption	None
1882	William D. Kelley	D-PA	Offensive utterance	None
1882	John D. White	R-KY	Offensive utterance	None
1883	John van Voorhis	R-NY	Offensive utterance	None
1884	William P. Kellogg	R-LA	Corruption	None
1890	William D. Bynum	D-IN	Offensive utterance	Censured

---

[4] Holbrook was a territorial delegate, not a representative.
[5] The House later rescinded part of the censure resolution against Brown.

Year	Member	Party/State	Charge/Grounds	Action/Sanction
1921	Thomas L. Blanton	D-TX	Abuse of leave to print	Censured
1924	John L. Langley	R-KY	Bribery	Suspended [6]
1924	Frederick W. Zihlman	R-MD	Bribery	Suspended[7]
1941	John M. Coffee	D-WA	Bribery/conflict of interest	None
1967	Adam Clayton Powell, Jr.	D-NY	Misuse of office/obstruction of legislative process	Excluded
1972	John V. Dowdy	D-TX	Bribery/conspiracy/perjury	Criminally convicted
1976	Robert L. F. Sikes	D-FL	Financial misconduct	Reprimanded[8]
1976	Wayne L. Hays	D-OH	Improper employment practices	None
1976	Andrew J. Hinshaw	R-CA	Bribery/embezzlement/misuse of public funds/misuse of office for campaign Criminal	Criminally convicted
1977	Thomas S. Foley	D-WA	Bribery/misuse of office	None
1977	Thomas P. O'Neill, Jr.	D-MA	Extortion	None
1977	Michael Harrington	D-MA	Breach of confidence	None
1978	Edward R. Roybal	D-CA	Lying to House Committee	Reprimanded
1978	John J. McFall	D-CA	Financial misconduct	Reprimanded
1978	Joshua Eilberg	D-PA	Conflict of interest/illegal compensation	Criminally convicted
1978	Edward Patten	D-NJ	Misuse of campaign funds	None
1979	Charles C. Diggs	D-MI	Misuse of clerk-hire funds	Censured/ Criminally convicted
1979	William H. Boner	D-TN	Misuse of campaign funds/ misuse of office/bribery	None

---

[6] Because of criminal conviction, no further action taken.

[7] Member temporarily suspended until acquitted on criminal charges.

[8] The only significant difference between censure and reprimand in the House is that Censured members must stand before the House as the Speaker reads the censure resolution. This is not required in reprimand cases.

Year	Member	Party/State	Charge/Grounds	Action/Sanction
1980	Michael J. Myers	D-PA	Corruption	Expelled/ Criminally convicted
1980	Charles H. Wilson	D-CA	Financial misconduct	Censured
1980	Raymond F. Lederer	D-PA	Bribery/influence peddling	None[9]
1980	John W. Jenrette, Jr.	D-SC	Bribery/influence peddling	None[10]
1980	Frank Thompson	D-NJ	Bribery/influence peddling/conspiracy/interstate travel to aid racketeering	Forfeited committee chair/Criminally convicted
1980	Daniel J. Flood	D-PA	Bribery/influence peddling	Criminally convicted
1981	John P. Murtha, Jr.	D-PA	Improper influence	None
1982	Frederick Richmond	D-NY	Tax evasion/improper influence/drug possession	Criminally convicted
1983	Gerry E. Studds	D-MA	Sexual misconduct	Censured
1983	Daniel B. Crane	R-IL	Sexual misconduct	Censured
1983	Ronald Dellums	D-CA	Drug use	None
1983	John Burton	D-CA	Drug use	None
1983	Frederic Richmond	D-NY	Drug use	None
1983	Barry Goldwater, Jr.	R-CA	Drug use	None
1984	George V. Hansen	R-ID	Financial misconduct	Reprimanded
1984	Geraldine A. Ferraro	D-NY	Disclosure	None
1984	Dan Daniel	D-VA	Illegitimate gifts/disclosure	None
1985	Anthony A. Coelho	D-CA	Misuse of office for campaign	None
1985	Michael A. Andrews	D-TX	Misuse of office for campaign	None

---

[9] Member resigned before vote on expulsion.
[10] Member resigned before vote on expulsion.

Year	Member	Party/State	Charge/Grounds	Action/Sanction
1985	Edward Feighan	D-OH	Misuse of office for campaign	None
1986	James J. Weaver	D-OR	Misuse of campaign funds/disclosure	None
1987	Austin J. Murphy	D-PA	Misuse of office	Reprimanded
1987	Richard H. Stallings	D-ID	Misuse of campaign funds	Letter of Rebuke
1987	Mary Rose Oakar	D-OH	Improper employment practices	Restitution
1987	Mario Biaggi	D-NY	Illegitimate gifts/improper influence/disclosure	Criminally convicted[11]
1987	David (Mac) Sweeney	R-TX	Misuse of office for campaign	None
1987	Fernand St Germain	D-RI	Bribery/tax fraud/illegitimate gifts/disclosure/improper intervention	None
1988	Robert Garcia	D-NY	Bribery/extortion	Forfeited committee chair/Criminally convicted
1988	James C. Wright, Jr.	D-TX	Conflict of interest/improper intervention/illegitimate outside income/illegitimate gifts	None[12]
1988	Charles G. Rose III	D-NC	Misuse of campaign funds/disclosure	Letter of Reproval
1988	Harold E. Ford	D-TN	Influence peddling/bank, mail, and tax fraud	Forfeited committee chair/Criminally convicted
1989	Patrick Swindall	R-GA	Improper intervention/perjury	None
1989	Jim Bates	D-CA	Sexual misconduct/misuse of office for campaigning	Letter of Reproval
1990	Barney Frank	D-MA	Discrediting House	Reprimanded
1990	Gus Savage	D-IL	Improper sexual conduct	None

---

[11] Member resigned before vote on expulsion.
[12] Member resignation prompted by Ethics Committee's preliminary findings.

Year	Member	Party/State	Charge/Grounds	Action/Sanction
1990	Donald E. Lukens	R-OH	Improper sexual conduct	Criminally convicted
1990	Newton L. Gingrich	R-GA	Illegitimate outside income/illegitimate gifts/misuse of office funds	None
1992	Nicholas Mavroules	D-MA	Bribery/tax fraud/influence peddling/illegitimate gifts	Forfeited committee chair/Criminallly convicted
1995	Mel Reynolds	D-IL	Criminal sexual assault and child pornography, campaign finance violation	None[13]
1996	Walter Tucker III	D-CA	Extortion and tax evasion	None[14]
1996	Donald Lukens	R-OH	Conspiracy and accepting bribes	None[15]
1997	Newton L. Gingrich	R-GA	Violation of House rules/ Illegitimate outside income	Reprimanded and fined ($300K)
1997	Corrine Brown	D-FL	Conflict of interest/misuse of campaign funds	None
1997	Barbara Rose-Collins	D-MI	Misuse of campaign funds	None
2000	E.G. (Bud) Shuster	R-PA	Serious official misconduct	Letter of reproval
2001	Earl F. Hilliard	D-AL	Improper use of campaign funds	Reprimanded

[13] Member resigned before any action taken.
[14] Member resigned after preliminary proceedings for expulsion.
[15] Member resigned before any action taken.

Sources:
Mary Ann Noyer. *Catalog of Congressional Ethics Cases.* Washington: Brookings Institution, 1993.
Dennis F. Thompson. *Ethics in Congress.* Washington: Brookings Institution, 1995.
Congressional Ethics: History Facts and Controversy. Washington, D.C.: Congressional Quarterly Press, 1992) pp.170–172.
Robert L. Tienken. *House of Representatives, Exclusion, Expulsion and Censure Cases from 1789 to 1973,* Committee Print, Joint Committee on Congressional Operations. Washington, D.C.: GPO. 1973.

Notes

1. A well-known quote cited everywhere, in which Mark Twain, the pen name of Samuel Langhorne Clemens, called Congress America's only native criminal class. "It could probably be shown by facts and figures that there is no distinctly native American criminal class except Congress," were his words. See Mark Twain, *Following the Equator* (London: Chatto & Windus, 1897).

2. Jim Wright, *Reflections of a Public Man* (Fort Worth, Tex.: Allied Printing, 1984). The book was primarily a collection of Wright's speeches. In the interest of full disclosure, it should be noted that Martin Tolchin acceded to Wright's request and gave the book a prepublication blurb.

3. Allen R. Myerson, "From One Fallen Speaker to Another," *The New York Times,* 12 December 1998: A22.

4. Byron York, "Never Mind, Newt," *The American Spectator,* April 1999: 28.

5. Roper Center at the University of Connecticut, *Public Opinion Online,* 11 November 1998.

6. York, *op. cit.*

7. *Ibid.*

8. John Rohr, *Ethics for Bureaucrats—An Essay on Law and Values,* 2nd ed. (New York: Marcel Dekker, 1989), p. 7.

9. Jock Friedly, "Hilliard Campaign Boosted His Business," *The Hill,* 3 December 1997: 1.

10. A Hastings Center report on ethics published in 1985 pointed out that in 1966 the Harris survey showed "42% of respondents [expressing] 'a great deal of confidence' in Congress," while by 1980, the figure had dropped to a "low point of 18 percent." See *The Ethics of Legislative Life* (The Hastings Center Institute of Society, Ethics, and the Life Sciences, 1985), p. 4.

11. Although the terms "chairman" and "chairwoman" are not gender neutral, they remain the terms recognized by the Congress in referring to the leaders of the subcommittees and committees. Accordingly, the text follows common congressional usage.

12. Andrew Stark, "Beyond Quid Pro Quo: What's Wrong with Private Gain from Public Office," *American Political Science Review* 91 (March 1997): 113.

13. Congressional Quarterly, *Congressional Ethics—History, Facts and Controversy* (Washington, D.C.: Congressional Quarterly Press, 1992), p. vii.

14. See Appendixes A and B for a list of Senate and House cases.

15. *Congressional Ethics, op. cit.,* p. 3.

16. Lizette Alvarez, "A Lawmaker Uses His Own Shame as a Guide," *The New York Times,* 12 December 1998: 45.

17. Michael Grunwald, "Senate's Surgeon Targeted on HMO Bill," *The Washington Post,* 5 October 1999: A1, A4.

18. U.S. Senate, 106th Congress, First Session, S1593, A bill to amend the Federal Election Campaign Act of 1971 to provide campaign reform. Cosponsored by John McCain and Russell Feingold (D-Wisc.), the bill never passed.

19. See Charles O. Jones, *The Presidency in a Separated System* (Washington, D.C.: Brookings Institution, 1994), for an excellent discussion of "divided government," and Susan J. Tolchin, *The Angry American—How Voter Rage Is Changing the Nation,* 2nd ed. (Boulder, Colo.: Westview Press, 1998), on "bipolarism" in government, pp. 36, 106–108, 122, and 127.

CHAPTER 2

1. Lincoln Steffens, "Los Angeles and the Apple," in John A. Gardiner and David J. Olson, eds. *Theft of the City—Readings on Corruption in Urban America* (Bloomington, Ind.: Indiana University Press, 1974), from Lincoln Steffens, *The Autobiography of Lincoln Steffens* (New York: Harcourt Brace Jovanovich, 1959), pp. 570–574.

2. All this occurred just prior to Jefferson's purchase of the Louisiana Territory. Prior to the U.S. purchase, Spain had ceded Louisiana back to France by virtue of a secret agreement, known as the Treaty of San Ildefonso.

3. See Congressional Quarterly, *Guide to Congress*, 4th ed. (Washington, D.C.: Congressional Quarterly Press, 1991), pp. 302–303; Congressional Research Service, *The Constitution of the United States—Analysis and Interpretation,* Johnny H. Killian, George A. Costello, eds. (Washington, D.C.: U.S. Government Printing Office, 1996), p. 584.

4. Raoul Berger, *Impeachment: The Constitutional Problems* (Cambridge, Mass.: Harvard University Press, 1973), p. 224.

5. John T. Noonan Jr., *Bribes* (Berkeley: University of California Press, 1984), pp. 429–430.

6. *Ibid.,* p. 435.

7. See Appendixes A and B for cases of expulsion, censure, and reprimand.

8. Donald C. Bacon, Roger H. Davidson, and Morton Keller, eds., "Ethics and Corruption in Congress," *The Encyclopedia of the United States Congress* (New York: Simon & Schuster, 1995), p. 776.

9. http://bioguide.congress.gov/scripts/biodisplay.pl?index=C000395. U.S. Congress, *Biographical Directory*, p. 814.

10. Robert V. Remini, *Daniel Webster: The Man and His Time* (New York: W. W. Norton, 1997), p. 402.

11. Congressional Quarterly, *Congressional Ethics—History, Facts, and Controversy* (Washington, D.C.: Congressional Quarterly Press, 1992), p. 51.

12. Susan J. Tolchin, *The Angry American—How Voter Rage Is Changing the Nation,* 2nd ed. (Boulder: Westview Press, 1998), pp. 90, 92.

13. *The Hill,* 28 July 1999: 28.

14. Carolyn Lochhead, "House Abolishes 'Slush Fund,'" *San Francisco Chronicle* 25 June 1992: A6.

15. David Brooks, "The Tragedy of SID: Status-Income Disequilibrium," *The Weekly Standard* 6 May 1996: 23–27.

CHAPTER 3

1. *Random House Webster's College Dictionary* (New York: Random House, 1997), p. 811.

2. Sam Tanenhaus, "Un-American Activities," *New York Review of Books* 47 (November 30, 2000): 25.

3. Congressional Quarterly, *Congressional Ethics—History, Facts, and Controversy* (Washington, D.C.: Congressional Quarterly Press, 1992), pp. 27–29.

4. A first person account by Arthur V. Watkins, former Senator from Utah, and Chairman of the Select Committee to Study Censure Charges Against the Senator from Wisconsin, Mr. McCarthy, *Enough Rope* (Englewood Cliffs, N.J.: Prentice Hall, and Salt Lake City, Utah: University of Utah Press, 1969).

5. Congressional Quarterly, *op. cit.*

6. U.S. Congress, Senate Congressional Record, 83rd Congress, 2nd session, 1954, 100, 16392, December 2, 1954.

7. Congressional Quarterly, *op. cit.*, p. 30. See also Congressional Record, "Daily Digest," Thursday, December 2, 1954, p. D739, and Congressional Record, Senate, November 8, 1954, pp. 15851–15921, for the full "Report on Resolution to Censure"; and Congressional Record, Senate, November 10, 1954, pp. 15922–15954, for a debate on the resolution including Senator McCarthy's defense.

8. Robert Griffith, *The Politics of Fear—Joseph R. McCarthy and the Senate* (Lexington, Ky.: The University Press of Kentucky, 1970), p. 317.

9. *Ibid.*, p. 317.

10. United States Senate, *Election, Expulsion and Censure Cases 1793–1990* (Washington, D.C.: U.S. Government Printing Office, 1995), p. xxx.

11. *Ibid.*, pp. 432–433.

12. Congressional Quarterly, *op. cit.*, pp. 12–14.

13. *Ibid.*, p. 12.

14. "Ethics Panel's Delay Has Consequences," *Hartford Courant* 3 January 1997: A20.

15. Thomas Oliphant, "Gingrich's Ethics Problems Won't Go Away," *Boston Globe* 15 September 1996: D7.

16. "Mr. Gingrich's Tainted Victory," *The New York Times* 8 January 1997: A14.

17. Dave Eisenstadt, "Dems Demand Ethics Big Quit Probe of Newt," *New York Daily News* 2 December 1995: 6.

18. Jonathan E. Fasman, "Connecticut 6: A Threat to Nancy Johnson's Reign?" *The Hill* 3 March 1998: 27.

19. Alison Mitchell, "New Rules Are Approved, Including a Ban on Outsiders' Complaints," *The New York Times* 19 September 1997: A27.

CHAPTER 4

1. The claim of "congressional privilege" took an interesting turn in the Abscam case, when Rep. Henry Helstoski (D-N.J.) attempted to exonerate himself in court by invoking the "speech and debate" clause of the Constitution. The clause protects "Senators and Representatives" from "Arrest" and from being "questioned" for "any Speech or Debate in either House" (Article I, Section 6, U.S. Constitution). The U.S. Court of Appeals agreed in part with Helstoski but would not dismiss his indictment. The Court agreed that his past legislative acts could not be introduced by government prosecutors in evidence against him. See *United States v. Helstoski*, No. 78–349, Argued March 27, 1979, Decided June 18, 1979, 442 U.S. 477, p. 1.

2. Milt Freudenheim, "Federal Jury Orders Keating to Pay Investors $3.3 Billion," *The New York Times* 11 July 1992: 33.

3. Congressional Record—Senate—Dec. 18, 1991, 102nd Cong., 1st Sess., 137 Cong Rec S 18828, Vol. 137, No. 179, p. 7.

4. *Ibid.*, p. 4.

5. *Ibid.*, p. 87.

6. Warren B. Rudman, *Combat: Twelve Years in the U.S. Senate* (New York: Random House, 1996), pp. 240–241.

7. Congressional Record, *op. cit.*, p. 7.

8. Dennis F. Thompson, "Mediated Corruption: The Case of the Keating Five," *American Political Science Review* 87 (June 1993): 372–373.

9. *Ibid.*, p. 374.

10. Congressional Record, *op. cit.*, p. 6.

11. Rudman, *op. cit.*, p. 241.

12. Alison Mitchell, "Republicans Pillory McCain in Debate Over Soft Money," *The New York Times* 10 October 1999: 30.

13. Jim Yardley, "Calls to Voters at Center Stage in G.O.P. Race," *The New York Times* 14 February 2000: 1, 42.

14. George C. S. Benson, *Political Corruption in America* (Lexington, Mass.: Lexington Books, D. C. Heath & Co., 1978), p. 138, quoting from Edmund Beard and Stephen Horn, *Congressional Ethics: The View from the House* (Washington, D.C.: The Brookings Institution, 1975).

15. Peter W. Morgan and Glenn H. Reynolds, *The Appearance of Impropriety—How the Ethics Wars Have Undermined American Government, Business, and Society* (New York: The Free Press, 1997), p. 33.

16. Referring to the opinion of Justice J. Potter Stewart, in *Jacobellis v. Ohio,* 378 U.S. 184, 197, (1973) on the test of the application of "contemporary community standards" when evaluating pornography. The exact quote reads: "Some condemn only 'hard-core pornography'; but even then a true definition is lacking. It has indeed been said of that definition, 'I could never succeed in (defining it) intelligibly,' but 'I know it when I see it.'"

17. Congressional Record, *op. cit.*, p. 4.

18. Rudman, *op. cit.*, p. 217. On the relationship between Keating and the deregulation of savings and loan institutions, see also Norma Riccucci, "William Black Tackles the Savings and Loan Debacle" in *Unsung Heroes—Federal Executives Making a Difference* (Washington, D.C.: Georgetown University Press, 1995), pp. 22–59.

19. Rudman, *op. cit.*, p. 203.

20. For a fuller discussion of entrapment, see Chapter 9.

21. Rudman, *op. cit.*, p. 219.

CHAPTER 5

1. Tip O'Neill, as told to Martin Tolchin. The story is also cited in Tip O'Neill and William Novak, *Man of the House* (New York: Random House, 1987), p. 132.

2. Pam Belluck, "Redemption to Rostenkowski Can Include Fun and Profit," *The New York Times* 18 March 1998: A1, 15. See also Richard E. Cohen's riveting book about the Chicago politician, *Rostenkowski: The Pursuit of Power and the End of the Old Politics* (Chicago, Ill.: Ivan R. Dee, 1999).

3. Bill Dedman, "They Changed the Rules 30 Times," *The New York Times* 10 October 1997: A14.

4. David E. Rosenbaum, "Guilty Plea and Jail Are Said to Be Near for Rostenkowski," *The New York Times* 9 April 1996: A1.

5. David Johnston, "Indictment of a Congressman," *The New York Times* 1 June 1994: A1.

6. Rosenbaum, *op. cit.*

7. Michael Remez, "Shays Formally Requests Ethics Investigation of Rostenkowski," *Hartford Courant* 2 July 1994: G12.

8. Martin Tolchin and Susan Tolchin, *To the Victor—Political Patronage from the Clubhouse to the White House* (New York: Random House, 1971), p. 18, based on William L. Riordan's *Plunkitt of Tammany Hall* (New York: McClure & Phillips, 1905).

9. E. Michael Myers, "Sen. Jesse Helms Recalls Another Senator Named Kennedy—JFK," *The Hill* 24 November 1999: 27.

10. Peter Egill Brownfeld, "For Most House Freshmen, Salaries Bring Boost in Pay," *The Hill* 23 June 1999: 1.

11. Larry Hugick, "Majority Disapproves of Congress," *The Gallup Poll Monthly* August 1991: 45.

12. Scott Shepard, "Decline in Respect Hampers Congress in Job, Experts Say," *Atlanta Constitution* 10 June 1994: A6.

13. The Roper Center at the University of Connecticut, *Public Opinion Online,* 11 November 1998.

14. George Gallup Jr., *The Gallup Poll, Public Opinion 1997*, p. 116.

15. The Roper Center at the University of Connecticut. *Public Opinion Online,* 20 September 1999; and George Gallup Jr., *The Gallup Poll, Public Opinion 1998,* p. 253.

16. George C. S. Benson, *Political Corruption in America* (Lexingon, Mass.: Lexington Books, D.C. Heath & Co., 1978), p. 2.

17. David C. Kimball and Samuel Patterson, "Living up to Expectations: Public Attitudes Toward Congress," *Journal of Politics* 59 (August 1997): 701–728.

18. The Roper Center at the University of Connecticut. *Public Opinion Online,* poll conducted by the Gallup Organization, 16 November 1999.

19. Richard E. Cohen, "Crack-up of the Committees," *National Journal* 31 July 1999: 2211–2217; see also Roger H. Davidson, "New Majority or Old Minority," in Nicol C. Rae and Colton C. Campbell, eds., *New Majority of Old Minority?* (Lanham, Md.: Rowman & Littlefield, 1999).

20. The witness was the coauthor, Susan J. Tolchin, testifying on the subject of foreign investment. See "Foreign Investment and Political Influence," Committee on Finance, U.S. Senate, September 19, 1990.

21. Dennis F. Thompson, *Ethics in Congress—From Individual to Institutional Corruption* (Washington, D.C.: The Brookings Institution, 1995), pp. 80, 133, and 141.

22. *Ibid.*, p. 141.

CHAPTER 6

1. Maxine Clark and Rudy Maxa, "Closed-Session Romance on the Hill," *The Washington Post* 23 May 1976: A1.

2. *Ibid.*

3. Richard L. Lyons, "Rep. Hays Quits Seat in Congress," *The Washington Post* 2 September 1976: A1.

4. Clark and Maxa, *op. cit.*

5. Alfred E. Lewis and Martin Weil, "Riders in Mills' Car Involved in a Scuffle," *The Washington Post* 10 October 1974: Al, A12.

6. Charles R. Babcock, "Rep. Studds of Massachusetts Will Not Seek Reelection," *The Washington Post* 29 October 1995: A31; and Suzanne Garment, *Scandal* (New York: Times Books, 1991), pp. 69, 191.

7. Hope Chamberlain, *A Minority of Members* (New York: Praeger, 1973), pp. 264–266.

8. The scandal involving the Jacksons is recounted in "Robert v Remini," in *Andrew Jackson and the Course of American Empire, 1767–1821* (New York: Harper & Row, 1977), pp. 57–69.

9. The Roper Center at the University of Connecticut, *Public Opinion Online,* 5 February 1999.

10. An interesting poll by Gallup-CNN indicated a split between those who answered "yes" to the statement "Bill Clinton's personal life doesn't matter to you, as long as he does a good job running the country," at 53 percent, and those who answered positively to "Bill Clinton's personal life does matter to you because the president's moral character is important," at 46 percent. The Roper Center, *Public Opinion Online,* 7 February 1999.

11. Richard L. Berke and Lisette Alvarez, "Impeachment: The Resignation; Professions of Shock and Support Aside, Livingston May Have Been in for a Push," *The New York Times* 20 December 1998: 33. For an excellent analysis of the Clinton scandal, see James P. Pfiffner, "Sexual Probity and Presidential Character," *Presidential Studies Quarterly* 28 (Fall): 881–886.

12. Actually, more people go to church each week than to all sporting events combined. See Garry Wills, *Under God: Religion and American Politics* (New York: Simon and Schuster, 1990), p. 16.

13. Garden City, N.Y.: Doubleday, 1959.

14. Michael Barone and Grant Ujifusa, *The Almanac of American Politics 1996* (Washington, D.C.: National Journal, 1995), pp. 649, 664.

15. Congressional Quarterly, *Congressional Ethics—History, Facts, and Controversy* (Washington, D.C.: Congressional Quarterly Press, 1992), pp. 43–44.

16. *Ibid.*

17. *Showdown at Gucci Gulch: Lawmakers, Lobbyists and the Unlikely Triumph of Tax Reform* (New York: Random House, 1987).

18. Before women's groups realized the true threats to *Roe v Wade*, the famous Supreme Court decision extrapolating a right to privacy in the U.S. Constitution. See *Roe et. al v. Wade*, No. 70–18, 410 U.S. 113; 93 S. Ct. 705; (1973) Lexis, 159; 35 L. Ed. 2d 147.

19. "Sen. Packwood Resigns in Disgrace," *Congressional Quarterly Almanac*, 1995, pp. 1–50.

20. The Senate Ethics Counsel, *The Packwood Report* (New York: Times Books, 1995).

21. *Ibid.*

22. "Sen. Packwood Resigns. . . ", *op. cit.*

23. *Ibid.*

24. U.S. Senate Select Committee on Ethics, "Resolution for Disciplinary Action," S. Rpt. 104–137, 104th Cong., 1st sess, September 8, 1995. p. 2.

25. *Ibid.*, p. 35.

26. *Ibid.*, p. 36.

27. *The Packwood Report, op. cit.*

28. *Ibid.*, p. 125.

29. U.S. Senate, "Documents Related to the Investigation of Senator Robert Packwood," U.S. Senate Select Committee on Ethics, 104th Cong., 1st sess., 1995, pp. 248, 892, 889, 886, 884, 900; Exhibits 116, 118, 119, 120, 121, 122.

30. *Ibid.*, p. 32.

31. *Ibid.*

32. *Mapp v Ohio*, No. 236, 367 US 643; 81 S. Ct. 1684; 197/61 U.S. Lexis, 812.

33. U.S. District Court for the District of Columbia, *Senate Select Committee on Ethics v Senator Bob Packwood*, Misc. No. 93–362, Memorandum of American Civil Liberties Union as *Amicus Curiae*, pp. 2,

34. Henry Campbell Black, *Black's Law Dictionary* (St. Paul, Minn.: West Publishing, 1991), p. 796.

35. *Resolution, op. cit.*, pp. 35, 55.

36. *Ibid.*

37. *Ibid.*

CHAPTER 7

1. *60 Minutes,* 6 November 1994.

2. Tim Weiner, "Guatemalan Agent of CIA Tied to Killing of American," *The New York Times* 23 March 1995: A1.

3. James Risen, "Secrets of History–The C.I.A. in Iran," *The New York Times* 17 April 2000: A1.

4. Weiner, *op. cit.*

5. Letter from Rep. Robert Torricelli to President Clinton on the Guatemala matter, March 22, 1995.

6. Kim Masters, "Truth and Consequences; Rep. Bob Torricelli Leaked the Goods on the CIA. Was It Loyalty or Betrayal?" *The Washington Post* 17 April 1995: C1.

7. *Congressional Quarterly* 14 April 1995.

8. Masters, *op. cit.*

9. *Ibid.*

10. Letter from Rep. Larry Combest (D-Tex.) to Hon. Nancy Johnson, April 7, 1995.

11. When the Gallup poll asked the question: "Does the U.S. have a moral obligation to keep/restore the peace in Kosovo?" 72 percent of the public supported the action. ABC News Poll, April 8, 1999, cited in Jack E. Leonard, "Ethics and National Security," unpublished paper, George Mason University, May 2000, p. 17.

12. Walter Pincus and R. Jeffrey Smith, "CIA Chief to Punish Employees, Deutch Cites Handling of Guatemala Efforts," *The Washington Post* 27 September 1995: A29.

13. Walter Pincus, "Inspector General Says CIA Made Mistakes in Guatemala," *The Washington Post* 26 July 1995: A19.

14. Central Intelligence Agency, "Summary of CIA Inspector General Report Relating to Agency Activities in Guatemala," 26 July 1995, p. 1.

15. James Risen, "C.I.A. Punishes 6 for Failure in Inquiry of Ex-Director," *The New York Times* 26 May 2000: A15.

16. Intelligence Oversight Board, "Report on the Guatemala Review," 28 June 1996, p. 8.

17. *Ibid.*, p. 11.

18. *Ibid.*, p. 9.

19. Central Intelligence Agency, Washington, D.C., Office of Public Affairs, "Former CIA Officer Terry Ward Recognized for Accomplishments Over 35-Year Career," 23 March 2000.

20. *Ibid.*

21. Tim Weiner, "A Secret Disclosed Imperils the Career Of State Dept. Aide," *The New York Times* 16 November 1996: 1.

22. Tim Weiner, "C.I.A. Chief Disciplines Official for Disclosure," *The New York Times* 6 December 1996: A20.

23. David M. Halbfinger and David Kocieniewski, "Torricelli Unified New Jersey's Democrats, but Against His Candidacy," *The New York Times* 2 August 2000: A24; and David Kocieniewski, "Torricelli, Opposed Within Party, Drops New Jersey Governor Bid," *The New York Times* 1 August 2000; A1, A23.

CHAPTER 8

1. Michael Barone and Grant Ujifusa, *The Almanac of American Politics 1996* (Washington, D.C.: National Journal, 1995), pp. 479–480, 1098.

2. Stephen Barr, "Nonprofit Groups Fault Restrictive GOP 'Riders,'" *The Washington Post* 29 September 1999: A27.

3. "Muzzling the Nonprofits," *The New York Times* 2 November 1995: A26.

4. John Yang, "Plan Limiting Nonprofits Is Labeled 'Extreme,'" *The Washington Post* 29 September 1995: A4.

5. Nan Aron, "No: The Bill Will Silence the Voices of Nonprofit Citizen Advocates," *Insight* 27 November 1995: 19.

6. *Ibid.*

7. Letter from President Nan Aron to the Committee on Standards of Official Conduct—The Ethics Committee—and addressed to chairs Nancy Johnson [R-Conn.] and Jim McDermott [D-Wash.], December 5, 1995, p. 2.

8. Alliance for Justice, "Factual Background," December 1995, pp. 2, 4.

9. Brian Francisco, "Amendment Out—For Now," *Muncie Star* 11 November 1995: 2A.

10. Henry Campbell Black, *Black's Law Dictionary* (St. Paul, Minn., West Publishing, 1968), p. 779.

11. "Faking It," *Legal Times* 2 October 1995: 5.

12. Anthony Lewis, "A Menacing Vendetta," *The New York Times* 2 October 1995: A17.

13. Yang, *op. cit.*, p. A4.

14. Katharine Q. Seelye, "Forgery Jolts G.O.P. Effort to Limit Some Lobbying," *The New York Times* 30 September 1995: 7.

15. "Ethics Complaint Against Representative David M. McIntosh," letter to the Honorable Nancy Johnson and Jim McDermott, U.S. House of Representatives, Committee on Standards of Official Conduct, December 5, 1995, p. 2; Nader's complaint, dated October 26, 1995, was titled: "Violation of the House Code of Official Conduct by Congressman David McIntosh" and was addressed to Nancy Johnson, Chairwoman of the Ethics Committee.

16. House Resolution, 104th Cong., lst sess., October 20, 1995.

17. *Congressional Record*, November 1, 1995, pp. H11662-11557.

18. Larry Margasak, "Ethics Committee Rebukes Lawmaker, Lets Him Announce It," Associated Press 21 March 1996.

19. Carl von Clausewitz, *On War,* translated by Michael Howard and Peter Paret (Princeton: Princeton University Press), p. 87.

CHAPTER 9

1. James Reston, *Deadlines—A Memoir* (New York: Random House, 1991), pp. 325–327.

2. *The New York Times Co. v Sullivan,* no. 39, 376 U.S. 254; 84 S. Ct. 710, 1964.

3. Thomas B. Edsall, "Nethercutt Abandons Campaign Pledge to Serve 3 Terms," *The Washington Post* 15 June 1999: A13. Another group, Americans for Term Limits, also lobbies for term limits. It is smaller and less vocal than U.S. Term Limits.

4. U.S. Term Limits, Washington, D.C., February 19, 1999.

5. *Ibid.*

6. Jim Camden, "Term-Limits Group Reminds Nethercutt of Vow," *Spokesman-Review* 17 February 1999: 9.

7. Arianna Huffington, "The Term-Limit Turncoats," *New York Post* 13 March 1999: 54.

8. Camden, *op. cit.*

9. "The Seduction of Seniority," *The Hill* 23 June 1999: 30.

10. Marianne Means, "Pols Reneging on Term-Limit Promises," *Cleveland Plain Dealer* 4 March 1999: 9B.

11. B. Drummond Ayres Jr., "Determined to Stay," *The New York Times* 5 May 2000: A22.

12. Francis X. Clines, "Public Lives: Keeping Politicians True to Their Inner Selves," *The New York Times* 15 March 1999: 14.

13. Susan J. Tolchin, *The Angry American—How Voter Rage Is Changing the Nation,* 2nd ed. (Boulder: Westview Press, 1998), p. 10.

14. Robert Shogan, "Lying Is an 'Occupational Disease.' Many Presidents Have Done It, Only Jimmy Carter Seems Squeaky Clean," *The Los Angeles Times* 23 August 1998: F4.

15. Albert R. Hunt, "Hamilton Jordan Survives Cancer—and Carter—with Wit and Dignity, *Wall Street Journal* 2 June 2000: W1.

16. Theodore J. Lowi, "The Intelligent Person's Guide to Political Corruption," *Public Affairs Government Research Bureau,* Series 81, 82 (September 1981): 2, and Sissela Bok, *Lying—Moral Choice in Public and Private Life,* 2nd ed. (New York: Vintage, 1999), p. 166.

17. Niccolò Machiavelli, *The Prince and the Discourses* (New York: McGraw-Hill, 1950).

18. Lowi, *op. cit.*, p. 3.

19. *Ibid.,* p. 2.

20. Patrick Anderson, *The President's Men* (Garden City, N.Y.: Anchor Books, 1969), pp. 40–41; Lord Acton's quote actually runs: "Power tends to corrupt, and absolute power corrupts absolutely. Great men are [almost] always bad men." See Lord Acton, letter to Bishop Mandell Creighton, April 3, 1887, in Louise Creighton, *Life and Letters of Mandell Creighton* (New York: Longmans, Green, 1905),Vol. 1, ch. 13.

21. Author Phillip Knightley identified the "first casualty" of any war as the truth in a book of the same name. See Phillip Knightley, *The First Casualty—From the Crimea to Vietnam: The War Correspondent as Hero, Propagandist and Mythmaker* (New York: Harcourt Brace Jovanovich, 1975). See also Robert Dallek, *Flawed Giant—Lyndon Johnson and His Times 1961–1973* (New York: Oxford University Press, 1998).

22. *Toyosabuko Korematsu v U.S.,* 319 US 432 (1943) and 323 US 214 (1944).

23. Lowi, *op. cit.,* p. 4.

24. Shogan, *op. cit.,* p. F5.

25. Bok, *op. cit.,* ch. 3, p. 32, quoting from Immanuel Kant, "The Doctrine of Virtue," part 2 of *The Metaphysic Morals,* translated by Mary Gregor (New York: Harper & Row, 1964).

26. Bok, *op. cit.,* pp. xxx, 141–142.

27. Jack Raymond, "Soviet Downs American Plane," *The New York Times* 6 May 1960: 1.

28. *Ibid.,* p. 7.

29. U.S. Department of State—Office of the Historian, "May–July 1960: The U-2 Airplane Incident,"Vol. X, Part 1, FRUS, 1958–1960: E. Europe Region; Soviet Union; Cyprus.

30. Shogan, *op. cit.*

31. Richard Norton-Taylor and Paul Lashmar, "Eden Vetoed U-2 Spy Flights," *The Guardian (London)* 7 March 1998: 10.

32. Bok, *op. cit.,* p. xxx, citing Cambridge Survey Research, 1975, 1976.

33. Tolchin, *op. cit.,* p. 108.

34. William Safire, "Hillary's Travels—Artful Deception Is Not a Crime," *The New York Times* 22 June 2000: A29; the original article, headlined "Blizzard of Lies," ran 8 January 1996: 27.

35. Bok, *op. cit.,* p. 28.

36. *Ibid.,* ch. 5, pp. 57–72.

37. John J. Coleman, "Police Ethics and Lawful Deception—A Conundrum of Principles," unpublished paper, George Mason University, May 2000, p. 6.

38. Black, Henry Campbell, *Black's Law Dictionary,* 4th ed. (St. Paul, Minn.: West Publishing, 1968), p. 627.

39. Bok, *op. cit.*, pp. 79, 168–169.

40. *Ibid.* p. 170.

41. Congressional Quarterly, *Congressional Ethics—History, Facts, and Controversy* (Washington, D.C.: Congressional Quarterly Press, 1992), pp. 41–42, 32.

CHAPTER 10

1. Dennis F. Thompson, *Ethics in Congress—From Individual to Institutional Corruption* (Washington, D.C.: Brookings Institution, 1995), p. 143.

2. *Ibid.*, p. 145.

3. Alison Mitchell, "New Ethics Rules Are Approved, Including a Ban on Outsiders' Complaints," *The New York Times* 19 September 1997: A27.

4. *Congressional Quarterly Almanac*, "Leaders Name New Ethics Chairman, But Little Action Taken in Either Chamber," 1999, pp. 8–17.

5. Albert Eisele and Mary Lynn Jones, "HHS Secretary Donna Shalala," Clinton Retrospective, *The Hill* 5 December 2000: 24.

6. David E. Price, *The Congressional Experience*, 2nd ed. (Boulder: Westview Press, 2000), pp. 221–222.

7. Flood resigned shortly after a mistrial was declared in 1979. Facing another trial, he pleaded guilty to a single misdemeanor charge and avoided a prison sentence. He was placed on probation. Congressional Quarterly, *Congressional Ethics— History, Facts, and Controversy* (Washington, D.C.: Congressional Quarterly Press, 1992), pp. 61–62.

8. Paul Simon, *The Glass House—Politics and Morality in the Nation's Capital* (New York: Continuum, 1984), p. 19.

9. Ian Miller, "Ethics Panel OKs Hillary's Disputed Fund," *The Hill* 28 March 2001: 1.

10. *Congressional Quarterly Almanac, op. cit.*

11. Sarah Pekkanen, "Ethics Committee Issues Scathing Report on Collins," *The Hill* 8 January 1997: 10.

12. Jock Friedly, "Hilliard Campaign Boosted His Business," *The Hill* 3 December 1997: 1.

13. Juliet Eilperin, "Ethics Panel Criticizes Shuster's Ties to Lobbyist," *The Washington Post* 6 October 2000: A1, A4. See also Amy Keller, "Ethics Report Reveals Inner Workings of Shuster's Office—Eppard Made Sure Her Lobbying Clients Got Audience with Chairman, Despite One-Year Prohibition," *Roll Call* 9 October 2000; and Tom Ichniowski, "House Ethics Panel Cites Shuster," *Engineering News-Record* 16 October 2000: 12.

14. David Stout, "Congressman Draws Rebuke But No Penalty," *The New York Times* 6 October 2000: A28.

References

BOOKS

Aaron, Henry J., Thomas E. Mann, and Timothy Taylor, eds. *Values and Public Policy*. Washington, D.C.: Brookings Institution, 1994.

Amer, Mildred. *The House Committee on Standards of Official Conduct: A Brief History of Its Evolution and Jurisdiction*. Washington, D.C.: Congressional Research Service, 1993.

Anderson, Patrick. *The President's Men*. Garden City, N.Y.: Anchor Books, 1969.

Anechiarico, Frank, and James B. Jacobs. *The Pursuit of Absolute Integrity—How Corruption Control Makes Government Ineffective*. Chicago: University of Chicago Press, 1996.

Bacon, Donald C., Roger H. Davidson, and Morton Keller, eds. *The Encyclopedia of the United States Congress*. New York: Simon and Schuster, 1995.

Barone, Michael, and Grant Ujifusa. *The Almanac of American Politics 1996*. Washington, D.C.: National Journal, 1995.

Beard, Edmund, and Stephen Horn. *Congressional Ethics: The View from the House*. Washington, D.C.: Brookings Institution, 1975.

Beauchamp, Tom L., ed. *Ethics and Public Policy*. Englewood Cliffs, N.J.: Prentice Hall, 1975.

Benson, George C. S. *Political Corruption in America*. Lexington, Mass.: Lexington Books, D.C. Heath & Co., 1978.

Berger, Raoul. *Impeachment: The Constitutional Problems*. Cambridge, Mass.: Harvard University Press, 1973.

Bianco, William T. *Trust: Representatives and Constituents*. Ann Arbor, Mich.: University of Michigan Press, 1994.

Birnbaum, Jeffrey H., and Alan S. Murray. *Showdown at Gucci Gulch: Lawmakers, Lobbyists and the Unlikely Triumph of Tax Reform*. New York: Random House, 1987.

Black, Henry Campbell. *Black's Law Dictionary: Definitions of the Terms and Phrases of American and British Jurisprudence, Ancient and Modern*. St. Paul, Minn.: West Publishing, 1968 and 1991.

Bok, Sissela. *Secrecy: On the Ethics of Concealment and Revelation.* New York: Pantheon Books, 1989.

———. *Lying—Moral Choice in Public and Private Life.* 2nd ed. New York: Vintage Books, 1999.

Butler, Anne M., and Wendy Wolff. *United States Senate—Election, Expulsion and Censure Cases 1793–1990.* Washington, D.C.: U.S. Government Printing Office, 1995.

Chamberlain, Hope. *A Minority of Members.* New York: Praeger, 1973.

Clausewitz, Carl von. *On War.* Translated by Michael Howard and Peter Paret. Princeton: Princeton University Press, 1976.

Cohen, Richard E. *Rostenkowski: The Pursuit of Power and the End of the Old Politics.* Chicago, Ill.: Ivan R. Dee, 1999.

Congressional Quarterly. *Congressional Ethics—History, Facts and Controversy.* Washington, D.C.: Congressional Quarterly Press, 1992.

———. *Guide to Congress.* 4th ed. Washington, D.C.: Congressional Quarterly Press, 1991.

Cooper, Joseph, ed. *Congress and the Decline of Public Trust.* Boulder: Westview Press, 1999.

Cooper, Joseph, and G. Calvin Mackenzie, eds. *The House at Work.* Austin, Tex.: University of Texas Press, 1981.

Corinthians. 11:31 (English, King James Version).

Creighton, Louise. *Life and Letters of Mandell Creighton. Vol. 1.* New York: Longmans, Green & Co., 1905.

Dallek, Robert. *Flawed Giant—Lyndon Johnson and His Times 1961–1973.* New York: Oxford Press, 1998.

DeLeon, Peter. *Thinking About Political Corruption.* New York: M. E. Sharpe, 1993.

Drury, Allen. *Advise and Consent.* Garden City, N.Y.: Doubleday, 1959.

Finch, Peter A. *Ethics in Government.* Englewood Cliffs, N.J.: Prentice Hall, 1983.

Fleishman, Joel, Lance Liebman, and Mark H. Moore, eds. *Public Duties: Moral Obligations of Government Officials.* Cambridge, Mass.: Harvard University Press, 1981.

Frederickson, H. George, ed. *Ethics and Public Administration.* Armonk, N.Y.: M. E. Sharpe, 1993.

Gardiner, John A., and David J. Olson, eds. *Theft of the City—Readings on Corruption in Urban America.* Bloomington, Ind.: Indiana University Press, 1974.

Garment, Suzanne. *Scandal.* New York: Times Books, 1991.

Graham, George A. *Morality in American Politics.* New York: Random House, 1952.

Griffith, Robert. *The Politics of Fear—Joseph R. McCarthy and the Senate.* Lexington, Ky.: The University Press of Kentucky, 1970.

Gutmann, Amy, and Dennis F. Thompson. *Ethics & Politics—Cases and Comments.* 3rd ed. Chicago: Nelson-Hall, 1997.

———. *Democracy and Disagreement.* Cambridge, Mass.: The Belknap Press of Harvard University Press, 1996.

Hastings Center. *The Ethics of Legislative Life.* Hastings-on-Hudson, N.Y. The Hastings Center Institute of Society, Ethics and the Life Sciences, 1985.

Heidenheimer, Arnold J., Michael Johnson, and Victor T. LeVine, eds. *Political Corruption: A Handbook.* New Brunswick, N.J.: Transaction Books, 1989.

Ingram, Helen, and Steven Rathgeb Smith, eds. *Public Policy for Democracy.* Washington, D.C.: Brookings Institution, 1993.

Jennings, Bruce, and Daniel Callahan, eds. *Representation and Responsibility—Exploring Legislative Ethics.* The Hastings Center Institute of Society, Ethics and the Life Sciences. New York: Plenum Press, 1985.

Johnston, Michael. *Political Corruption and Public Policy in America.* Monterey, Calif.: Cole, 1982.

Jones, Charles O. *The Presidency in a Separated System.* Washington, D.C.: Brookings Institution, 1994.

Kant, Immanuel. *The Foundations of the Metaphysics of Morals.* Translated by Lewis White Beck. Indianapolis, Ind.: Bobbs-Merrill, 1959.

Killian, Johnny H., and George A. Costello, eds. *The Constitution of the United States—Analysis and Interpretation.* Congressional Research Service. Washington, D.C.: U.S. Government Printing Office, 1996.

Knightley, Phillip. *The First Casualty—From the Crimea to Vietnam: The War Correspondent as Hero, Propagandist and Mythmaker.* New York: Harcourt Brace Jovanovich, 1975.

Lasswell, Harold D., and Abraham Kaplan. *Power and Society.* New Haven: Yale University Press, 1950.

Lewis, Carol W. *The Ethics Challenge in Public Service—A Problem-Solving Guide.* San Francisco: Jossey-Bass Publishers, 1991.

Lewis, Charles. *The Buying of Congress—How Special Interests Have Stolen Your Right to Life, Liberty, and the Pursuit of Happiness.* New York: Avon Books, 1998.

Machiavelli, Niccolò. *The Prince and the Discourses.* New York: McGraw-Hill, 1950.

Maskell, Jack. *Expulsion and Censure Actions Taken by the Full Senate Against Members.* Washington, D.C.: Congressional Research Service, 1990.

———. *Reports Concerning Investigations and/or Disciplinary Recommendations from the House Committee on Standards of Official Conduct Since Its Inception in 1968.* Washington, D.C.: Congressional Research Service, 1989.

Morgan, Peter W., and Glenn H. Reynolds. *The Appearance of Impropriety—How the Ethics Wars Have Undermined American Government, Business and Society.* New York: The Free Press, 1997.

Noonan, John T. *Bribes.* Berkeley: University of California Press, 1984.

O'Neill, Tip, and William Novak. *Man of the House.* New York: Random House, 1987.

Price, David E. *The Congressional Experience.* 2nd ed. Boulder: Westview Press, 2000.

Rae, Nicol C., and Colton C. Campbell. *New Majority or Old Minority?: The Impact of Republicans on Congress.* Lanham, Md.: Rowman & Littlefield, 1999.

Remini, Robert V. *Andrew Jackson and the Course of American Empire 1767–1821.* New York: Harper & Row, 1977.

———. *Henry Clay: Statesman for the Union.* New York: W. W. Norton, 1991.

———. *Daniel Webster: The Man and His Time.* New York: W. W. Norton, 1997.

Reston, James. *Deadlines—A Memoir.* New York: Random House, 1991.

Riccucci, Norma. *Unsung Heroes—Federal Executives Making a Difference.* Washington, D.C.: Georgetown University Press, 1995.

Rogers, Joseph M. *The True Henry Clay.* Philadelphia: J. B. Lippincott, 1904.

Rogow, Arnold A., and Harold D. Lasswell. *Corruption, Power and Rectitude.* Englewood Cliffs, N.J.: Prentice Hall, 1963.

Rohr, John. *Ethics for Bureaucrats—An Essay on Law and Values.* 2nd ed. New York: Marcel Dekker, 1989.

———. *Public Service, Ethics, and Constitutional Practice.* Lawrence, Kans.: University Press of Kansas, 1998.

Rose-Ackerman, Susan. *Corruption: A Study in Political Economy.* New York: Academic Press, 1978.

Rosenberg, Morton, and Jack H. Maskell. *Congressional Intervention in the Administrative Process: Legal and Ethical Considerations.* Washington, D.C.: Congressional Research Service, 1990.

Rudman, Warren B. *Combat: Twelve Years in the U.S. Senate.* New York: Random House, 1996.

Sandel, Michael. *Democracy's Discontent—America in Search of a Public Philosophy.* Cambridge, Mass.: The Belknap Press of Harvard University Press, 1996.

Scott, Sir Walter. *Marmion: A Poem in Six Cantos.* New York: Crowell & Co., 1884.

Senate Ethics Counsel. *The Packwood Report.* New York: Times Books, 1995.

Simon, Paul. *The Glass House—Politics and Morality in the Nation's Capital.* New York: Continuum, 1984.

Steffens, Lincoln. *The Autobiography of Lincoln Steffens.* New York: Harcourt Brace Jovanovich, 1959.

Tang, Rosemary. *Ethics for Public Policy Analysis.* Englewood Cliffs, N.J.: Prentice Hall, 1986.

Thompson, Dennis F. *Ethics in Congress—From Individual to Institutional Corruption* Washington, D.C.: Brookings Institution, 1995.

Timberg, Robert. *The Nightingale's Song.* New York: Simon and Schuster, 1995.

Tolchin, Martin, and Susan J. Tolchin. *To the Victor—Political Patronage from the Clubhouse to the White House.* New York: Random House, 1971.

———. *Dismantling America—The Rush to Deregulate.* Boston: Houghton Mifflin, 1983.

———. *Buying into America—How Foreign Money Is Changing the Face of Our Nation.* New York: Times Books, 1988.

———. *Clout—Womanpower and Politics.* New York: Coward, McCann & Geoghegan, 1973.

———. *Selling Our Security—The Erosion of America's Assets.* New York: Alfred A. Knopf, 1992.

Tolchin, Susan J. *The Angry American—How Voter Rage Is Changing the Nation.* 2nd ed. Boulder: Westview Press, 1998.

Uslaner, Eric. *The Decline of Comity in Congress.* Ann Arbor, Mich.: University of Michigan Press, 1993.

Watkins, Arthur V. *Enough Rope.* Englewood Cliffs, N.J., and Salt Lake City, Utah: Prentice Hall and University of Utah Press, 1969.

Williams, Bernard. *Ethics and the Limits of Philosophy.* Cambridge, Mass.: Harvard University Press, 1985.

Wilson, H. H. *Congress: Corruption and Compromise.* New York: Rinehart & Co., 1951.

Wills, Garry. *Under God—Religion and American Politics.* New York: Simon and Schuster, 1990.

Winsten, Stephan. *Days with Bernard Shaw.* New York: Vanguard Press, 1949.

Wright, Jim. *Reflections of a Public Man.* Fort Worth, Tex.: Allied Printing, 1984.

ARTICLES, ESSAYS, PAPERS, AND MONOGRAPHS

Alford, John, Holly Teeters, Daniel S. Ward, and Rick K. Wilson. "Overdraft: The Political Cost of Congressional Malfeasance." *Journal of Politics* 56 (August 1994): 788–801.

Alvarez, Lizette. "A Lawmaker Uses His Own Shame as a Guide." *The New York Times* 12 December 1998: 45.

Aron, Nan. "No: The Bill Will Silence the Voices of Nonprofit Citizen Advocates." *Insight* 27 November 1995: 19.

Ayres, B. Drummond, Jr. "Determined to Stay." *The New York Times* 5 May 2000: A22.

Babcock, Charles R. "Rep. Studds of Massachusetts Will Not Seek Reelection." *The Washington Post* 29 October 1995: A31.

Baker, Richard Allen. "The History of Congressional Ethics." In *Representation and Responsibility*. Edited by Bruce Jennings and Daniel Callahan. New York: Plenum Press, 1985.

Barr, Stephen. "Nonprofit Groups Fault Restrictive GOP 'Riders'." *The Washington Post* 29 September 1999: A27.

Belluck, Pam. "Redemption to Rostenkowski Can Include Fun and Profit." *The New York Times* 18 March 1998: A1, A15.

Berke, Richard L. "The Confusing Case of the Keating 5." *The New York Times* 28 October 1990: 4:5.

———. "In New Climate, More Politicians Surmount Imperfect Private Lives." *The New York Times* 19 April 1998: 1, 30.

Berke, Richard L., and Lisette Alvarez. "Impeachment: The Resignation; Professions of Shock and Support Aside, Livingston May Have Been in for a Push." *The New York Times* 20 December 1998: 33.

Brooks, David. "The Tragedy of SID: Status-Income Disequilibrium." *Weekly Standard* 6 May 1996: 23–27.

Brownfeld, Peter Egill. "For Most House Freshmen, Salaries Bring Boost in Pay." *The Hill* 23 June 1999: 1.

Camden, Jim. "Term-Limits Groups Reminds Nethercutt of Vow." *Spokesman-Review* 17 February 1999: 9.

Clark, Maxine, and Rudy Maxa. "Closed-Session Romance on the Hill." *The Washington Post* 23 May 1976: A1.

Clines, Francis X. "Public Lives: Keeping Politicians True to Their Inner Selves." *The New York Times* 15 March 1999: 14.

Cohen, Richard E. "Crack-up of the Committees." *National Journal* 31 July 1999: 2211–2217.

Coleman, John J. "Police Ethics and Lawful Deception—A Conundrum of Principles." Unpublished paper, George Mason University, May 2000.

Dedman, Bill. "They Changed the Rules 30 Times." *The New York Times* 10 October 1997: A14.

Dimock, Michael A., and Gary Jacobson. "Checks and Choices: The House Bank Scandal's Impact on Voters in 1992." *Journal of Politics* 57 (November 1995): 1143–1159.

Edsall, Thomas B. "Nethercutt Abandons Campaign Pledge to Serve 3 Terms." *The Washington Post* 15 June 1999: A13.

Eilperin, Juliet. "Ethics Panel Criticizes Shuster's Ties to Lobbyist." *The Washington Post* 6 October 2000: A1, A4.

Eisele, Albert, and Mary Lynn Jones. "HHS Secretary Donna Shalala." Clinton Retrospective, *The Hill* 5 December 2000: 24.

Eisenstadt, Dave. "Dems Demand Ethics Big Quit Probe of Newt." *New York Daily News* 2 December 1995: 6.

"Ethics Panel's Delay Has Consequences." *Hartford Courant* 3 January 1997: A20.

"Faking It." *Legal Times* 2 October 1995: 5.

Fasman, Jonathan E. "Connecticut 6: A Threat to Nancy Johnson's Reign?" *The Hill* 3 March 1998: 27.

Francisco, Brian. "Amendment Out—For Now." *Muncie Star* 11 November 1995: A2.

Freudenheim, Milt. "Federal Jury Orders Keating to Pay Investors $3.3 Billion." *The New York Times* 11 July 1992: 33.

Friedly, Jock. "Hilliard Campaign Boosted His Business." *The Hill* 3 December 1997: 1.

Grunwald, Michael. "Senate's Surgeon Targeted on HMO Bill." *The Washington Post* 5 October 1999: A1, A4.

Gutmann, Amy, and Dennis F. Thompson. "The Theory of Legislative Ethics." In *Representation and Responsibility*. Edited by Bruce Jennings and Daniel Callahan. New York: Plenum Press, 1985.

Halbfinger, David M., and David Kocieniewski. "Torricelli Unified New Jersey's Democrats, but Against His Candidacy." *The New York Times* 2 August 2000: A24.

Huffington, Arianna. "The Term-Limit Turncoats." *New York Post* 13 March 1999: 54.

Hugick, Larry. "Majority Disapproves of Congress." *Gallup Poll Monthly* August 1991: 45.

Hunt, Albert R. "Hamilton Jordan Survives Cancer—and Carter—with Wit and Dignity." *The Wall Street Journal* 2 June 2000: W1.

Ichniowski, Tom. "House Ethics Panel Cites Shuster." *Engineering News-Record* 16 October 2000: 12.

Johnston, David. "Indictment of a Congressman." *The New York Times* 1 June 1994: A1.

Katz, Allan J. "The Politics of Congressional Ethics." In *The House at Work*. Edited by Joseph Cooper and G. Calvin Mackenzie. Austin, Tex.: University of Texas Press, 1981.

Keller, Amy. "Ethics Report Reveals Inner Workings of Shuster's Office—Eppard Made Sure Her Lobbying Clients Got Audience with Chairman, Despite One-Year Prohibition." *Roll Call* 9 October 2000: 1.

Kimball, David C., and Samuel Patterson. "Living Up to Expectations: Public Attitudes Toward Congress." *Journal of Politics* 59 (August 1997): 701–728.

King, Stephen M. "Ethics. Speaking the Truth." *Pennsylvania Times* September 2000: 3.

Kirby, James C. "The Role of the Electorate in Congressional Ethics." In *Representation and Responsibility.* Edited by Bruce Jennings and Daniel Callahan. New York: Plenum Press, 1985.

Kocieniewski, David. "Torricelli Opposed Within Party, Drops New Jersey Governor Bid." *The New York Times* 1 August 2000: A1, A23.

Koszczuk, Jackie. "Filing Complaints in House: Now for Members Only?" *Congressional Quarterly* 20 September 1997: 2199–2201.

"Leaders Name New Ethics Chairman, but Little Action Taken in Either Chamber." *Congressional Quarterly Almanac* 1999: 8–17.

Leonard, Jack E. "Ethics and National Security." Unpublished paper, George Mason University, May 2000.

Lewis, Alfred E., and Martin Weil. "Riders in Mills' Car Involved in a Scuffle." *The Washington Post* 10 October 1974: A1, A12.

Lewis, Anthony. "A Menacing Vendetta." *The New York Times* 2 October 1995: A17.

Lochhead, Carolyn. "House Abolishes 'Slush Fund'." *San Francisco Chronicle* 25 June 1992: A6.

Lowi, Theodore J. "The Intelligent Person's Guide to Political Corruption." Public Affairs, Governmental Research Bureau, Series 81, Number 82, September 1981: 1–8.

Lyons, Richard L. "Rep. Hays Quits Seat in Congress." *The Washington Post* 2 September 1976: A1.

Malec, Kathryn L. "Public Attitudes Toward Corruption: Twenty-five Years of Research." In *Ethics and Public Administration.* Edited by H. George Frederickson. Armonk, N.Y.: M. E. Sharpe, 1993.

Margasak, Larry. "Ethics Committee Rebukes Lawmaker, Lets Him Announce It." Associated Press 21 March 1966.

Masters, Kim. "Truth and Consequences: Rep. Bob Torricelli Leaked the Goods on the CIA. Was It Loyalty or Betrayal?" *The Washington Post* 17 April 1995: C1.

Means, Marianne. "Pols Reneging on Term-Limit Promises." *Cleveland Plain Dealer* 4 March 1999: 9B.

Mitchell, Alison. "New Ethics Rules Are Approved, Including a Ban on Outsider's Complaints." *The New York Times* 19 September 1997: A27.

———. "Republicans Pillory McCain in Debate over Soft Money." *The New York Times* 10 October 1999: 30.

Mondac, Jeffrey J. "Competence, Integrity, and the Electoral Success of Congressional Incumbents." *Journal of Politics* 57 (November 1995): 1043–1069.

Morgan, Peter W. "The Appearance of Impropriety: Ethics Reform and the Blifil Paradoxes." *Stanford Law Review* February 1992: 593.

"Mr. Gingrich's Tainted Victory." *The New York Times* 8 January 1997: A14.

"Muzzling the Nonprofits." *The New York Times* 2 November 1995: A26.

Myers, E. Michael. "Sen. Jesse Helms Recalls Another Senator Named Kennedy— JFK." *The Hill* 24 November 1999: 27.

Myerson, Allen R. "From One Fallen Speaker to Another." *The New York Times* 12 December 1998: A22.

Norton-Taylor, Richard, and Paul Lashmar. "Eden Vetoed U–2 Spy Flights." *The Guardian (London)* 7 March 1998: 10.

Oliphant, Thomas. "Gingrich's Ethics Problems Won't Go Away." *Boston Globe* 15 September 1996; D7.

Pekkanen, Sarah. "Ethics Committee Issues Scathing Report on Collins." *The Hill* 8 January 1997: 10.

Peters, John G., and Susan Welch. "Political Corruption in America: A Search for Definitions and the Theory, or if Political Corruption Is in the Mainstream of Politics, Why Is It Not in the Mainstream of American Politics Research?" *American Political Science Review* 72 (September 1978): 974–984.

Pfiffner, James P. "Sexual Probity and Presidential Character." *Presidential Studies Quarterly* 28 (Fall 1998): 881–886.

Pincus, Walter. "Inspector General Says CIA Made Mistakes in Guatemala." *The Washington Post* 26 July 1995: A19.

Pincus, Walter, and R. Jeffrey Smith. "CIA Chief to Punish Employees, Deutch Cites Handling of Guatemala Efforts." *The Washington Post* 27 September 1995: A29.

Price, David E. "Legislative Ethics in the New Congress." In *Representation and Responsibility.* Edited by Bruce Jennings and Daniel Callahan. New York: Plenum Press, 1985.

Raymond, Jack. "Soviet Downs American Plane." *The New York Times* 6 May 1960: 1.

Remez, Michael. "Shays Formally Requests Ethics Investigation of Rostenkowski." *Hartford Courant* 2 July 1994; G12.

Risen, James. "C.I.A. Punishes 6 for Failure in Inquiry of Ex-Director." *The New York Times* 26 May 2000: A15.

———. "Secrets of History—The C.I.A. In Iran." *The New York Times* 17 April 2000: A1.

Rohr, John. "On Achieving Ethical Behavior in Government." *The Public Manager—The New Bureaucrat* Spring 1992: 47–51.

Rosenbaum, David E. "Guilty Plea and Jail Are Said to Be Near for Rostenkowski." *The New York Times* 9 April 1996: A1.

Safire, William. "Blizzard of Lies." *The New York Times* 8 January 1996: 27.

———. "Hillary's Travels—Artful Deception Is Not a Crime." *The New York Times* 22 June 2000: A29.

"The Seduction of Seniority." *The Hill* 23 June 1999: 30.

Seelye, Katharine Q. "Forgery Jolts G.O.P. Effort to Limit Some Lobbying." *The New York Times* 30 September 1995: 7.

"Sen. Packwood Resigns in Disgrace." *Congressional Quarterly Almanac* 1995: 1–50.

Shepard, Scott. "Decline in Respect Hampers Congress in Job, Experts Say." *Atlanta Constitution* 10 June 1994: A6.

Shogan, Robert. "Lying Is an 'Occupational Disease.' Many Presidents Have Done It, Only Jimmy Carter Seems Squeaky Clean." *The Los Angeles Times* 23 August 1998: F4.

Stark, Andrew. "Beyond Quid Pro Quo: What's Wrong with Private Gain from Public Office." *American Political Science Review* 91 (March 1997): 108–119.

Steffens, Lincoln. "Los Angeles and the Apple." In *Theft of the City—Readings on Corruption in Urban America.* Edited by John A. Gardiner and David J. Olson. Bloomington, Ind.: Indiana University Press, 1974.

Stout, David. "Congressman Draws Rebuke but No Penalty." *The New York Times* 6 October 2000: A28.

Tanenhaus, Sam. "Un-American Activities." *New York Review of Books* 47 (November 30, 2000): 25.

Thompson, Dennis F. "Mediated Corruption: The Case of the Keating Five." *American Political Science Review* 87 (June 1993): 369–379.

Weiner, Tim. "A Secret Disclosed Imperils the Career of State Dept. Aide." *The New York Times* 16 November 1996: 1.

———. "C.I.A. Chief Disciplines Official for Disclosure." *The New York Times* 6 December 1996: A20.

———. "Guatemalan Agent of CIA Tied to Killing of American." *The New York Times* 23 March 1995: A1.

Welch, Susan, and John R. Hibbing. "The Effects of Charges of Corruption on Voting Behavior in Congressional Elections 1982–1990." *Journal of Politics* 59 (February 1997): 226–239.

Yang, John. "Plan Limiting Nonprofits Is Labeled 'Extreme'." *The Washington Post* 29 September 1995: A4.

Yardley, Jim. "Calls to Voters at Center Stage in G.O.P. Race." *The New York Times* 14 February 2000: 1.

York, Byron. "Never Mind, Newt." *The American Spectator* April 1999: 28.

GOVERNMENT DOCUMENTS,
REPORTS, CONGRESSIONAL HEARINGS,
TESTIMONY, AND COURT CASES

Central Intelligence Agency. *Summary of CIA Inspector General Report Relating to Agency Activities in Guatemala.* Washington, D.C.: Central Intelligence Agency, 1995.

Committee on Standards of Official Conduct, House Ethics Manual, 102nd Cong., 2nd sess. Washington, D.C.: U.S. Government Printing Office, 1992.

Congressional Accountability Project. "Ethics Complaint Against Representative Bud Shuster and Call for Investigation into Possible Violations of Criminal Law and House Rules." Submitted to House Committee on Standards of Official Conduct, September 5, 1996.

Congressional Record. "Daily Digest." Thursday, December 2, 1954, p. D 739.

Congressional Record, House of Representatives. 25th Cong., 2nd sess., May 10, 1838. "Death of Mr. Cilley—Duel," Rep. No. 825. pp. 1–25.

Congressional Record, Senate. 83rd Cong., 2nd sess., December 2, 1954. 100, 16392.

Congressional Record, Senate. November 8, 1954. "Report on the Resolution to Censure." [Senator Joseph McCarthy]. pp. 15851–15921.

Congressional Record, Senate. November 10, 1954. pp. 15922–15954.

Congressional Record, Senate. 102nd Cong., 1st sess., December 18, 1991. 137 Cong. Rec. S 18828, Volume 137, Number 179, p. 7.

"Ethics Complaint Against Representative David M. McIntosh," letter to the Honorable Nancy Johnson and Jim McDermott, U.S. House of Representatives, Committee on Standards of Official Conduct, December 5, 1995.

Intelligence Oversight Board. *Report on the Guatemala Review.* Washington, D.C.: Central Intelligence Agency, 1996.

Jacobellis v Ohio, 378 US 184, 197 (1973).

Mapp v Ohio, No. 236, 367 US 643; 81 S. Ct. 1684; 197/61 U.S. Lexis 812 (1961).

Office of Public Affairs. "Former CIA Officer Terry Ward Recognized for Accomplishments over 35-Year Career." Washington, D.C.: Central Intelligence Agency, 2000.

Office of the Historian. "The U-2 Airplane Incident." Volume X, Part 1, FRUS, 1958–1960: E. Europe Region; Soviet Union; Cyprus. Washington, D.C.: U.S. Department of State, 1960.

Roe et. al. v Wade, No. 70–18, 410 US 113; 93 S. Ct. 705; 1973 Lexis, 159; 35 L. Ed. 2nd 147 (1973).

Select Committee on Ethics, U.S. Senate. 104th Cong., 2nd sess. Washington, D.C.: U.S. Government Printing Office, 1996.

Select Committee on Ethics, U.S. Senate. 104th Cong., 1st sess., 1995. Documents Related to the Investigation of Senator Robert Packwood.

Select Committee on Ethics, U.S. Senate. 102nd Cong., 1st sess., 1991. Investigation of Senator Alan Cranston.

Tienken, Robert L. *House of Representatives Exclusion, Expulsion and Censure Cases from 1789 to 1973.* Joint Committee on Congressional Operations. Washington, D.C.: Government Printing Office, 1973.

Toyosabuko Korematsu v U.S., 319 US 432 (1943) and 323 US 214 (1944).

United States Office of Government Ethics. *Standards of Ethical Conduct for Employees of the Executive Branch.* Washington, D.C.: U.S. Government Printing Office, 1997.

United States v Helstoski, No. 78–349, 442 US 477 (June 18, 1979).

U.S. District Court for the District of Columbia, *Senate Select Committee on Ethics v. Senator Bob Packwood.* Misc. No. 93–362, Memorandum of American Civil Liberties Union as *Amicus Curiae.*

U.S. House of Representatives, Committee on the Judiciary. 93rd Cong., 1st sess., October, 1973. "Impeachment—Selected Materials." Washington, D.C.: U.S. Government Printing Office, 1973.

U.S. House of Representatives. 102nd Cong., 2nd sess., April 1992. "Ethics Manual for Members, Officers, and Employees of the U.S. House of Representatives." Washington, D.C.: U.S. Government Printing Office, 1992.

U.S. House of Representatives, House Committee on Standards of Official Conduct. "A Report. Summary of Activities—One Hundred Fourth Congress." Washington, D.C.: Government Printing Office, 1997.

U.S. House of Representatives, House Committee on Standards of Official Conduct. "A Report. Summary of Activities—One Hundred Fifth Congress." Washington, D.C.: Government Printing Office, 1999.

U.S. House of Representatives, House Committee on Standards of Official Conduct. "Highlights of House Ethics Rules." Revised November 1996.

U.S. House of Representatives, House Committee on Standards of Official Conduct. *Historical Summary of Conduct Cases in the House of Representatives.* Washington, D.C.: Government Printing Office, April 1992.

U.S. House of Representatives, House Ethics Reform Task Force. 105th Cong., 1st sess., March 4 and June 20, 1997. "Revisions to the Rules of the House and the Rules of the Committee on Standards of Official Conduct: Hearings Before the Ethics Reform Task Force."

U.S. House of Representatives, House Permanent Select Committee on Intelligence. March 17, 1997. "Report on the Guatemala Review." Washington, D.C.: U.S. Government Printing Office, 1997.

U.S. House of Representatives, House Select Committee on Ethics. January 17, 1997. "In the Matter of Representative Newt Gingrich." Washington, D.C.: Congressional Information Service, 1997.

U.S. Senate. *Election, Expulsion and Censure Cases 1793–1990.* Washington, D.C.: U.S. Government Printing Office, 1995.

U.S. Senate, 104th Congress. "Documents Related to the Investigation of Senator Robert Packwood." U.S. Senate 104th Congress Select Committee on Ethics, First Session, 24, 892, 889, 886, 884, 900, Exhibits 116, 118, 119, 120, 121, 122, 1995.

U.S. Senate, 106th Congress, 1st Session, S 1593. "A Bill to Amend the Federal Election Campaign Act of 1971."

U.S. Senate Select Committee on Ethics. "Resolution for Disciplinary Action," Senate S. Rpt. 104–137 104th Cong., 1st sess., September 8, 1995.

"Violation of the House Code of Official Conduct by Congressman David McIntosh," ethics complaint from Ralph Nader, addressed to Rep. Nancy Johnson, Chair of the Ethics Committee, October 26, 1995.

INDEX

About the Authors

Martin Tolchin, founder, publisher, and editor-in-chief of *The Hill* newspaper, reported on Congress during most of his forty-year career at *The New York Times.* **Susan J. Tolchin** is professor of public policy at George Mason University's School of Public Policy and the author of *The Angry American: How Voter Rage Is Changing the Nation* (1996 and 1998). Together, the Tolchins have written five previous books—*Selling Our Security: The Erosion of America's Assets* (1992), *Buying Into America: How Foreign Money Is Changing the Face of Our Nation* (1988), *Dismantling America: The Rush to Deregulate* (1983), *Clout: Womanpower and Politics* (1974), and *To the Victor: Political Patronage from the Clubhouse to the White House* (1971).